François Guizot

History of Civilization in Europe

From the Fall of the Roman Empire to the French Revolution

François Guizot

History of Civilization in Europe
From the Fall of the Roman Empire to the French Revolution

ISBN/EAN: 9783744773454

Printed in Europe, USA, Canada, Australia, Japan

Cover: Foto ©ninafisch / pixelio.de

More available books at **www.hansebooks.com**

IN

EUROPE,

FROM

HE FALL OF THE ROMAN EMPIRE TO THE
FRENCH REVOLUTION.

BY M. GUIZOT.

PRIME MINISTER OF FRANCE, AUTHOR OF "A HISTORY OF FRANCE," ETC.

NEW YORK:
JOHN B. ALDEN, PUBLISHER,
1885.

ANALYTICAL TABLE OF CONTENTS.

LECTURE I.

CIVILIZATION IN GENERAL.

	PAGE.		PAGE.
ct of the course	7	That these two facts are necessarily connected to one another, and sooner or later produce one another	17
ry of European civilization	8		
taken in it by France	8		
ization may be recounted	9		
is the most general and intersting fact of history	9	The entire destiny of man not contained in his present or social condition	21
lar and usual meaning of the 'ord civilization	11	Two ways of considering and writing the history of civilization	21
zation consists of two principal acts:—1st, the progress of society; 2d, the progress of individuals	16	A few words upon the plan of this course	22
ts of this assertion	17	Of the actual state of opinion, and of the future, as regards civilization	23

LECTURE II.

EROPEAN CIVILIZATION:—IN PARTICULAR ITS DISTINGUISHED CHARACTERISTICS—ITS SUPERIORITY—ITS ELEMENTS.

ct of the lecture	25	existed down to the fifth century	37
y of ancient civilization	26		
ty of modern civilization	27	The clergy possessed of municipal offices	38
riority of the latter	29		
of Europe at the Fall of the oman Empire	30	Good and evil influence of the Church	41
onderance of cities	31	THE BARBARIANS	41
npts at political reform made y the emperors	33	They introduce into the modern world the sentiments of personal independence and loyalty	43
ipts of Honorius and Theodous II	33	Sketch of the various elements of civilization at the beginning of the fifth century	44
r in the name of empire	35		
CHRISTIAN CHURCH	35		
various states in which it had			

LECTURE III.

OLITICAL LEGITIMACY—CO-EXISTENCE OF ALL THE SYSTEMS OF GOVERNMENT IN THE FIFTH CENTURY—ATTEMPTS TO RE-ORGANIZE SOCIETY.

he various systems of civilization lay claim to legitimacy	46	The elementary principles of civilization have been,	
anation of political legitimacy	49	1. The want of order	57
cistence of all the various systems of government in the fifth entury	51	2. Remembrances of the empire	57
		3. The Christian Church	58
		4. The barbarians	58
bility of the state of persons, states, domains, and institutions	52	Attempts at organization	59
		1. By the barbarians	59
		2. By the cities	59
causes—one material, the coninuation of the invasions	53	3. By the Church of Spain	60
		4. By Charlemagne—Alfred	61, 62
nd moral, the sentiment of egoist individualism, peculiar to he barbarians	56	The German and Saracen invasion arrested	63
		The feudal system begins	63

LECTURE IV.

THE FEUDAL SYSTEM.

	PAGE		PAGE
Necessary alliance of facts and theories	66	Impossibility of regular organization of the feudal system	77
Preponderance of country life	70	1st. No great authority	78
Organization of a little feudal society	71	2d. No public power	79
Influence of feudalism upon the disposition of a proprietor of a fief	72	3d. Difficulties of the federative system	80
Upon the spirit of family	72	Right of resistance inherent in the feudal system	82
Hatred of the people for the feudal system	75	Influence of feudalism good for the development of individual man	83
Priests could do but little for the serfs	76	Bad for social order	83

LECTURE V.

THE CHRISTIAN CHURCH.

Religion a principle of association	86	It failed in the second condition by the unlawful extension of the principle of authority	97
Force not essential to government	92		
Conditions necessary to the legitimacy of a government	94	And by its abusive employment of force	98
1. Power in the hands of the most worthy	94	Activity and liberty of mind within the Church	100
2. Respect for the liberties of the governed	94	Connexion of the Church with princes	101
The Church being a corporation and not a caste, answered to the first of these conditions	94	Principle of the independence of spiritual authority	103
Various modes of nomination and election in the Church	96	Claims of the Church to dominion over temporal powers	103

LECTURE VI.

THE CHRISTIAN CHURCH.

Separation of the governing and the governed in the Church	106	the fifth to the twelfth century	120
		1. The imperial church	120
Indirect influence of the laity upon the Church	109	2. The barbarian church—development of the principle of the separation of the two powers	121
The clerical body recruited from all ranks of society	110	The monastic orders	121
Influence of the Church on public order and legislation	112	3. The feudal church	123
Its system of penitence	114	Attempts at organization	123
The progress of the human mind purely theological	116	Want of reform	124
		Gregory VII	124
The Church ranges itself on the side of authority	117	4. The theocratic church	124
		Revival of free inquiry	125
Not astonishing—the object of religion is to regulate human liberty	117	Abelard, etc.	125
		Agitation in the municipalities	126
Various states of the Church from		No connexion between these two facts	127

LECTURE VII.

RISE OF FREE CITIES.

A sketch of the different states of cities in the twelfth and eighteenth centuries	128	Social and moral effects of the affranchisement of the cities	140
Twofold question:—		2d. Of the interior government of cities	146
1st. Affranchisement of cities	132	Assemblies of the people	146
State of cities from the fifth to the tenth centuries	133	Magistrates	146
Their decline and revival	134	High and low burghers	146
Insurrection of the commons	137	Diversity in the state of the commons in various countries	147
Charters	138		

CONTENTS. 5

LECTURE VIII.

SKETCH OF EUROPEAN CIVILIZATION—THE CRUSADES.

General view of the civilization of Europe... 148
Its distinctive and fundamental character... 150
When this character began to appear 150
State of Europe from the twelfth to the sixteenth century... 150
THE CRUSADES:
Their character... 152
Their moral and social causes... 154
These causes cease at the end of the thirteenth century... 155
Effects of the crusades upon civilization... 157

LECTURE IX.

MONARCHY.

Important part of monarchy in the history of Europe... 167
In the history of the world... 169
True causes of its importance... 169
Twofold point of view under which monarchy should be considered. 169
1st. Its peculiar and permanent character... 169
It is the personification of legitimate sovereignty... 170
Within what limits... 171
2d. Its flexibility and diversity... 174
The European monarchy seems the result of the various species of monarchy... 174
Of the barbarian monarchy... 174
Of the imperial monarchy... 176
Of the feudal monarchy... 179
Of modern monarchy, properly so called, and of its true character. 181

LECTURE X.

ATTEMPTS AT ORGANIZATION.

Attempts to reconcile the various social elements of modern Europe, so as to make them live and act in common—to form one society under one same central power.. 183
1st. Attempt at theocratic organization... 186
Why it failed... 186
Four principal obstacles... 186
Faults of Gregory VII... 189
Reaction against the dominion of the Church... 190
On the part of the people... 190
On the part of the sovereigns... 190
2d. Attempts at republican organization... 190
Italian republics—their vices... 192
Cities of the south of France... 194
Crusade against the Albigenses... 194
The Swiss confederacy... 194
Free cities of Flanders and the Rhine... 195
Hanseatic League... 195
Struggle between the feudal nobility and the cities... 195
3d. Attempts at mixed organization. 196
The States-general of France... 196
The Cortes of Spain and Portugal. 197
The Parliament of England... 198
Bad success of all these attempts... 199
Causes of their failure... 199
General tendency of Europe... 199

LECTURE XI.

CENTRALIZATION, DIPLOMACY, ETC.

Particular character of the fifteenth century... 200
Progressive centralizations of nations and governments... 201
1st. Of France... 202
Formation of the national spirit of France... 203
Formation of the French territory... 203
Louis XI., manner of governing... 204
2d. Of Spain... 205
3d. Of Germany... 206
4th. Of England... 206
5th. Of Italy... 207
Rise of the exterior relations of states and of diplomacy... 208
Agitation of religious opinions... 210
Attempt at aristocratic reform in the Church... 211
Councils of Constance and Bale... 212
Attempt at popular reform... 213
John Huss... 214
Revival of ancient literature... 214
Admiration for antiquity... 214
Classic school... 215
General activity... 216
Voyages, travels, inventions, etc... 216
Conclusion... 216

LECTURE XII.

THE REFORMATION.

	PAGE		PAGE
Difficulty of unravelling general facts in modern history	217	against absolute power in intellectual affairs	224
Picture of Europe in the sixteenth century	218	Proofs of this fact	226
Danger of precipitate generalizations	222	Progress of the reformation in different countries	228
Various causes assigned for the reformation	223	Weak side of the reformation	228
Its predominant characteristic—the insurrection of the human mind		The Jesuits	231
		Analogy between the revolutions of civil and religious society	232

LECTURE XIII.

THE ENGLISH REVOLUTION.

General character of the English revolution	234	3d. The republican party	242
Its principal causes	235	They all fail	243
Rather political than religious	236	Cromwell	244
Three great parties succeed one another in its progress	240	Restoration of the Stuarts	246
1st. The pure monarchy reform party	240	The legitimate administration	246
2d. The constitutional reform party	241	Profligate administrations	247
		National administration	248
		Revolution of 1688 in England and Europe	250

LECTURE XIV.

THE FRENCH REVOLUTION.

Differences and resemblances in the progress of civilization in England and on the continent	252	Louis XIV	257
Preponderance of France in Europe in the seventeenth and eighteenth centuries	256	Of his wars	258
		Of his diplomacy	260
		Of his administration	262
In the seventeenth by the French government	256	Of his legislation	263
		Causes of its prompt decline	264
In the eighteenth by the country itself	257	France in the eighteenth century	267
		Essential characteristics of the philosophical revolution	267
		Conclusion	270

GENERAL

HISTORY OF CIVILIZATION

IN MODERN EUROPE.

FROM THE FALL OF THE ROMAN EMPIRE TO THE FRENCH REVOLUTION.

LECTURE I.

CIVILIZATION IN GENERAL.

BEING called upon to give a course of lectures, and having considered what subject would be most agreeable and convenient to fill up the short space allowed us from now to the close of the year, it has occurred to me that a general sketch of the History of Modern Europe, considered more especially with regard to the progress of civilization—that a general survey of the history of European civilization, of its origin, its progress, its end, its character, would be the most profitable subject upon which I could engage your attention.

I say European civilization, because there is evidently so striking a uniformity (*unité*) in the civilization of the different states of Europe, as fully to warrant this appellation. Civilization has flowed to them all from sources so much alike—it is so connected in them all, notwithstanding the great differences of time, of place, and circumstances, by the same principles, and it so tends in them all to bring about the same results, that no one will doubt the fact of there being a civilization essentially European.

At the same time it must be observed that this civilization cannot be found in—its history cannot be collected from, the history of any single state of Europe. However similar in its general appearance throughout the whole, its variety is not less remarkable, nor has it ever yet developed itself completely in any particular country. Its characteristic features are widely spread, and we shall be obliged to seek, as occasion may require, in England, in France, in Germany, in Spain, for the elements of its history.

The situation in which we are placed, as Frenchmen, affords us a great advantage for entering upon the study of European civilization; for, without intending to flatter the country to which I am bound by so many ties, I cannot but regard France as the centre, as the focus, of the civilization of Europe. It would be going too far to say that she has always been, upon every occasion, in advance of other nations. Italy, at various epochs, has outstripped her in the arts; England, as regards political institutions, is by far before her; and, perhaps, at certain moments, we may find other nations of Europe superior to her in various particulars; but it must still be allowed, that whenever France has set forward in the career of civilization, she has sprung forth with new vigor, and has soon come up with, or passed by, all her rivals.

Not only is this the case, but those ideas, those institutions which promote civilization, but whose birth must be referred to other countries, have, before they could become general, or produce fruit—before they could be transplanted to other lands, or benefit the common stock of European civilization, been obliged to undergo in France a new preparation: it is from France, as from a second country more rich and fertile, that they have started forth to make the conquest of Europe. There is not a single great idea, not a single great principle of civilization, which, in order to become universally spread, has not first passed through France.

There is, indeed, in the genius of the French, something of a sociableness, of a sympathy—something which spreads itself with more facility and energy, than in the genius of any other people: it may be in the language, or the particular turn of mind of the French nation; it may be in their manners, or that their ideas, being more popular, present themselves more clearly to the masses, penetrate among them with greater ease; but, in a word, clearness, sociability, sympathy, are the particular characteristics of France, of its civilization; and these qualities render it eminently qualified to march at the head of European civilization.

In studying, then, the history of this great fact, it is neither an arbitrary choice, nor convention, that leads us to make France the central point from which we shall study it;

but it is because we feel that in so doing, we in a manner place ourselves in the very heart of civilization itself—in the heart of the very fact which we desire to investigate.

I say *fact*, and I say it advisedly: civilization is just as much a fact as any other—it is a fact which like any other may be studied, described, and have its history recounted.

It has been the custom for some time past, and very properly, to talk of the necessity of confining history to facts; nothing can be more just; but it would be almost absurd to suppose that there are no facts but such as are material and visible: there are moral, hidden facts, which are no less real than battles, wars, and the public acts of government. Besides these individual facts, each of which has its proper name, there are others of a general nature, without a name, of which it is impossible to say that they happened in such a year, or on such a day, and which it is impossible to confine within any precise limits, but which are yet just as much facts as the battles and public acts of which we have spoken.

That very portion, indeed, which we are accustomed to hear called the philosophy of history—which consists in showing the relation of events with each other—the chain which connects them—the *causes* and *effects* of events—this is history just as much as the description of battles, and all the other exterior events which it recounts. Facts of this kind are undoubtedly more difficult to unravel; the historian is more liable to deceive himself respecting them; it requires more skill to place them distinctly before the reader; but this difficulty does not alter their nature; they still continue not a whit the less, for all this, to form an essential part of history.

Civilization is just one of these kind of facts; it is so general in its nature that it can scarcely be seized; so complicated that it can scarcely be unravelled; so hidden as scarcely to be discernible. The difficulty of describing it, of recounting its history, is apparent and acknowledged; but its existence, its worthiness to be described and to be recounted, is not less certain and manifest. Then, respecting civilization, what a number of problems remain to be solved! It may be asked, it is even now disputed, whether civilization be a good or an evil? One party decries it as teeming with mischief to man, while another lauds it as the means by which he will attain his highest dignity and excellence. Again, it is asked whether this *fact* is universal— whether there is a general civilization of the whole human race—a course for humanity to run—a destiny for it to accomplish; whether nations have not transmitted from age to age something to their successors which is never lost, but which grows and continues as a common stock, and will thus be carried on to the end of all things. For my part, I feel assured that human nature has such a destiny; that a general civilization pervades the human race; that at every epoch it augments; and that there, consequently, is a universal history of civilization to be written. Nor have I any hesitation in asserting that this history is the most noble, the most interesting of any, and that it comprehends every other.

Is it not indeed clear that civilization is the great fact in which all others merge; in which they all end, in which they are all condensed, in which all others find their importance? Take all the facts of which the history of a nation is composed, all the facts which we are accustomed to consider as the elements of its existence—take its institutions, its commerce, its industry, its wars, the various details of its government; and if you would form some idea of them as a whole, if you would see their various bearings on each other, if you would appreciate their value, if you would pass a judgment upon them, what is it you desire to know? Why, what they have done to forward the progress of civilization—what part they have acted in this great drama—what influence they have exercised in aiding its advance. It is not only by this that we form a general opinion of these facts, but it is by this standard that we try them, that we estimate their true value. These are, as it were, the rivers of whom we ask how much water they have carried to the ocean. Civilization is, as it were, the grand emporium of a people, in which all its wealth—all the elements of its life—all the powers of its existence are stored up. It is so true that we judge of minor facts accordingly as they affect this greater one, that even some which are naturally detested and hated, which prove a heavy calamity to the nation upon which they fall—say, for instance, despotism, anarchy, and so forth—even these are partly forgiven, their evil nature is partly overlooked, if they have aided in any considerable degree the march of civilization. Wherever the progress of this principle is visible, together with the facts which have urged it forward, we are tempted to forget the price it has cost—we overlook the dearness of the purchase.

Again, there are certain facts which, properly speaking, cannot be called social—individual facts which rather concern the human intellect than public life: such are religious doctrines, philosophical opinions, literature, the sciences and arts. All these seem to offer themselves to individual man for his improvement, instruction, or amusement; and to be directed rather to his intellectual melioration and pleasure, than to his social condition. Yet still, how often do these facts come before us—how often are we compelled to consider them as influencing civilization! In all times, in all countries, it has been the boast of religion, that it has civilized the people among whom it has dwelt. Literature, the arts, and sciences, have put in their claim for a share of this glory; and mankind has been ready to laud and honor them whenever it has felt that this praise was fairly their due. In the same manner, facts the most important—facts of themselves, and independently of their exterior consequences, the most sublime in their nature, have increased in importance, have reached a higher degree of sublimity, by their connexion with civilization. Such is the worth of this great principle, that it gives a value to all it touches. Not only so, but there are even cases, in which the facts of which we have spoken, in which philosophy, literature, the sciences, and the arts, are especially judged, and condemned or applauded, according to their influence upon civilization.

Before, however, we proceed to the history of this fact, so important, so extensive, so precious, and which seems, as it were, to imbody the entire life of nations, let us consider it for a moment in itself, and endeavor to discover what it really is.

I shall be careful here not to fall into pure philosophy; I shall not lay down a certain rational principle, and then, by deduction, show the nature of civilization as a consequence; there would be too many chances of error in pursuing this method. Still, without this, we shall be able to find a fact to establish and to describe.

For a long time past, and in many countries, the word civilization has been in use; ideas more or less clear, and of wider or more contracted signification, have been attached to it; still it has been constantly employed and generally understood. Now, it is the popular, common signification of this word that we must investigate. In the usual, general acceptation of terms, there will nearly always be found more truth than in the seemingly more precise and rigorous definitions of science. It is common sense which gives to words their popular signification, and common sense is the genius of humanity. The popular signification of a word is formed by degrees, and while the facts it repesents are themselves present. As often as a fact comes before us which seems to answer to the signification of a known term, this term is naturally applied to it, its signification gradually extending and enlarging itself, so that at last the various facts and ideas which, from the nature of things, ought to be brought together and imbodied in this term, will be found collected and imbodied in it. When, on the contrary, the signification of a word is determined by science, it is usually done by one or a very few individuals, who, at the time, are under the influence of some fact which has taken possession of their imagination. Thus it comes to pass that scientific definitions are, in general, much narrower, and, on that very account, much less correct, than the popular significations given to words. So, in the investigation of the meaning of the word *civilization* as a fact—by seeking out all the ideas it comprises, according to the common sense of mankind, we shall arrive much nearer to the knowledge of the fact itself, by than attempting to give our own scientific definition of it, though this might at first appear more clear and precise.

I shall commence this investigation by placing before you a series of hypotheses. I shall describe society in various conditions, and shall then ask if the state in which I so describe it is, in the general opinion of mankind, the state of a people advancing in civilization—if it answers to the signification which mankind generally attaches to this word.

First, imagine a people whose outward circumstances are easy and agreeable; few taxes, few hardships; justice is fairly administered; in a word, physical existence, taken altogether, is satisfactorily and happily regulated. But with all this the moral and intellectual energies of this people are studiously kept in a state of torpor and inertness. It can hardly be called oppression; its tendency is not of that character—it is rather compression. We are not without examples of this state of society. There have been a great number of little aristocratic republics, in which the people have been thus treated like so many flocks of sheep, carefully tended, physically happy, but without the least intellectual and moral activity. Is this civilization? Do we recognize here a people in a state of moral and social advancement?

Let us take another hypothesis. Let us imagine a people whose outward circumstances are less favorable and agreeable; still, however, supportable. As a set-off, its intellectual and moral cravings have not here been entirely neglected. A certain range has been allowed them—some few pure and elevated sentiments have been here distributed; religious and moral notions have reached a certain degree of improvement; but the greatest care has been taken to stifle every principle of liberty. The moral and intellectual wants of this people are provided for in the way that, among some nations, the physical wants have been provided for; a certain portion of truth is doled out to each, but no one is permitted to help himself—to seek for truth on his own account. Immobility is the character of its moral life; and to this condition are fallen most of the populations of Asia, in which theocratic government restrains the advance of man; such, for example, is the state of the Hindoos. I again put the same question as before—Is this a people among whom civilization is going on?

I will change entirely the nature of the hypothesis: suppose a people among whom there reigns a very large stretch of personal liberty, but among whom also disorder and inequality almost everywhere abound. The weak are oppressed, afflicted, destroyed; violence is the ruling character of the social condition. Every one knows that such has been the state of Europe. Is this a civilized state? It may without doubt contain germs of civilization which may progressively shoot up; but the actual state of things which prevails in this society is not, we may rest assured, what the common sense of mankind would call civilization.

I pass on to a fourth and last hypothesis. Every individual here enjoys the widest extent of liberty; inequality is rare, or, at least, of a very slight character. Every one does as he likes, and scarcely differs in power from his neighbor. But then here scarcely such a thing is known as a general interest; here exist but few public ideas; hardly any public feeling; but little society: in short, the life and faculties of individuals are put forth and spent in an isolated state, with but little regard to society, and with scarcely a sentiment of its influence. Men here exercise no influence upon one another; they leave no traces of their existence. Generation after generation pass away, leaving society just as they found it. Such is the condition of the various tribes of savages; liberty and equality dwell among them, but no touch of civilization.

I could easily multiply these hypotheses; but I presume that I have gone far enough to show what is the popular and natural signification of the word civilization.

It is evident that none of the states which I have just described will correspond with the common notion of mankind respecting this term. It seems to me that the first idea comprised in the word *civilization* (and this may be gathered from the various examples which I have placed before you) is the notion of progress, of development. It calls up within us the notion of a people advancing, of a people in a course of improvement and melioration.

Now what is this progress? What is this development? In this is the great difficulty. The etymology of the word seems sufficiently obvious—it points at once to the improvement of civil life. The first notion which strikes us in pronouncing it is the progress of society; the melioration of the social state; the carrying to higher perfection the relations between man and man. It awakens within us at once the notion of an increase of national prosperity, of a greater activity and better organization of the social relations. On one hand there is a manifest increase in the power and wellbeing of society at large; and on the other a more equitable distribution of this power and this well-being among the individuals of which society is composed.

But the word civilization has a more extensive signification than this, which seems to confine it to the mere outward, physical organization of society. Now, if this were all, the human race would be little better than the inhabitants of an ant-hill or bee-hive; a society in which nothing was sought for beyond order and well-being—in which the highest, the sole aim, would be the production of the means of life, and their equitable distribution.

But our nature at once rejects this definition as too narrow. It tells us that man is formed for a higher destiny than this. That this is not the full development of his character—that civilization comprehends something more extensive, something more complex, something superior to the perfection of social relations, of social power and well-being.

That this is so, we have not merely the evidence of our nature, and that derived from the signification which the common sense of mankind has attached to the word; but we have likewise the evidence of facts.

No one, for example, will deny that there are communities in which the social state of man is better—in which the means of life are better supplied, are more rapidly produced, are better distributed, than in others, which yet will be pronounced by the unanimous voice of mankind to be superior in point of civilization.

Take Rome, for example, in the splendid days of the republic, at the close of the second Punic war; the moment of her greatest virtues, when she was rapidly advancing to the empire of the world—when her social condition was evidently improving. Take Rome again under Augustus, at the commencement of her decline, when, to say the least, the progressive movement of society halted, when bad principles seemed ready to prevail; but is there any person who would not say that Rome was more civilized under Augustus than in the days of Fabricius or Cincinnatus?

Let us look further: let us look at France in the seventeenth and eighteenth centuries. In a merely social point of view, as respects the quantity and the distribution of wellbeing among individuals, France, in the seventeenth and eighteenth centuries, was decidedly inferior to several of the other states of Europe; to Holland and England in particular. Social activity, in these countries, was greater, increased more rapidly, and distributed its fruits more equitably among individuals. Yet consult the general opinion of mankind, and it will tell you that France in the seventeenth and eighteenth centuries was the most civilized country of Europe. Europe has not hesitated to acknowledge this fact, and evidence of its truth will be found in all the great works of European literature.

It appears evident, then, that all that we understand by this term is not comprised in the simple idea of social wellbeing and happiness; and, if we look a little deeper, we discover that, besides the progress and melioration of social life, another development is comprised in our notion of civilization: namely, the development of individual life, the development of the human mind and its faculties—the development of man himself.

It is this development which so strikingly manifested itself in France and Rome at these epochs; it is this expansion of human intelligence which gave to them so great a degree of superiority of civilization. In these countries the godlike principle which distinguishes man from the brute exhibited itself with peculiar grandeur and power; and compensated in the eyes of the world for the defects of their social system. These communities had still many social conquests to make; but they had already glorified themselves by the intellectual and moral victories they had achieved. Many of the conveniences of life were here wanting; from a considerable portion of the community were still withheld their natural rights and political privileges; but see the number of

illustrious individuals who lived and earned the applause and
approbation of their fellow-men. Here, too, literature, science, and art, attained extraordinary perfection, and shone
in more splendor than perhaps they had ever done before.
Now, wherever this takes place, wherever man sees these
glorious idols of his worship displayed in their full lustre—
wherever he sees this fund of rational and refined enjoyment for the godlike part of his nature called into existence,
there he recognizes and adores civilization.

Two elements, then, seem to be comprised in the great
fact which we call civilization;—two circumstances are necessary to its existence—it lives upon two conditions—it reveals
itself by two symptoms: the progress of society, the progress of individuals; the melioration of the social system,
and the expansion of the mind and faculties of man.
Wherever the exterior condition of man becomes enlarged,
quickened, and improved; wherever the intellectual nature
of man distinguishes itself by its energy, brilliancy, and its
grandeur; wherever these two signs concur, and they often
do so, notwithstanding the gravest imperfections in the social system, there man proclaims and applauds civilization.

Such, if I mistake not, would be the notion mankind in
general would form of civilization, from a simple and rational inquiry into the meaning of the term. This view of
it is confirmed by History. If we ask of her what has been
the character of every great crisis favorable to civilization,
if we examine those great events which all acknowledge to
have carried it forward, we shall always find one or other of
the two elements which I have just described. They have
all been epochs of individual or social improvement; events
which have either wrought a change in individual man, in
his opinions, his manners; or in his exterior condition, his
situation as regards his relations with his fellow-men. Christianity, for example: I allude not merely to the first moment
of its appearance, but to the first centuries of its existence—
Christianity was in no way addressed to the social condition
of man; it distinctly disclaimed all interference with it. It
commanded the slave to obey his master. It attacked none
of the great evils, none of the gross acts of injustice, by
which the social system of that day was disfigured; yet who
but will acknowledge that Christianity has been one of the
greatest promoters of civilization? And wherefore? Because it has changed the interior condition of man, his opinions, his sentiments: because it has regenerated his moral,
his intellectual character.

We have seen a crisis of an opposite nature; a crisis affecting not the intellectual, but the outward condition of man, which has changed and regenerated society. This also we may rest assured is a decisive crisis of civilization. If we search history through, we shall everywhere find the same result; we shall meet with no important event, which had a direct influence in the advancement of civilization, which has not exercised it in one of the two ways I have just mentioned.

Having thus, as I hope, given you a clear notion of the two elements of which civilization is composed, let us now see whether one of them alone would be sufficient to constitute it: whether either the development of the social condition, or the development of the individual man taken separately, deserves to be regarded as civilization? or whether these two events are so intimately connected, that. if they are not produced simultaneously, they are nevertheless *so intimately connected*, that, sooner or later, one uniformly produces the other?

There are three ways, as it seems to me, in which we may proceed in deciding this question. *First:* we may investigate the nature itself of the two elements of civilization, and see whether by that they are strictly and necessarily bound together. *Secondly:* we may examine historically whether, in fact, they have manifested themselves separately, or whether one has always produced the other. *Thirdly:* we may consult common sense, *i.e.*, the general opinion of mankind. Let us first address ourselves to the general opinion of mankind—to common sense.

When any great change takes place in the state of a country—when any great development of social prosperity is accomplished within it—any revolution or reform in the powers and privileges of society, this new event naturally has its adversaries. It is necessarily contested and opposed. Now what are the objections which the adversaries of such revolutions bring against them?

They assert that this progress of the social condition is attended with no advantage; that it does not improve in a corresponding degree the moral state—the intellectual powers of man; that it is a false, deceitful progress, which proves detrimental to his moral character, to the true interests of his better nature. On the other hand, this attack is repulsed with much force by the friends of the movement. They maintain that the progress of society necessarily leads to the progress of intelligence and morality; that, in proportion as the social life is better regulated, individual life becomes more refined and virtuous. Thus the question rests in abeyance between the opposers and partisans of the change.

But reverse this hypothesis; suppose the moral development in progress. What do the men who labor for it generally hope for?—What, at the origin of societies, have the founders of religion, the sages, poets, and philosophers, who have labored to regulate and refine the manners of mankind, promised themselves? What but the melioration of the social condition: the more equitable distribution of the blessings of life? What, now, let me ask, should be inferred from this dispute and from those hopes and promises? It may, I think, be fairly inferred that it is the spontaneous, intuitive conviction of mankind, that the two elements of civilization—the social and moral development—are intimaely connected; that, at the approach of one, man looks for the other. It is to this natural conviction we appeal when, to second or combat either one or the other of the two elements, we deny or attest its union with the other. We know that if men were persuaded that the melioration of the social condition would operate against the expansion of the intellect, they would almost oppose and cry out against the advancement of society. On the other hand, when we speak to mankind of improving society by improving its individual members, we find them willing to believe us, and to adopt the principle. Hence we may affirm that it is the intuitive belief of man, that these two elements of civilization are intimately connected, and that they reciprocally produce one another.

If we now examine the history of the world we shall have the same result. We shall find that every expansion of human intelligence has proved of advantage to society; and that all the great advances in the social condition have turned to the profit of humanity. One or other of these facts may predominate, may shine forth with greater splendor for a season, and impress upon the movement its own particular character. At times, it may not be till the lapse of a long interval, after a thousand transformations, a thousand obstacles, that the second shows itself, and comes, as it were, to complete the civilization which the first had begun; but when we look closely we easily recognize the link by which they are connected. The movements of Providence are not restricted to narrow bounds: it is not anxious to deduce to-day the consequence of the premises it laid down yesterday. It may defer this for ages, till the fullness of time shall come. Its logic will not be less conclusive for reasoning slowly. Providence moves through time, as the gods of Homer through space—it makes a step, and ages have rolled away! How long a time, how many circumstances intervened, before the regeneration of the moral powers of man, by Christianity, exercised its great, its legitimate influence upon his social condition? Yet who can doubt or mistake its power?

If we pass from history to the nature itself of the two facts which constitute civilization, we are infallibly led to the same result. We have all experienced this. If a man makes a mental advance, some mental discovery, if he acquires some new idea, or some new faculty, what is the desire that takes possession of him at the very moment he makes it? It is the desire to promulgate his sentiment to the exterior world—to publish and realize his thought. When a man acqures a new truth—when his being in his own eyes has made an advance, has acquired a new gift, immediately there becomes joined to this acquirement the notion of a mission. He feels obliged, impelled, as it were, by a secret interest, to extend, to carry out of himself the change, the melioration which has been accomplished within him. To what, but this, do we owe the exertions of great reformers? The exertions of those great benefactors of the human race, who have changed the face of the world, after having first been changed themselves, have been stimulated and governed by no other impulse than thus.

So much for the change which takes place in the intellectual man. Let us now consider him in a social state. A revolution is made in the condition of society. Rights and property are more equitably distributed among individuals: this is as much as to say, the appearance of the world is purer—is more beautiful. The state of things, both as respects governments, and as respects men in their relations with each other, is improved. And can there be a question whether the sight of this goodly spectacle, whether the melioration of this external condition of man, will have a corresponding influence upon his moral, his individual character—upon humanity? Such a doubt would belie all that is said of the authority of example and of the power of habit, which is founded upon nothing but the conviction that exterior facts and circumstances, if good, reasonable, well-regulated, are followed, sooner or later, more or less completely, by intellectual results of the same nature, of the same beauty: that a world better governed, better regulated, a world in which justice more fully prevails, renders man himself more just. That the intellectual man then is instructed and improved by the superior condition of society and his social condition, his external well-being, meliorated and refined by increase of intelligence in individuals: that the two elements of civilization are strictly connected: that ages, that obstacles of all kinds, may interpose between them—that it is possible they may undergo a thousand transformations before they meet together; but that sooner or later this union will take place is certain; for it is a law of their nature that they should do so—the great facts of history bear witness that such is really the case—the instinctive belief of man proclaims the same truth.

Thus, though I have not by a great deal advanced all that might be said upon this subject, I trust I have given a tolerably correct and adequate notion, in the foregoing cursory account, of what civilization is, of what are its offices, and what its importance. I might here quit the subject; but I cannot part with it, without placing before you another question, which here naturally presents itself—a question not purely historical, but rather, I will not say hypothetical, but conjectural; a question which we can see here but in part; but which, however, is not less real, but presses itself upon our notice at every turn of thought.

Of the two developments, of which we have just now spoken, and which together constitute civilization—of the development of society on one part, and of the expansion of human intelligence on the other—which is the end? which are the means? Is it for the improvement of the social condition, for the melioration of his existence upon the earth, that man fully developes himself, his mind, his faculties, his sentiments, his ideas, his whole being? Or is the melioration of the social condition, the progress of society—is indeed society itself merely the theatre, the occasion, the motive and excitement for the development of the individual? In a word, is society formed for the individual, or the individual for society? Upon the reply to this question depends our knowledge of whether the destiny of man is purely social, whether society exhausts and absorbs the entire man, or whether he bears within him something foreign, something superior to his existence in this world?

One of the greatest philosophers and most distinguished men of the present age, whose words become indelibly engraved upon whatever spot they fall, has resolved this question; he has resolved it, at least, according to his own conviction. The following are his words: "Human societies are born, live, and die, upon the earth; there they accomplish their destinies. But they contain not the whole man. After his engagement to society there still remains in him the more noble part of his nature; those high faculties by which he elevates himself to God, to a future life, and to the unknown blessings of an invisible world. We, individuals, each with a separate and distinct existence, with an identical person, we, truly beings endowed with immortality, we have a higher destiny than that of states."

I shall add nothing on this subject; it is not my province to handle it; it is enough for me to have placed it before you. It haunts us again at the close of the history of civilization. Where the history of civilization ends, when there is no more to be said of the present life, man invincibly demands if all is over—if that be the end of all things? This, then, is the last problem, and the grandest, to which the history of civilization can lead us. It is sufficient that I have marked its place, and its sublime character.

From the foregoing remarks, it becomes evident that the history of civilization may be considered from two different points of view—may be drawn from two different sources. The historian may take up his abode during the time prescribed, say a series of centuries, in the human soul, or with some particular nation. He may study, describe, relate, all the circumstances, all the transformations, all the revolutions, which may have taken place in the intellectual man; and when he had done this he would have a history of the civilization among the people, or during the period which he had chosen. He might proceed differently: instead of entering into the interior of man, he might take his stand in the external world. He might take his station in the midst of the great theatre of life; instead of describing the change of ideas, of the sentiments of the individual being, he might describe his exterior circumstances, the events, the revolutions of his social condition. These two portions, these two histories of civilization, are strictly connected with each

other; they are the counterpart, the reflected image of one
another. They may, however, be separated. Perhaps it is
necessary, at least in the beginning, in order to be exposed
in detail and with clearness, that they should be. For my
part I have no intention, upon the present occasion, to
enter upon the history of civilization in the human mind;
the history of the exterior events of the visible and social world
is that to which I shall call your attention. It would give
me pleasure to be able to display before you the phenomenon of civilization in the way I understand it, in all its bearings, in its widest extent—to place before you all the vast
questions to which it gives rise. But, for the present, I
must restrain my wishes; I must confine myself to a narrower field: it is only the history of the social state that I
shall attempt to narrate.

My first object will be to seek out the elements of European civilization at the time of its birth, at the fall of the
Roman empire—to examine carefully society such as it was
in the midst of these famous ruins. I shall endeavor to pick
out these elements, and to place them before you, side by
side; I shall endeavor to put them in motion, and to follow
them in their progress through the fifteen centuries which
have rolled away since that epoch.

We shall not, I think, proceed far in this study, without
being convinced that civilization is still in its infancy. How
distant is the human mind from the perfection to which it
may attain—from the perfection for which it was created!
How incapable are we of grasping the whole future destiny
of man! Let any one even descend into his own mind—let
him picture there the highest point of perfection to which
man, to which society may attain, that he can conceive, that
he can hope;—let him then contrast this picture with the
present state of the world, and he will feel assured that society and civilization are still in their childhood: that however
great the distance they have advanced, that which they have
before them is incomparably, is infinitely greater. This,
however, should not lessen the pleasure with which we contemplate our present condition. When you have run over
with me the great epochs of civilization during the last fifteen centuries, you will see, up to our time, how painful, how
stormy, has been the condition of man; how hard has been
his lot, not only outwardly as regards society, but internally,
as regards the intellectual man. For fifteen centuries the
human mind has suffered as much as the human race. You
will see that it is only lately that the human mind, perhaps

for the first time, has arrived, imperfect though its condition still be, to a state where some peace, some harmony, some freedom is found. The same holds with regard to society— its immense progress is evident—the condition of man, compared with what it has been, is easy and just. In thinking of our ancestors we may almost apply to ourselves the verses of Lucretius:

> "Suave mari magno, turbantibus æquora ventis,
> E terrà magnum alterius spectare laborem."

Without any great degree of pride we may, as Sthenelas is made to do in Homer, Ημεις τοὶ πατὲρων μεγ' ἀμεινονες ευχομεθ' ειναν, "Return thanks to God that we are infinitely better than our fathers."

We must, however, take care not to deliver ourselves up too fully to a notion of our happiness and our improved condition. It may lead us into two serious evils, pride and inactivity;—it may give us an overweening confidence in the power and success of the human mind, of its present attainments; and, at the same time, dispose us to apathy, enervated by the agreeableness of our condition. I know not if this strikes you as it does me, but in my judgment we continually oscillate between an inclination to complain without sufficient cause, and to be too easily satisfied. We have an extreme susceptibility of mind, an inordinate craving, an ambition in our thoughts, in our desires, and in the movements of our imagination; yet when we come to practical life— when trouble, when sacrifices, when efforts are required for the attainment of our object, we sink into lassitude and inactivity. We are discouraged almost as easily as we had been excited. Let us not, however, suffer ourselves to be invaded by either of these vices. Let us estimate fairly what our abilities, our knowledge, our power enable us to do lawfully; and let us aim at nothing that we cannot lawfully, justly, prudently—with a proper respect to the great principles upon which our social system, our civilization is based —attain. The age of barbarian Europe, with its brute force, its violence, its lies and deceit—the habitual practice under which Europe groaned during four or five centuries are passed away for ever, and has given place to a better order of things. We trust that the time now approaches when man's condition shall be progressively improved by the force of reason and truth, when the brute part of nature shall be crushed, that the godlike spirit may unfold. In the meantime let us be cautious that no vague desires, that no extravagant theories, the time for which may not yet be come, carry us beyond the bounds of prudence, or beget in us a discontent with our present state. To us much has been given, of us much will be required. Posterity will demand a strict account of our conduct—the public, the government, *all* is now open to discussion, to examination. Let us then attach ourselves firmly to the principles of our civilization, to justice, to the laws, to liberty: and never forget, that, if we have the right to demand that all things shall be laid open before us, and judged by us, we likewise are before the world, who will examine us, and judge us according to our works.

LECTURE II.

OF EUROPEAN CIVILIZATION IN PARTICULAR: ITS DISTINGUISHING CHARACTERISTICS—ITS SUPERIORITY—ITS ELEMENTS.

In the preceding lecture, I endeavored to give an explanation of civilization in general. Without referring to any civilization in particular, or to circumstances of time and place, I essayed to place it before you in a point of view purely philosophical. I purpose now to enter upon the History of the Civilization of Europe; but before doing so, before going into its proper history, I must make you acquainted with the peculiar character of this civilization—with its distinguishing features, so that you may be able to recognize and distinguish European civilization from every other.

When we look at the civilizations which have preceded that of modern Europe, whether in Asia or elsewhere, including even those of Greece and Rome, it is impossible not to be struck with the unity of character which reigns among them. Each appears as though it had emanated from a single fact, from a single idea. One might almost assert that society was under the influence of one single principle, which universally prevailed and determined the character of its institutions, its manners, its opinions—in a word, all its developments.

In Egypt, for example, it was the theocratic principle that took possession of society, and showed itself in its manners, in its monuments, and in all that has come down to us of Egyptian civilization. In India the same phenomenon occurs—it is still a repetition of the almost exclusively prevailing influence of theocracy. In other regions a different organization may be observed—perhaps the domination of a conquering caste: and where such is the case, the principle of force takes entire possession of society, imposing upon it its laws and its character. In another place, perhaps, we discover society under the entire influence of the democratic principle; such was the case in the commercial republics which covered the coasts of Asia Minor and Syria—in

Ionia and Phœnicia. In a word, whenever we contemplate the civilizations of the ancients, we find them all impressed with one ever-prevailing character of unity, visible in their institutions, their ideas, and manners—one sole, or at least one very preponderating influence, seems to govern and determine all things.

I do not mean to aver that this overpowering influence of one single principle, of one single form, prevailed without any exception in the civilization of those states. If we go back to their earliest history, we shall find that the various powers which dwelt in the bosom of the societies frequently struggled for mastery. Thus among the Egyptians, the Etruscans, even among the Greeks and others, we may observe the warrior caste struggling against that of the priests. In other places we find the spirit of clanship stuggling against the spirit of free association, the spirit of aristocracy against popular rights. These struggles, however, mostly took place in periods beyond the reach of history, and no evidence of them it left beyond a vague tradition.

Sometimes, indeed, these early struggles broke out afresh at a later period in the history of the nations; but in almost every case they were quickly terminated by the victory of one of the powers which sought to prevail, and which then took sole possession of society. The war always ended by the domination of some special principle, which, if not exclusive, at least greatly predonderated. The co-existence and strife of various principles among these nations were no more than a passing, an accidental circumstance.

From this cause a remarkable unity characterizes most of the civilizations of antiquity, the results of which, however, were very different. In one nation, as in Greece, the unity of the social principle led to a development of wonderful rapidity; no other people ever ran so brilliant a career in so short a time. But Greece had hardly become glorious, before she appeared worn out: her decline, if not quite so rapid as her rise, was strangely sudden. It seems as if the principle which called Greek civilization into life was exhausted. No other came to invigorate it, or supply its place.

In other states, say, for example, in India and Egypt, where again only one principle of civilization prevailed, the result was different. Society here became stationary; simplicity produced monotomy; the country was not destroyed; society continued to exist; but there was no progression; it remained torpid and inactive.

To this same cause must be attributed that character of tyranny which prevailed, under various names, and the most opposite forms, in all the civilizations of antiquity. Society belonged to one *exclusive* power, which could bear with no other. Every principle of a different tendency was proscribed. The governing principle would nowhere suffer by its side the manifestation and influence of a rival principle.

This character of simplicity, of unity, in their civilization, is equally impressed upon their literature and intellectual productions. Who that has run over the monuments of Hindoo literature lately introduced into Europe, but has seen that they are all struck from the same die? They all seem the result of one same fact; the expression of one same idea. Religious and moral treatises, historical traditions, dramatic poetry, epics, all bear the same physiognomy. The same character of unity and monotony shines out in these works of mind and fancy, as we discover in their life and institutions. Even in Greece, notwithstanding the immense stores of knowledge and intellect which it poured forth, a wonderful unity still prevailed in all relating to literature and the arts.

How different to all this is the case as respects the civilization of modern Europe! Take ever so rapid a glance at this, and it strikes you at once as diversified, confused, and stormy. All the principles of social organization are found existing together within it; powers temporal, powers spiritual, the theocratic, monarchic, aristocratic, and democratic elements, all classes of society, all the social situations, are jumbled together, and visible within it; as well as infinite gradations of liberty, of wealth, and of influence. These various powers, too, are found here in a state of continual struggle among themselves, without any one having sufficient force to master the others, and take sole possession of society. Among the ancients, at every great epoch, all communities seem cast in the same mould: it was now pure monarchy, now theocracy or democracy, that became the reigning principle, each in its turn reigning absolutely. But modern Europe contains examples of all these systems, of all the attempts at social organization; pure and mixed monarchies, theocracies, republics more or less aristocratic, all live in common, side by side, at one and the same time; yet, notwithstanding their diversity, they all bear a certan resemblance to each other, a kind of family likeness which it is impossible to mistake, and which shows them to be essentially European.

In the moral character, in the notions and sentiments of Europe, we find the same variety, the same struggle. Theocratical opinions, monarchical opinions, aristocratic opinions, democratic opinions, cross and jostle, struggle, become interwoven, limit, and modify each other. Open the boldest treatises of the middle age: in none of them is an opinion carried to its final consequences. The advocates of absolute power clinch, almost unconsciously, from the results to which their doctrine would carry them. We see that the ideas and influences around them frighten them from pushing it to its uttermost point. Democracy felt the same control. That imperturable boldness, so striking in ancient civilizations, nowhere found a place in the European system. In sentiments we discover the same contrasts, the same variety; an indomitable taste for independence dwelling by the side of the greatest aptness for submission; a singular fidelity between man and man, and at the same time an imperious desire in each to do his own will, to shake off all restraint, to live alone, without troubling himself with the rest of the world. Minds were as much diversified as society.

The same characteristic is observable in literature. It cannot be denied that in what relates to the form and beauty of art, modern Europe is very inferior to antiquity; but if we look at her literature as regards depth of feeling and ideas, it will be found more powerful and rich. The human mind has been employed upon a greater number of objects, its labors have been more diversified, it has gone to a greater depth. Its imperfection in form is owing to this very cause. The more plenteous and rich the materials, the greater is the difficulty of forcing them into a pure and simple form. That which gives beauty to a composition, that which in works of art we call form, is the clearness, the simplicity, the symbolical unity of the work. With the prodigious diversity of ideas and sentiments which belong to European civilization, the difficulty to attain this grand and chaste simplicity has been increased.

In every part, then, we find this character of variety to prevail in modern civilization It has undoubtedly brought with it this inconvenience, that when we consider separately any particular development of the human mind in literature, in the arts, in any of the ways in which human intelligence may go forward, we shall generally find it inferior to the corresponding development in the civilization of antiquity;

but, as a set-off to this, when we regard it as a whole, European civilization appears incomparably more rich and diversified: if each particular fruit has not attained the same perfection, it has ripened an infinitely greater variety. Again, European civilization has now endured fifteen centuries, and in all that time it has been in a state of progression. It may be true that it has not advanced so rapidly as the Greek; but, catching new impulses at every step, it is still advancing. An unbounded career is open before it; and from day to day it presses forward to the race with increasing rapidity, because increased freedom attends upon all its movements. While in other civilizations the exclusive domination, or at least the excessive preponderance of a single principle, of a single form, led to tyranny, in modern Europe the diversity of the elements of social order, the incapability of any one to exclude the rest, gave birth to the liberty which now prevails. The inability of the various principles to exterminate one another compelled each to endure the others, made it necessary for them to live in common, for them to enter into a sort of mutual understanding. Each consented to have only that part of civilizaion which fell to its share. Thus, while everywhere else the predominance of one principle has produced tyranny, the variety of elements of European civilization, and the constant warfare in which they have been engaged, have given birth in Europe to that liberty which we prize so dearly.

It is this which gives to European civilization its real, its immense superiority—it is this which forms its essential, its distinctive character. And if, carrying our views still further, we penetrate beyond the surface into the very nature of things we shall find that this superiority is legitimate—that it is acknowledged by reason as well as proclaimed by facts. Quitting for a moment European civilization, and taking a glance at the world in general, at the common course of earthly things, what is the character we find it to bear? What do we here perceive? Why just that very same diversity, that very same variety of elements, that very same struggle which is so strikingly evinced in European civilization. It is plain enough that no single principle, no particular organization, no simple idea, no special power has ever been permitted to obtain possession of the world, to mould it into a durable form, and to drive from it every opposing tendency, so as to reign itself supreme. Various powers, principles, and systems here intermingle, modify one another, and struggle incessantly—now subduing, now subdued—never wholly conquered, never conquering. Such is apparently the general state of the world, while diversity of forms, of ideas, of principles, their struggles and their energies, all tend toward a certain unity, a certain ideal, which, though perhaps it may never be attained, mankind is constantly approaching by dint of liberty and labor. Hence European civilization is the reflected image of the world—like the course of earthly things, it is neither narrowly circumscribed, exclusive, nor stationary. For the first time, civilization appears to have divested itself of its special character; its development presents itself for the first time under as diversified, as abundant, as laborious an aspect as the great theatre of the universe itself.

European civilization has, if I may be allowed the expression, at last penetrated into the ways of eternal truth—into the scheme of Providence;—it moves in the ways which God has prescribed. This is the rational principle of its superiority.

Let it not, I beseech you, be forgotten—bear in mind, as we proceed with these lectures, that it is in this diversity of elements, and their constant struggle, that the essential character of our civilization consists. At present I can do no more than assert this; its proof will be found in the facts I shall bring before you. Still I think you will acknowledge it to be a confirmation of this assertion, if I can show you that the causes, and the elements of the character which I have just attributed to it, can be traced to the very cradle of our civilization. If, I say, at the very moment of her birth, at the very hour in which the Roman empire fell, I can show you, in the state of the world, the circumstances which, from the beginning, have concurred to give to European civilization that agitated and diversified, but at the same time prolific character which distinguishes it, I think I shall have a strong claim upon your assent to its truth. In order to accomplish this, I shall begin by investigating the condition of Europe at the fall of the Roman empire, so that we may discover in its institutions, in its opinions, its ideas, its sentiments, what were the elements which the ancient world bequeathed to the modern. And upon these elements you will see strongly impressed the character which I have just described.

It is necessary that we should first see what the Roman empire was, and how it was formed.

Rome in its origin was a mere municipality, a corporation. The Roman government was nothing more than an assemblage of institutions suitable to a population enclosed within the walls of a city; that is to say, they were *municipal* institutions;—this was their distinctive character.

This was not peculiar to Rome. If we look, in this period, at the part of Italy, which surrounded Rome we find nothing but cities. What were then called nations were nothing more than confederations of cities. The Latin nation was a confederation of Latin cities. The Etrurians, the Samnites, the Sabines, the nations of Magna Græcia, were all composed in the same way.

At this time there were no country places, no villages; at least the country was nothing like what it is in the present day. It was cultivated, no doubt, but it was not peopled. The proprietors of lands and of country estates dwelt in cities; they left these occasionally to visit their rural property, where they usually kept a certain number of slaves; but that which we now call the country, that scattered population, sometimes in lone houses, sometimes in hamlets and villages, and which everywhere dots our land with agricultural dwellings, was altogether unknown in ancient Italy.

And what was the case when Rome extended her boundaries? If we follow her history, we shall find that she conquered or founded a host of cities. It was with cities she fought, it was with cities she treated, it was into cities she sent colonies. In short, the history of the conquest of the world by Rome is the history of the conquest and foundation of a vast number of cities. It is true that in the East the extension of the Roman dominion bore somewhat of a different character; the population was not distributed there in the same way as in the western world; it was under a social system, partaking more of the patriarchal form, and was consequently much less concentrated in cities. But, as we have only to do with the population of Europe, I shall not dwell upon what relates to that of the East.

Confining ourselves, then, to the West, we shall find the fact to be such as I have described it. In the Gauls, in Spain, we meet with nothing but cities. At any distance from these, the country consisted of marshes and forests. Examine the character of the monuments left us of ancient Rome—the old Roman roads. We find great roads extending from city to city; but the thousands of little by-paths, which now intersect every part of the country, were then unknown. Neither do we find any traces of that immense number of lesser objects—of churches, castles, country-seats, and villages, which were spread all over the country during the middle ages. Rome has left no traces of this kind; her only bequest consists of vast monuments impressed with a municipal character, destined for a numerous population, crowded into a single spot. In whatever point of view you consider the Roman world, you meet with this almost exclusive preponderance of cities, and an absence of country populations and dwellings. This municipal character of the Roman world evidently rendered the unity, the social tie of a great state, extremely difficult to establish and maintain.

A municipal corporation like Rome might be able to conquer the world, but it was a much more difficult task to govern it, to mould it into one compact body. Thus, when the work seemed done, when all the West, and a great part of the East, had submitted to the Roman yoke, we find an immense host of cities, of little states formed for separate existence and independence, breaking their chains, escaping on every side. This was one of the causes which made the establishment of the empire necessary; which called for a more concentrated form of government, one better able to hold together elements which had so few points of cohesion. The empire endeavored to unite and to bind together this extensive and scattered society; and to a certain point it succeeded. Between the reigns of Augustus and Dioclesian, during the very time that her admirable civil legislation was being carried to perfection, that vast and despotic administration was established, which, spreading over the empire a sort of chain-work of functionaries subordinately arranged, firmly knit together the people and the imperial court, serving at the same time to convey to society the will of the government, and to bring to the government the tribute and obedience of society.

This system, besides rallying the forces, and holding together the elements, of the Roman world, introduced with wonderful celerity into society a taste for despotism, for central power. It is truly astonishing to see how rapidly this incoherent assemblage of little republics, this association of municipal corporations, sunk into an humble and obedient respect for the sacred name of emperor. The necessity for establishing some tie between all these parts of the Roman world must have been very apparent and powerful, otherwise we can hardly conceive how the spirit of despotism could so easily have made its way into the minds and almost into the affections of the people.

It was with this spirit, with this administrative organization, and with the military system connected with it, that the Roman empire struggled against the dissolution which was working within it, and against the barbarian who attacked it from without. But, though it struggled long, the day at length arrived when all the skill and power of despotism, when all the pliancy of servitude, was insufficient to prolong its fate. In the fourth century, all the ties which had held this immense body together seem to have been loosened or snapped; the barbarians broke in on every side; the province no longer resisted, no longer troubled themselves with the general destiny. At this crisis an extraordinary idea entered the minds of one or two of the emperors: they wished to try whether the hope of general liberty, whether a confederation, a system something like what we now call the representative system, would not better defend the Roman empire than the despotic administration which already existed. There is a mandate of Honorius and the younger Theodosius, addressed, in the year 418, to the prefect of Gaul, the object of which was to establish a sort of representative government in the south of Gaul, and by its aid still to preserve the unity of empire.

Rescript of the Emperors Honorius and Theodosius the Younger, addressed, in the year 418, to the Prefect of the Gauls, residing at Arles.

"Honorius and Theodosius, Augusti, to Agricoli, Prefect of the Gauls.

"In consequence of the very salutary representation which your Magnificence has made to us, as well as upon other information obviously advantageous to the republic, we decree, in order that they may have the force of a perpetual law, that the following regulations should be made, and that obedience should be paid to them by the inhabitants of our seven provinces, and which are such as they themselves should wish for and require. Seeing that from motives, both of public and private utility, responsible persons of special deputies should be sent, not only by each province, but by each city, to your Magnificence, not only to render up accounts, but also to treat of such matters as concern the interest of landed proprietors, we have judged that it would be both convenient and highly advanantageous to have annually, at a fixed period, and to date from the present year, an assembly for the inhabitants of the seven provinces held in the Metropolis, that is to say, in the city of Arles. By this institution our desire is to provide both for public and private interests. First, by the union of the most influential inhabitants in the presence of their illustrious Prefect, (unless he should be absent from causes affecting public order,) and by their deliberations, upon every subject brought before them, the best possible advice will be obtained. Nothing which shall have been treated of and determined upon, after a mature discussion, shall be kept from the knowledge of the rest of the provinces; and such as have not assisted at the assembly shall be bound to follow the same rules of justice and equity. Furthermore, by ordaining that an assembly should be held every year in the city of Constantine, we believe that we are doing not only what will be advantageous to the public welfare, but what will also multiply its social relations. Indeed, this city is so favorably situated, foreigners resort to it in such large numbers, and it possesses so extensive a commerce, that all the varied productions and manufactures of the rest of the world are to be seen within it. All that the opulent East, the perfumed Arabia, the delicate Assyria, the fertile Africa, the beautiful Spain, and the courageous Gaul, produce worthy of note, abound here in such profusion, that all things admired as magnificent in the different parts of the world seem the productions of its own climate. Further, the union of the Rhone and the Tuscan sea so facilitate intercourse, that the countries which the former traverses, and the latter waters in its winding course, are made almost neighbors. Thus, as the whole earth yields up its most esteemed productions for the service of this city, as the particular commodities of each country are transported to it by land, by sea, by rivers, by ships, by rafts, by wagons, how can our Gaul fail of seeing the great benefit we confer upon it by convoking a public assembly to be held in this city, upon which, by a special gift, as it were, of Divine Providence, has been showered all the enjoyments of life, and all the facilities for commerce?

"The illustrious Prefect Petronius did, some time ago, with a praiseworthy and enlightened view, ordain that this custom should be observed; but as its practice was interrupted by the troubles of the times and the reign of usurpers, we have resolved to put it again in force, by the prudent exercise of our authority. Thus, then, dear and wellbeloved cousin Agricoli, your Magnificence, conforming to our present ordinance and the custom established by your predecessors, will cause the following regulations to be observed in the provinces:—

"It will be necessary to make known unto all persons honored with public functions or proprietors of domains, and to all the judges of provinces, that they must attend in council every year in the city of Arles, between the Ides of August and September, the days of convocation and of session to be fixed at pleasure.

"Novempopulana and the second Aquitaine, being the most distant provinces, shall have the power, according to custom, to send, if their judges should be detained by indispensable duties, deputies in their stead.

"Such persons as neglect to attend at the place appointed, and within the prescribed period, shall pay a fine: viz., judges, five pounds of gold; members of the curiæ and other dignitaries, three pounds.

"By this measure we conceive we are granting great advantages and favor to the inhabitants of our provinces. We have also the certainty of adding to the welfare of the city of Arles, to the fidelity of which, according to our father and countryman, we owe so much.

"Given the 15th of the calends of May; received at Arles the 10th of the calends of June."

Notwithstanding this call, the provinces and cities refused the proffered boon; nobody would name deputies, none would go to Arles. This centralization, this unity, was opposed to the primitive nature of this society. The spirit of locality, and of municipality, everywhere reappeared; the impossibility of reconstructing a general society, of building up the whole into one general state, became evident. The cities, confining themselves to the affairs of their own corporations, shut themselves up within their own walls, and the empire fell, because none would belong to the empire; because citizens wished but to belong to their city. Thus the Roman empire, at its fall, was resolved into the elements of which it had been composed, and the preponderance of municipal rule and government was again everywhere visible. The Roman world had been formed of cities, and to cities again it returned.

This municipal system was the bequest of the ancient Roman civiliation to modern Europe. It had no doubt become feeble, irregular, and very inferior to what it had been at an earlier period; but it was the only living principle, the only one that retained any form, the only one that survived the general destruction of the Roman world.

When I say the *only* one, I mistake. There was another phenomenon, another idea, whch likewise outlived it. I mean the remembrance of the empire, and the title of the emperor—the idea of imperial majesty, and of absolute power attached to the name of emperor. It must be observed, then, that the two elements which passed from the Roman civilization into ours were, *first*, the system of municipal corporations, its habits, its regulations, its principle of liberty—a general civil legislation, common to all; *secondly*, the idea of absolute power;—the principle of order and the principle of servitude.

Meanwhile, within the very heart of Roman society, there had grown up another society of a very different nature, founded upon different principles, animated by different sentiments, and which has brought into European civilization elements of a widely different character: I speak of the *Christian Church*. I say the Christian Church, and not Christianity, between which a broad distinction is to be made. At the end of the fourth century, and the beginning of the fifth, Christianity was no longer a simple belief, it was an institution—it had formed itself into a corporate body. It had its government, a body of priests; a settled ecclesiastical polity for the regulation of their different functions; revenues; independent means of influence. It had the rallying points suitable to a great society, in its provincial, national, and general councils, in which were wont to be debated in common the affairs of society. In a word, the Christian religion, at this epoch, was no longer merely a religion, it was a church.

Had it not been a church, it is hard to say what would have been its fate in the general convulsion which attended the overthrow of the Roman empire. Looking only to worldly means, putting out of the question the aids and superintending power of Divine Providence, and considering only the natural effects of natural causes, it would be difficult to say how Christianity, if it had continued what it was at first, a mere belief, an individual conviction, could have withstood the shock occasioned by the dissolution of the Roman empire and the invasion of the barbarians. At a later period, when it had even become an institution, an established church, it fell in Asia and the North of Africa, upon an invasion of a like kind—that of the Mohammedans; and circumstances seem to point out that it was still more likely such would have been its fate at the fall of the Roman empire. At this time there existed none of those means by which in the present day moral influences become established or rejected without the aid of institutions; none of those means by which an abstract truth now makes way, gains an authority over mankind, governs their actions, and directs their movements. Nothing of this kind existed in the fourth century; nothing which could give to simple ideas, to personal opinions, so much weight and power. Hence I think it may be assumed, that only a society firmly established, under a powerful government and rules of discipline, could hope to bear up amid such disasters—could hope to weather so violent a storm. I think, then, humanly speaking, that it is not too much to aver, that in the fourth and fifth centuries it was the Christian Church that saved Christianity; that it was the Christian Church, with its institutions, its magistrates, its authority—the Christian Church, which struggled so vigorously to prevent the interior dissolution of the empire, which struggled against the barbarian, and which, in fact, overcame the barbarian;—it was this Church, I say, that became the great connecting link—the principle of civilization between the Roman and the barbarian world. It is *the state* of the Church, then, rather than religion strictly understood—rather than that pure and simple faith of the Gospel which all true believers must regard as its highest triumph—that we must look at in the fifth century, in order to discover what influence Christianity had from this time upon modern civilization, and what are the elements it has introduced into it.

Let us see what at this epoch the Christian Church really was.

If we look, still in an entirely worldly point of view—if we look at the changes which Christianity underwent from its first rise to the fifth century—if we examine it (still, I repeat, not in a religious, but solely in a political sense) we shall find that it passed through three essentially different states.

In infancy, in its very babyhood, Christian society presents itself before us as a simple association of men possessing the same faith and opinions, the same sentiments and feelings. The first Christians met to enjoy together their common emotions, their common religious convictions. At this time we find no settled form of doctrine, no settled rules of discipline, no body of magistrates.

Still, it is perfectly obvious, that no society, however young, however feebly held together, or whatever its nature, can exist without some moral power which animates and guides it; and thus, in the various Christian congregations, there were men who preached, who taught, who *morally governed* the congregation. Still there was no settled magistrate, no discipline; a simple association of believers in a common faith, with common sentiments and feelings, was the first condition of Christian society.

But the moment this society began to advance, and almost at its birth, for we find traces of them in its earliest documents, there gradually became moulded a form of doctrine, rules of discipline, a body of magistrates: of magistrates called πρεσβύτεροι, or *elders*, who afterward became priests; of ἐπίσκοποι, inspectors or overseers, who became bishops; and of διάκονοι, or deacons, whose office was the care of the poor and the distribution of alms.

It is almost impossible to determine the precise functions of these magistrates; the line of demarcation was probably very vague and wavering; yet here was the embryo of institutions. Still, however, there was one prevailing character in this second epoch: it was that the power, the authority, the preponderating influence, still remained in the hands of the general body of believers. It was they who decided in the election of magistrates, as well as in the adoption of rules of discipline and doctrine. No separation had as yet taken place between the Christian government and the Christian people; neither as yet existed apart from, or independently of, of the other, and it was still the great body of Christian believers who exercised the principal influence in the society.

In the third period all this was entirely changed. The clergy were separated from the people, and now formed a distinct body, with its own wealth, its own jurisdiction, its own constitution; in a word, it had its own government, and formed a complete society of itself—a society, too, provided with all the means of existence, independently of the society to which it applied itself, and over which it extended its influence. This was the third state of the Christian Church, and in this state it existed at the opening of the fifth century. The government was not yet completely separated from the people; for no such government as yet existed, and less so in religious matters than in any other; but, as respects the relation between the clergy and Christians in general, it was the clergy who governed, and governed almost without control.

But, besides the influence which the clergy derived from their spiritual functions, they possessed considerable power over society, from their having become chief magistrates in the city corporations. We have already seen, that, strictly speaking, nothing had descended from the Roman empire, except its municipal system. Now it had fallen out that by the vexations of despotism, and the ruin of the cities, the curiales, or officers of the corporations, had sunk into insignificance and inanity; while the bishops and the great body of the clergy, full of vigor and zeal, were naturally prepared to guide and watch over them. It is not fair to accuse the clergy of usurpation in this matter, for it fell out according to the common course of events: the clergy alone possessed moral strength and activity, and the clergy everywhere succeeded to power—such is the common law of the universe.

The change which had taken place in this respect shows itself in every part of the legislation of the Roman emperors at this period. In opening the Theodosian and Justinian codes, we find innumerable enactments, which place the management of the municipal affairs in the hands of the clergy and bishops. I shall cite a few.

Cod. Just., L. I., tit. iv., *De Episcopali audientia*, § 26.—With regard to the yearly affairs of the cities, (whether as respects the ordinary city revenues, the funds arising from the city estates, from legacies or particular gifts, or from any other source; whether as respects the management of the public works, of the magazines of provisions, of the aqueducts; of the maintenance of the public baths and the city gates, of the building of walls or towers, the repairing of bridges and roads, or of any lawsuit in which the city may be engaged on account of public or private interests,) we ordain as follows:—The right reverend bishop, and three men of good report, from among the chiefs of the city, shall assemble together; every year they shall examine the works done; they shall take care that those who conduct, or have conducted them, measure them correctly, give a true account of them, and cause it to be seen that they have fulfilled their contracts, whether in the care of the public monuments, in the moneys expended in provisions and the public baths, of all that is expended for the repairs of the roads, aqueducts, and all other matters.

Ibid., § 30.—With respect to the guardianship of youth, of the first and second age, and of all those to whom the law gives *curators*, if their fortune is not more than 5000 *aurei*, we ordain that the nomination of the president of the province should not be waited for, on account of the great expense it would occasion, especially if the president should not reside in the city in which it becomes necessary to provide for the guardianship. The nomination of the curators or tutors shall, in this case, be made by the magistrate of the city . . . . in concert with the right reverend bishop and other persons invested with public authority, if more than one should reside in the city.

Ibid., L. I., tit. v., *De Defensoribus*, § 8.—We desire the defenders of cities, well instructed in the holy mysteries of the orthodox faith, should be chosen and instituted into their office by the reverend bishops, the clerks, notables, proprietors, and the curiales. With regard to their installation, it must be committed to the glorious power of the prefects of the prætorium, in order that their authority should have all the stability and weight which the letters of admission granted by his Magnificence are likely to give.

I could cite numerous other laws to the same effect, and in all of them you would see this one fact very strikingly prevail: namely, that between the Roman municipal system, and that of the free cities of the middle ages, there intervened an *ecclesiastical* municipal system; the preponderance of the clergy in the management of the affairs of the city corporations succeeded to that of that of the ancient Roman municipal magistrates, and paved the way for the organization of our modern free communities.

It will at once be seen what an amazing accession of power the Christian Church gained by these means, not only in its own peculiar circle, by its increased influence on the body of Christians, but also by the part which it took in temporal matters. And it is from this period we should date its powerful co-operation in the advance of modern civilization, and the extensive influence it has had upon its character. Let us briefly run over the advantages which it introduced into it.

And, first, it was of immense advantage to European civilization that a moral influence, a moral power—a power resting entirely upon moral convictions, upon moral opinions and sentiments—should have established itself in society, just at this period, when it seemed upon the point of being crushed by the overwhelming physical force which had taken possession of it. Had not the Christian Church at this time existed, the whole world must have fallen a prey to mere brute force. The Christian Church alone possessed a moral power, it maintained and promulgated the idea of a precept, of a law superior to all human authority; it proclaimed that great truth which forms the only foundation of our hope for humanity: namely, that there exists a law above all human law, which, by whatever name it may be called, whether reason, the law of God, or what not, is, in all times and in all places, the same law under different names.

Finally, the Church commenced an undertaking of great importance to society—I mean the separation of temporal and spiritual authority. This separation is the only true source of liberty of conscience; it was based upon no other principle than that which serves as the groundwork for the strictest and most extensive liberty of conscience. The separation of temporal and spiritual power rests solely upon the idea that physical, that brute force, has no right or authority over the mind, over convictions, over truth. It flows from the distinction established between the world of thought and the world of action, between our inward and intellectual nature and the outward world around us. So that, however parodoxical it may seem, that very principle of liberty of conscience for which Europe has so long struggled, so much suffered, which has only so lately prevailed, and that, in many instances, against the will of the clergy—that very principle was acted upon under the name of a separation of the temporal and spiritual power, in the infancy of European civilization. It was, moreover, the Christian Church itself, driven to assert it by the circumstances in which it was placed, as a means of defence against barbarism, that introduced and maintained it.

The establishment, then, of a moral influence, the maintenance of this divine law, and the separation of temporal and spiritual power, may be enumerated as the great benefits which the Christian Church extended to European society in the fifth century.

Unfortunately, all its influences, even at this period, were not equally beneficial. Already, even before the close of the fifth century, we discover some of those vicious principles which have had so baneful an effect on the advancement of our civilization. There already prevailed in the bosom of the Church a desire to separate the governing and the governed. The attempt was thus early made to render the government entirely independent of the people under its authority—to take possession of their mind and life, without the conviction of their reason or the consent of their will. The Church, moreover, endeavored with all her might to establish the principle of theocracy, to usurp temporal authority, to obtain universal dominion. And when she failed in this, when she found she could not obtain absolute power for herself, she did what was almost as bad: to obtain a share of it, she leagued herself with temporal rulers and enforced, with all her might, their claim to absolute power at the expense of the liberty of the subject.

Such then, I think, were the principal elements of civilization which Europe deprived, in the fifth century, from the Church and from the Roman empire. Such was the state of the Roman world when the barbarians came to make it their prey; and we have now only to study the barbarians themselves, in order to be acquainted with the elements which were united and mixed together in the cradle of our civilization.

It must be here understood that we have nothing to do with the history of the barbarians. It is enough for our purpose to know, that with the exception of a few Slavonian tribes, such as the Alans, they were all of the same German origin: and that they were all in pretty nearly the same state of civilization. It is true that some little difference might exist in this respect, accordingly as these nations had more or less intercourse with the Roman world; and there is no doubt but the Goths had made a greater progress, and had become more refined than the Franks; but in a general point of view, and with regard to the matter before us, these little differences are of no consequence whatever.

A general notion of the state of society among the barbarians, such, at least, as will enable us to judge of what they have contributed toward modern civilization, is all that we require. This information, small as it may appear, it is now almost impossible to obtain. Respecting the municipal system of the Romans and the state of the Church we may form a tolerably accurate idea. Their influence has lasted to the present times; we have vestiges of them in many of our institutions, and possess a thousand means of becoming acquainted with them; but the manners and social state of the barbarians have completely perished, and we are driven to conjecture what they were, either from a very few ancient historical remains, or by an effort of the imagination.

There is one sentiment, one in particular, which it is neccessary to understand before we can form a true picture of a barbarian; it is the pleasure of personal independence —the pleasure of enjoying, in full force and liberty, all his powers in the various ups and downs of fortune; the fondness for activity without labor; for a life of enterprise and adventure. Such was the prevailing character and disposition of the barbarians; such were the moral wants which put these immense masses of men into motion. It is extremely difficult for us, in the regulated society in which we move, to form anything like a correct idea of this feeling, and of the influence which it exercised upon the rude barbarians of the fourth and fifth centuries. There is, however, a history of the Norman conquest of England, written by M. Thierry, in which the character and disposition of the barbarian are depicted with much life and vigor. In this admirable work, the motives, the inclinations and impulses that stir men into action in a state of life bordering on the savage, have been felt and described in a truly masterly manner. There is nowhere else to be found so correct a likeness of what a barbarian was, or of his course of life. Something of the same kind, but, in my opinion, much inferior, is found in the novels of Mr. Cooper, in which he depicts the manners of the savages of America. In these scenes, in the sentiments and social relations which these savages hold in the midst of their forests, there is unquestionably something which, to a certain point, calls up before

us the manners of the ancient Germans. No doubt these
pictures are a little imaginative, a little poetical; the worst
features in the life and manners of the barbarians are not
given in all their naked coarseness. I allude not merely to
the evils which these manners forced into the social condition, but to the inward individual condition of the barbarian
himself. There is in this passionate desire for personal
independence something of a grosser, more material character than we should suppose from the work of M. Thierry; a
degree of brutality, of headstrong passion, of apathy, which
we do not discover in his details. Still, notwithstanding
this alloy of brutal and stupid selfishness, there is, if we
look more profoundly into the matter, something of a noble
and moral character, in this taste for independence, which
seems to derive its power from our moral nature. It is the
pleasure of feeling one's self a man; the sentiment of per-
sonality; of human spontaneity in its unrestricted development.

It was the rude barbarians of Germany who introduced
this sentiment of personal independence, this love of individual liberty, into European civilization; it was unknown
among the Romans, it was unknown in the Christian Church,
it was unknown in nearly all the civilizations of antiquity.
The liberty which we meet with in ancient civilizations is
political liberty; it is the liberty of the citizen. It was not
about his personal liberty that man troubled himself, it was
about his liberty as a citizen. He formed part of an association, and to this alone he was devoted. The case was the
same in the Christian Church. Among its members a devoted
attachment to the Christian body, a devotedness to its laws,
and an earnest zeal for the extension of its empire, were
everywhere conspicuous; the spirit of Christianity wrought a
change in the moral character of man, opposed to this principle of independence; for under its influence his mind
struggled to extinguish its own liberty, and to deliver itself up
entirely to the dictates of his faith. But the feeling of personal independence, a fondness for genuine liberty displaying itself without regard to consequences, and with scarcely
any other aim than its own satisfaction—this feeling, I
repeat, was unknown to the Romans and to the Christians.
We are indebted for it to the barbarians, who introduced it
into European civilization, in which, from its first rise, it has
played so considerable a part, and has produced such lasting
and beneficial results, that it must be regarded as one of its fundamental principles, and could not be passed without notice.

There is another, a second element of civilization, which we likewise inherit from the barbarians alone: I mean military patronage, the tie which became formed between individuals, between warriors, and which, without destroying the liberty of any, without even destroying in the commencement the equality up to a certain point which existed between them, laid the foundation of a graduated subordination, and was the origin of that aristocratical organization which, at a later period, grew into the feudal system. The germ of this connexion was the attachment of man to man; the fidelity which united individuals, without apparent necessity, without any obligation arising from the general principles of society. In none of the ancient republics do you see any example of individuals particularly and freely attached to other individuals. They were all attached to the city. Among the barbarians this tie was formed between man and man; first by the relationship of companion and chief, when they came in bands to overrun Europe; and at a later period, by the relationship of sovereign and vassal. This second principle, which has had so vast an influence in the civilization of modern Europe—this devotedness of man to man—came to us entirely from our German ancestors; it formed part of their social system, and was adopted into ours.

Let me ask if I was not fully justified in stating, as I did at the outset, that modern civilization, even in its infancy, was diversified, agitated, and confused? Is it not true that we find at the fall of the Roman empire nearly all the elements which are met with in the progressive career of our civilization? We have found at this epoch three societies all different; first, municipal society, the last remains of the Roman empire; secondly, Christian society; and lastly, barbarian society. We find these societies very differently organized; founded upon principles totally opposite; inspiring men with sentiments altogether different. We find the love of the most absolute independence by the side of the devoted submission; military patronage by the side of ecclesiastical domination; spiritual power and temporal power everywhere together; the canons of the Church, the learned legislation of the Romans, the almost unwritten customs of the barbarians; everywhere a mixture or rather co-existence of nations, of languages, of social situations, of manners, of ideas, of impressions, the most diversified. These, I think, afford a sufficient proof of the truth of the general character which I have endeavored to picture of our civilization.

There is no denying that we owe to this confusion, this diversity, this tossing and jostling of elements, the slow progress of Europe, the storms by which she has been buffeted, the miseries to which ofttimes she has been a prey. But, however dear these have cost us, we must not regard them with unmingled regret. In nations, as well as in individuals, the good fortune to have all the faculties called into action, so as to ensure a full and free development of the various powers both of mind and body, is an advantage not too dearly paid for by the labor and pain with which it is attended. What we might call the hard fortune of European civilization—the trouble, the toil it has undergone—the violence it has suffered in its course—have been of infinitely more service to the progress of humanity than that tranquil, smooth simplicity, in which other civilizations have run their course. I shall now halt. In the rude sketch which I have drawn, I trust you will recognize the general features of the world such as it appeared upon the fall of the Roman empire, as well as the various elements which conspired and mingled together to give birth to European civilization. Henceforward these will move and act under our notice. We shall next put these in motion, and see how they work together. In the next lecture I shall endeavor to show what they became and what they performed in the epoch which is called the Barbarous Period; that is to say, the period during which the chaos of invasion continued.

LECTURE III.

OF POLITICAL LEGITIMACY—CO-EXISTENCE OF ALL THE SYSTEMS OF GOVERNMENT IN THE FIFTH CENTURY—ATTEMPTS TO REORGANIZE SOCIETY.

In my last lecture, I brought you to what may be called the porch to the history of modern civilization. I briefly placed before you the primary elements of European civilization, as found when, at the dissolution of the Roman empire, it was yet in its cradle. I endeavored to give you a preliminary sketch of their diversity, their continual struggles with each other, and to show you that no one of them succeeded in obtaining the mastery in our social system; at least such a mastery as would imply the complete subjugation or expulsion of the others. We have seen that these circumstances form the distinguishing character of European civilization. We will to-day begin the history of its childhood in what is commonly called the dark or middle age, the age of barbarism.

It is impossbile for us not to be struck, at the first glance at this period, with a fact which seems quite contradictory to the statement we have just made. No sooner do we seek for information respecting the opinions that have been formed relative to the ancient condition of modern Europe, than we find that the various elements of our civilization, that is to say, monarchy, theocracy, aristocracy, and democracy, each would have us believe that originally, European society belonged to it alone, and that it has only lost the power it then possessed by the usurpation of the other elements. Examine all that has been written, all that has been said on this subject, and you will find that every author who has attempted to build up a system which should represent or explain our origin, has asserted the exclusive predominance of one or other of these elements of European civilization.

First, there is the school of civilians, attached to the feudal system, among whom we may mention Boulainvilliers as the most celebrated, who boldly asserts, that, at the downfall of the Roman empire, it was the conquering nation, forming afterward the nobility, who alone possessed authority, or right, or power. Society, it is said, was their domain, of which kings and people have since despoiled them; and hence, the aristocratic organization is affirmed to have been in Europe the primitive and genuine form.

Next to this school we may place the advocates of monarchy, the Abbe Dubois, for example, who maintains, on the other side, that it was to royalty that European society belonged. According to him, the German kings succeeded to all the rights of the Roman emperors; they were even invited in by the ancient nations, among others by the Gauls and Saxons; they alone possessed legitimate authority, and all the conquests of the aristocracy were only so many encroachments upon the power of the monarchs.

The liberals, republicans, or democrats, whichever you may choose to call them, form a third school. Consult the Abbe de Mably. According to this school, the government by which society was ruled in the fifth century, was composed of free institutions; of assemblies of freedom, of the nation properly so called. Kings and nobles enriched themselves by the spoils of this primitive Liberty; it has fallen under their repeated atacks, but it reigned before them.

Another power, however, claimed the right of governing society, and upon much higher grounds than any of these. Monarchical, aristocratic, and popular pretensions were all of a worldly nature: the Church of Rome founded her pretensions upon her sacred mission and divine right. By her labors, Europe, she said, had attained the blessings of civilization and truth, and to her alone belonged the right to govern it.

Here then is a difficulty which meets us at the very outset. We have stated our belief that no one of the elements of European civilization obtained an exclusive mastery over it, in the whole course of its history, that they lived in a constant state of proximity, of amalgamation, of strife, and of compromise; yet here, at our very first step, we are met by the directly opposite opinion, that one or the other of these elements, even in the very infancy of civilization, even in the very heart of barbarian Europe, took entire possession of society. And it is not in one country alone, it is in every nation of Europe, that the various principles of our civilization, under forms a little varied, at epochs a little apart, have displayed these irreconcilable pretensions. The historic schools which I have enumerated are met with everywhere.

This fact is important, not in itself, but because it reveals some other facts which make a great figure in our history. By this simultaneous advancement of claims the most opposed to the exclusive possession of power, in the first stage of modern Europe, two important facts are revealed: first, the principle, the idea of political legitimacy; an idea which has played a considerable part in the progress of European civilization. The second is the particular, the true character of the state of barbarian Europe during that period, which now more expressly demands attention.

It is my task, then, to explain these two facts; and to show you how they may be fairly deduced from the early struggle of the pretensions which I have just called to your notice.

Now what do these various elements of our civilization—what do theocracy, monarchy, aristocracy, and democracy aim at, when they each endeavor to make out that it alone was the first which held possession of European society? Is it anything beyond the desire of each to establish its sole claim to legitimacy? For what is political legitimacy? Evidently nothing more than a right founded upon antiquity, upon duration, which is obvious from the simple fact, that priority of time is pleaded as the source of right, as proof of legitimate power. But, observe again, this claim is not peculiar to one system, to one element of our civilization, but is made alike by all. The political writers of the Continent have been in the habit, for some time past, of regarding legitimacy as belonging, exclusively, to the monarchical system. This is an error; legitimacy may be found in all the systems. It has already been shown that, of the various elements of our civilization, each wished to appropriate it to itself. But advance a few steps further into the history of Europe, and you will see social forms of government, the most opposed in principles, alike in possession of this legitimacy. The Italian and Swiss aristocracies and democracies, the little republic of San Marino, as well as the most powerful monarchies, have considered themselves legitimate, and have been acknowledged as such; all founding their claim to this title upon the antiquity of their institutions; upon the historical priority and duration of their particular system of government.

If we leave modern Europe, and turn our attention to other times and to other countries, we shall everywhere find this same notion prevail respecting political legitimacy. It everywhere attaches itself to some portion of government; to some institution; to some form, or to some maxim. There is no country, no time, in which you may not discover some portion of the social system, some public authority, that has assumed, and been acknowledged to possess, this character of legitimacy, arising from antiquity, prescription, and duration.

Let us for a moment see what this legitimacy is? of what it is composed? what it requires? and how it found its way into European civilization?

You will find that all power—I say all, without distinction—owes its existence in the first place partly to force. I do not say that force alone has been, in all cases, the foundation of power, or that this, without any other title, could in every case have been established by force alone. Other claims undoubtedly are requisite. Certain powers become established in consequence of certain social expediencies, of certain relations with the state of society, with its customs or opinions. But it is impossible to close our eyes to the fact, that violence has sullied the birth of all the authorities in the world, whatever may have been their nature or their form.

This origin, however, no one will acknowledge. All authorities, whatever their nature, disclaim it. None of them will allow themselves to be considered as the offspring of force. Governments are warned by an invincible instinct that force is no title—that might is not right—and that, while they rest upon no other foundation than violence, they are entirely destitute of right. Hence, if we go back to some distant period, in which the various systems, the various powers, are found struggling one against the other, we shall hear them each exclaiming, " I existed before you; my claim is the oldest; my claim rests upon other grounds than force; society belonged to me before this state of violence, before this strife in which you now find me. I was legitimate; I have been opposed, and my rights have been torn from me."

This fact alone proves that the idea of violence is not the foundation of political legitimacy—that it rests upon some other basis. This disavowal of violence made by every system, proclaims, as plainly as facts can speak, that there is another legitimacy, the true foundation of all the others, the legitimacy of reason, of justice, of right. It is to this origin that they seek to link themselves. As they feel scandalized at the very idea of being the offspring of force, they pretend to be invested, by virtue of their antiquity, with a different title. The first characteristic, then, of political legitimacy, is to disclaim violence as the source of authority, and to associate it with a moral notion, a moral force—with the notion of justice, of right, of reason. This is the primary element from which the principle of political legitimacy has sprung forth. It has issued from it, aided by time, aided by prescription. Let us see how.

Violence presides at the birth of governments, at the birth of societies; but time rolls on. He changes the works of violence. He corrects them. He corrects them, simply because society endures, and because it is composed of men. Man bears within himself certain notions of order, of justice, of reason, with a certain desire to bring them into play—he wishes to see them predominate in the sphere in which he moves. For this he labors unceasingly; and if the social system in which he lives, continues, his labor is not in vain. Man naturally brings reason, morality, and legitimacy into the world in which he lives.

Independently of the labor of man, by a special law of Providence which it is impossible to mistake, a law analogous to that which rules the material world, there is a certain degree of order, of intelligence, of justice, indispensable to the duration of human society. From the simple fact of its duration we may argue, that a society is not completely irrational, savage, or iniquitous; that it is not altogether destitute of intelligence, truth, and justice, for without these, society cannot hold together. Again, as society develops itself, it becomes stronger, more powerful; if the social system is continually augmented by the increase of individuals who accept and approve its regulations, it is because the action of time gradually introduces into it more right, more intelligence, more justice; it is because a gradual approximation is made in its affairs to the pinciples of true legitimacy.

Thus forces itself into the world, and from the world into the mind of man, the notion of political legitimacy. Its foundation in the first place, at least to a certain extent, is moral legitimacy—is justice, intelligence, and truth; it next obtains the sanction of time, which gives reason to believe that affairs are conducted by reason, that the true legitimacy has been introduced. At the epoch which we are about to study, you will find violence and fraud hovering over the cradle of monarchy, aristocracy, democracy, and even over the Church itself; you will see this violence and fraud everywhere gradually abated; and justice and truth taking their place in civilization. It is this introduction of justice and truth into our social system, that has nourished and gradually matured political legitimacy; and it is thus that it has taken firm root in modern civilization.

All those then who have attempted at various times to set up this idea of legitimacy as the foundation of absolute power, have wrested it from its true origin. It has nothing to do with absolute power. It is under the name of justice and righteousness that it has made its way into the world and found footing. Neither is it exclusive. It belongs to no party in partciular; it springs up in all systems where truth and justice prevail. Political legitimacy is as much attached to liberty as to power; to the rights of individuals as to the forms under which are exercised the public functions. As we go on we shall find it, as I said before, in systems the most opposed; in the feudal system; in the free cities of Flanders and Germany; in the republics of Italy, as well as in monarchy. It is a quality which appertains to all the divers elements of our civilization, and which it is necessary should be well understood before entering upon its history.

The second fact revealed to us by that simultaneous advancement of claims, of which I spoke at the beginning of this lecture, is the true character of what is called the period of barbarism. Each of the elements of European civilization pretends, that at this epoch Europe belonged to it alone; hence we may conclude that it really belonged to no one of them. When any particular kind of government prevails in the world, there is no difficulty in recognizing it. When we come to the tenth century, we acknowledge, without hesitation, the preponderance of feudalism. At the seventeenth we have no hesitation in asserting, that the monarchical principle prevails. If we turn our eyes to the free communities of Flanders, to the republics of Italy, we confess at once the predominance of democracy. Whenever, indeed, any one principle really bears sway in society, it cannot be mistaken.

The dispute, then, that has risen among the various systems which hold a part in European civilization, respecting which bore chief sway at is origin, proves that they all existed there together, without any one of them having prevailed so generally as to give society its form or its name.

This is, indeed, the character of the dark age: it was a chaos of all the elements; the childhood of all the systems; a universal jumble, in which even strife itself was neither permanent nor systematic. By an examination of the social system of this period under its various forms, I could show you that in no part of them is there to be found anything like a general principle, anything like stability. I shall, however, confine myself to two essential particulars—the state of persons, the state of institutions. This will be sufficient to give a general picture of society.

We find at this time four classes of persons: 1st, Freemen, that is to say, men who, depending upon no superior, upon no patron, held their property and life in full liberty, without being fettered by any obligation toward another individual; 2d, The *Luedes, Fideles, Antrustions*, etc., who were connected at first by the relationship of companion and chief, and afterward by that of vassal and lord, toward another individual to whom they owed fealty and service, in consequence of a grant of lands, or some other gifts; 3d, Freedmen; 4th, Slaves.

But were these various classes fixed? Were men once placed in a certain rank bound to it? Were the relations, in which the different classes stood toward each other, regular or permanent? Not at all. Freemen were continually changing their condition, and becoming vassals to nobles, in consideration of some gift which these might have to bestow; while others were falling into the class of slaves or serfs. Vassals were continually struggling to shake off the yoke of patronage, to regain their independence, to return to the class of freemen. Every part of society was in motion. There was a continual passing and repassing from one class to the other. No man continued long in the same rank; no rank continued long the same.

Property was in much the same state. I need scarcely tell you, that possessions were distinguished into *allodial*, or entirely free, and *beneficiary*, or such as were held by tenure, with certain obligations to be discharged toward a superior. Some writers attempt to trace out a regular and established system with respect to the latter class of proprietors, and lay it down as a rule that benefices were at first bestowed for a determinate number of years; that they were afterward granted for life; and finally, at a later period, became hereditary. The attempt is vain. Lands were held in all these various ways at the same time, and in the same places. Benefices for a term of years, benefices for life, hereditary benefices, are found in the same period; even the same lands, within a few years, passed through these different states. There was nothing more settled, nothing more general, in the state of lands than in the state of persons. Everything shows the difficulties of the transition from the wandering life to the settled life; from the simple personal relations which existed among the barbarians as invading migratory hordes, to the mixed relations of persons and property. During this transition all was confused, local, and disordered.

In institutions we observe the same unfixedness, the same chaos. We find here three different systems at once before us:—1st, Monarchy; 2d, Aristocracy, or the proprietorship of men and lands, as lord and vassal; and, 3dly, Free institutions, or assemblies of free men deliberating in common. No one of these systems entirely prevailed. Free institutions existed; but the men who should have formed part of these assemblies seldom troubled themselves to attend them. Baronial jurisdiction was not more regularly exercised. Monarchy, the most simple institution, the most easy to determine, here had no fixed character; at one time it was elective, at another hereditary—here the son succeeded to his father, there the election was confined to a family; in another place it was open to all, purely elective, and the choice fell on a distant relation, or perhaps a stranger. In none of these systems can we discover anything fixed; all the institutions, as well as the social conditions, dwelt together, continually confounded, continually changing.

The same unsettledness existed with regard to states; they were created, suppressed, united, and divided; no governments, no frontiers, no nations; a general jumble of situations, principles, events, races, languages; such was barbarian Europe.

Let us now fix the limits of this extraordinary period. Its origin is strongly defined; it began with the fall of the Roman empire. But where did it close? To settle this question, we must find out the cause of this state of society; we must see what were the causes of barbarism.

I think I can point out two:—one material, arising from exterior circumstances, from the course of events; the other, moral, arising from the mind, from the intellects of man.

The material, or outward cause, was the continuance of invasion; for it must not be supposed that the invasions of the barbarian hordes stopped all at once, in the fifth century. Do not believe that because the Roman empire was fallen, and kingdoms of barbarians founded upon its ruins, that the movement of nations was over. There are plenty of facts to prove that this was not the case, and that this movement lasted a long time after the destruction of the empire.

If we look to the Franks, or French, we shall find even the first race of kings continually carrying on wars beyond the Rhine. We see Clotaire, Dagobert, making expedition after expedition into Germany, and engaged in a constant struggle with the Thuringians, the Danes, and the Saxons who occupied the right bank of that river. And why was this but because these nations wished to cross the Rhine and get a share in the spoils of the empire? How came it to pass that the Franks, established in Gaul, and principally the Eastern, or Austrasian Franks, much about the same time, threw themselves in such large bodies upon Switzerland, and invaded Italy by crossing the Alps? It was because they were pushed forward by new populations from the north-east. These invasions were not mere pillaging inroads, they were not expeditions undertaken for the purpose of plunder, they were the result of necessity. The people, disturbed in their own settlements, pressed forward to better their fortune and find new abodes elsewhere. A new German nation entered upon the arena, and founded the powerful kingdom of the Lombards in Italy. In Gaul, or France, the Merovinginian dynasty gave way to the Carlovingian; a change which is now generally acknowledged to have been, properly speaking, a new irruption of Franks into Gaul—a movement of nations, which substituted the Eastern Franks for the Western. Under the second race of kings, we find Charlemagne playing the same part against the Saxons, which the Merovinginian princes played against the Thuringians: he carried on an unceasing war against the nations beyond the Rhine, who were precipitated upon the west by the Wiltzians, the Swabians, the Bohemians, and the various tribes of Slavonians, who trod on the heels of the German race. Throughout the north-east emigrations were going on and changing the face of affairs.

In the south, a movement of the same nature took place. While the German and Slavonian tribes pressed along the Rhine and Danube, the Saracens began to ravage and conquer the various coasts of the Mediterranean.

The invasion of the Saracens, however, had a character peculiarly its own. In them the spirit of conquest was united with the spirit of proselytism; the sword was drawn as well for the promulgation of a faith as the acquisition of territory. There is a vast difference between their invasion and that of the Germans. In the Christian world spiritual force and temporal force were quite distinct. The zeal for the propagation of a faith and the lust of conquest are not inmates of the same bosom. The Germans, after their conversion, preserved the same manners, the same sentiments, the same tastes, as before; they were still guided by passions and interests of a worldly nature. They had become Christians, but not missionaries. The Saracens, on the contrary, were both conquerors and missionaries. The power of the Koran and of the sword was in the same hands. And it was this peculiarity which, I think, gave to Mohammedan civilization the wretched character which it bears. It was in this union of the temporal and spiritual powers, and the confusion which it created between moral authority and physical force, that that tyranny was born which seems inherent in their civilization. This I believe to be the principal cause of that stationary state into which it has everywhere fallen. This effect, however, did not show itself upon the first rise of Mohammedanism; the union, on the contrary, of military ardor and religious zeal, gave to the Saracen invasion a prodigious power. Its ideas and moral passions had at once a brilliancy and splendor altogether wanting in the Germanic invasions; it displayed itself with more energy and enthusiasm, and had a correspondent effect upon the minds and passions of men.

Such was the situation of Europe from the fifth to the ninth century. Pressed on the south by the Mohammedans, and on the north by the Germans and Slavonians, it could not be otherwise than that the reaction of this double invasion should keep the interior of Europe in a state of continual ferment. Populations were incessantly displaced, crowded one upon another; there was no regularity, nothing permanent or fixed. Some differences undoubtedly prevailed between the various nations. The chaos was more general in Germany than in the other parts of Europe. Here was the focus of movement. France was more agitated than Italy. But nowhere could society become settled and regulated; barbarism everywhere continued, and from the same cause that introduced it.

Thus much for the material cause depending upon the course of events; let us now look to the moral cause, founded on the intellectual condition of man, which, it must be acknowledged, was not less powerful.

For, certainly, after all is said and done, whatever may be the course of external affairs, it is man himself who makes our world. It is according to the ideas, the sentiments, the moral and intellectual dispositions of man himself, that the world is regulated, and marches onward. It is upon the intellectual state of man that the visible form of society depends.

Now let us consider for a moment what is required to enable men to form themselves into a society somewhat durable, somewhat regular? It is evidently necessary, in the first place, that they should have a certain number of ideas sufficiently enlarged to settle upon the terms by which this society should be formed; to apply themselves to its wants, to its relations. In the second place, it is necessary that these ideas should be common to the greater part of the members of the society; and, finally, that they should put some constraint upon their own inclinations and actions.

It is clear that where men possess no ideas extending beyond their own existence, where their intellectual horizon is bounded in self, if they are still delivered up to their own passions, and their own wills—if they have not among them a certain number of notions and sentiments common to them all, round which they may all rally, it is clear that they cannot form a society: without this each individual will be a principle of agitation and dissolution in the social system of which he forms a part.

Wherever individualism reigns nearly absolute, wherever man considers but himself, wherever his ideas extend not beyond himself, wherever he only yields obedience to his own passions, there society—that is to say, society in any degree extended or permanent—becomes almost impossible. Now this was just the moral state of the conquerors of Europe at the epoch which engages our attention. I remarked, in the last lecture, that we owe to the Germans the powerful sentiment of personal liberty, of human individualism. Now, in a state of extreme rudeness and ignorance, this sentiment is mere selfishness, in all its brutality, with all its unsociability. Such was its character from the fifth to the eighth century, among the Germans. They cared for nothing beyond their own interest, for nothing beyond the gratification of their own passions, their own inclinations; how, then, could they accommodate themselves, in any tolerable degree, to the social condition? The attempt was made to bring them into it; they endeavored of themselves to enter into it; but an act of improvidence, a burst of passion, a lack of intelligence, soon threw them back to their old position. At every instant we see attempts made to form man into a social state, and at every instant we see them overthrown by the failings of man, by the absence of the moral conditions necessary to its existence.

Such were the two causes which kept our forefathers in a state of barbarism; so long as these continued, so long barbarism endured. Let us see if we can discover when and from what causes it at last ceased.

Europe labored to emerge from this state. It is contrary to the nature of man, even when sunk into it by his own fault, to wish to remain in it. However rude, however ignorant, however selfish, however headstrong, there is yet in him a still small voice, an instinct, which tells him he was made for something better;—that he has another and higher destiny. In the midst of confusion and disorder, he is haunted and tormented by a taste for order and improvement. The claims of justice, of prudence, of development, disturb him, even under the yoke of the most brutish egotism. He feels himself impelled to improve the material world, society, and himself; he labors to do this, without attempting to account to himself for the want which urges him to the task. The barbarians aspired to civilization, while they were yet incapable of it—nay, more—while they even detested it whenever its laws restrained their selfish desires.

There still remained, too, a considerable number of wrecks and fragments of Roman civilization. The name of the empire, the remembrance of that great and glorious society still dwelt in the memory of many, and especially among the senators of cities, bishops, priests, and all those who could trace their origin to the Roman world.

Among the barbarians themselves, or their barbarian ancestors, many had witnessed the greatness of the Roman empire: they had served in its armies; they had conquered it. The image, the name of Roman civilization dazzled them; they felt a desire to imitate it; to bring it back again, to preserve some portion of it. This was another cause which ought to have forced them out of the state of barbarism which I have described.

A third cause, and one which readily presents itself to every one, was the Christian Church. The Christian Church was a regularly constituted society; having its maxims, its rules, its discipline, together with an ardent desire to extend its influence, to conquer its conquerors. Among the Christians of this period, in the Catholic clergy, there were men of profound and varied learning; men who had thought deeply, who were versed in ethics and politics; who had formed definite opinions and vigorous notions, upon all subjects; who felt a praiseworthy zeal to propagate information, and to advance the cause of learning. No society ever made greater efforts than the Christian Church did from the fifth to the tenth century, to influence the world around it, and to assimilate it to itself. When its history shall become the particular object of our examination, we shall more clearly see what it attempted—it attacked, in a manner, barbarism at every point, in order to civilize it and rule over it.

Finally, a fourth cause of the progress of civilization, a cause which it is impossible strictly to appreciate, but which is not therefore the less real, was the appearance of great men. To say why a great man appears on the stage at a certain epoch, or what of his own individual development he imparts to the world at large, is beyond our power; it is the secret of Providence; but the fact is still certain. There are men to whom the spectacle of society, in a state of anarchy or immobility, is revolting and almost unbearable; it occasions them an intellectual shudder, as a thing that should not be; they feel an unconquerable desire to change it; to restore order; to introduce something general, regular and permanent, into the world which is placed before them. Tremendous power! often tyrannical, committing a thousand iniquities, a thousand errors, for human weakness accompanies it. Glorious and salutary power! nevertheless, for it gives to humanity, and by the hand of man, a new and powerful impulse.

These various causes, these various powers working together, led to several attempts, between the fifth and ninth centuries, to draw European society from the barbarous state into which it had fallen.

The first of these was the compilation of the barbarian laws; an attempt which, though it effected but little, we cannot pass over, because it was made by the barbarians themselves. Between the sixth and eighth centuries, the laws of nearly all the barbarous nations (which, however, were nothing more than the rude customs by which they had been regulated, before their invasion of the Roman empire) were reduced to writing. Of these there are enumerated the codes of the Burgundians, the Salii, and Ripuarian Franks, the Visigoths, the Lombards, the Saxons, the Frisons, the Bavarians, the Germans, and some others. This was evidently a commencement of civilization—an attempt to bring society under the authority of general and fixed principles. Much, however, could not be expected from it. It published the laws of a society which no longer existed; the laws of the social system of the barbarians before their establishment in the Roman territory—before they had changed their wandering life for a settled one; before the nomad warriors became lost in the landed proprietors. It is true, that here and there may be found an article respecting the lands conquered by the barbarians, or respecting their relations with the ancient inhabitants of the country; some few bold attempts were made to regulate the new circumstances in which they were placed. But the far greater part of these laws were taken up with their ancient life, their ancient condition in Germany; were totally inapplicable to the new state of society, and had but a small share in its advancement.

In Italy and the south of Gaul, another attempt of a different character was made about this time. In these places Roman society had not been so completely rooted out as elsewhere; in the cities, especially, there still remanied something of order and civil life; and in these civilization seemed to make a stand. If we look, for example, at the kingdom of the Ostrogoths in Italy under Theodoric, we shall see, even under the dominion of a barbarous nation and king, the municipal form taking breath, as it were, and exercising a considerable influence upon the general tide of events. Here Roman manners had modified the Gothic, and brought them in a great degree to assume a likeness to their own. The same thing took place in the south of Gaul. At the opening of the sixth century, Alaric, a Visigothic king of Toulouse, caused a collection of the Romans laws to be made, and published under the name of *Breviarum Aniani*, a code for his Roman subjects.

In Spain, a different power, that of the Church, endeavored to restore the work of civilization. Instead of the ancient German assemblies of warriors, the assembly that had most influence in Spain was the Council of Toledo; and in this council the bishops bore sway, although it was attended by the higher order of the laity. Open the laws of the Visigoths, and you will discover that it is not a code compiled by barbarians, but bears convincing marks of having been drawn up by the philosophers of the age —by the clergy. It abounds in general views, in theories, and in theories, indeed, altogether foreign to barbarian manners. Thus, for example, we know that the legislation of the barbarians was a personal legislation; that is to say, the same law only applied to one particular race of men. The Romans were judged by the old Roman laws, the Franks were judged by the Salian or Ripuarian code; in short, each people had its separate laws, though united under the same government, and dwelling together in the same territory. This is what is called personal legislation, in contradistinction to real legislation, which is founded upon territory. Now this is exactly the case with the legislation of the Visigoths; it is not personal, but territorial. All the inhabitants of Spain, Romans, Visigoths, or what not, were compelled to yield obedience to one law. Read a little further, and you will meet with still more striking traces of philosophy. Among the barbarians a fixed price was put upon man, according to his rank in society—the life of the barbarian, the Roman; the freeman, and vassal, were not valued at the same amount—there was a graduated scale of prices. But the principle that all men's lives are of equal worth in the eyes of the law, was established by the code of the Visigoths. The same superiority is observable in their judicial proceedings :—instead of the ordeal, the oath of compurgators, or trial by battle, you will find the proofs established by witnesses, and a rational examination made of the fact, such as might take place in a civilized society. In short, the code of the Visigoths bore throughout evident marks of learning, system, and polity. In it we trace the hand of the same clergy that acted in the Council of Toledo, and which exercised so large and beneficial an influence upon the government of the country.

In Spain then, up to the time of the great invasion of the Saracens, it was the hierarchy which made the greatest efforts to advance civilization.

In France the attempt was made by another power. It was the work of great men, and above all of Charlemagne. Examine his reign under its different aspects; and you will see that the darling object of his life was to civilize the nations he governed. Let us regard him first as a warrior. He was always in the field; from the south to the northeast, from the Ebro to the Elbe and Weser. Perhaps you imagine that these expeditions were the effect of choice, and sprung from a pure love of conquest? No such thing. I will not assert that he pursued any very regular system, or that there was much diplomacy or strategy in his plans; but what he did sprang from necessity, and a desire to repress barbarism. From the beginning to the end of his reign he was occupied in staying the progress of a double invasion—that of the Mohammedans in the south, and that of the Germanic and Slavonic tribes in the north. This is what gave the reign of Charlemagne its military cast. I have already said that his expeditions against the Saxons were undertaken for the same pupose. If we pass on from his wars to his government, we shall find the case much the same: his leading object was to introduce order and unity in every part of his extensive dominions. I have not said *kingdom* or *state*, because these words are too precise in their signification, and call up ideas which bear but little relation to the society of which Charlemagne stood at the head. Thus much, however, seems certain, that when he found himself master of this vast territory, it mortified and grieved him to see all within it so precarious and unsettled—to see anarchy and brutality everywhere prevailing—and it was the first wish of his heart to better this wretched condition of society. He endeavored to do this at first by his *missi regii*, whom he sent into every part of his dominions to find out and correct abuses; to amend the mal-administration of justice, and to render him an account of all that was wrong; and afterward by the general assemblies or parliaments as they have been called of the Champ de Mars, which he held more regularly than any of his predecessors. These assemblies he made nearly every considerable person in his dominions to attend. They were not assemblies formed for the preservation of the liberty of the subject, there was nothing in them bearing any likeness to the deliberations of our own days. But Charlemagne found them a means by which he could become well informed of facts and circumstances, and by which he could introduce some regulation, some unity, into the restless and disorganized populations he had to govern.

In whatever point of view, indeed, we regard the reign of Charlemagne, we always find its leading characteristic to be a desire to overcome barbarism, and to advance civilization. We see this conspicuously in his foundation of schools, in his collecting of libraries, in his gathering about him the learned of all countries; in the favor he showed toward the influence of the Church, for everything, in a word, which seemed likely to operate beneficially upon society in general, or the individual man.

An attempt of the same nature was made very soon afterward in England, by ALFRED THE GREAT

These are some of the means which were in operation, from the fifth to the ninth century, in various parts of Europe, which seemed likely to put an end to barbarism.

None of them succeeded. Charlemagne was unable to establish his great empire, and the system of government by which he wished to rule it. The Church succeeded no better in its attempt in Spain to found a system of theocracy. And though in Italy and the south of France, Roman civilization made several attempts to raise its head, it was not till a later period, till toward the end of the tenth century, that it in reality acquired any vigor. Up to this time, every effort to put an end to barbarism failed: they supposed men more advanced than they in reality were. They all desired, under various forms, to establish a society more extensive, or better regulated, than the spirit of the age was prepared for. The attempts, however, were not lost to mankind. At the commencement of the tenth century, there was no longer any visible appearance of the great empire of Charlemagne, nor of the glorious councils of Toledo, but barbarism was drawing nigh its end. Two great results were obtained:

1. The movement of the invading hordes had been stopped both in the north and in the south. Upon the dismemberment of the empire of Charlemagne, the states, which became formed upon the right bank of the Rhine, opposed an effectual barrier to the tribes which advanced from the west. The Danes and Normans are an incontestable proof of this. Up to this time, if we except the Saxon attacks upon England, the invasions of the German tribes by sea had not been very considerable: but in the course of the

ninth century they became constant and general. And this happened, because invasions by land had become exceedingly difficult; society had acquired, on this side, frontiers more fixed and secure; and that portion of the wandering nations, which could not be pressed back, were at least turned from their ancient course, and compelled to proceed by sea. Great as undoubtedly was the misery occasioned to the west of Europe by the incursions of these pirates and marauders, they still were much less hurtful than the invasions by land, and disturbed much less generally the newly-forming society. In the south, the case was much the same. The Arabs had settled in Spain; and the struggle between them and the Christians still continued; but this occasioned no new emigration of nations. Bands of Saracens still, from time to time, infested the coasts of the Mediterranean, but the great career of Islamism was arrested.

· 2. In the interior of Europe we begin at this time to see the wandering life decline: populations became fixed; estates and landed possessions became settled; the relations between man and man no longer varied from day to day under the influence of force or chance. The interior and moral condition of man himself began to undergo a change; his ideas, his sentiments, began, like his life, to assume a more fixed character. He began to feel an attachment to the place in which he dwelt; to the connexions and associations which he there formed; to those domains which he now calculated upon leaving to his children; to that dwelling which hereafter became his castle; to that miserable assemblage of serfs and slaves, which was one day to become a village. Little societies everywhere began to be formed; little states to be cut out according to the measure, if I may so say, of the capacities and prudence of men. There, societies gradually became connected by a tie, the origin of which is to be found in the manners of the German barbarians: the tie of a confederation which would not destroy individual freedom. On one side we find every considerable proprietor settling himself in his domains, surrounded only by his family and retainers; on the other, a certain graduated subordination of services and rights existing among all these military proprietors scattered over the land. Here we have the feudal system oozing at last out of the bosom of barbarism. Of the various elements of our civilizations, it was natural enough that the Germanic element should first prevail. It was already in possession of power; it had conquered Europe: from it European civilization was to receive its first form—its first social organization.

The character of this form—the character of feudalism, and the influence it had exercised upon European civilization—will be the object of my next lecture; while in the very bosom of this system, in its meridian, we shall, at every step, meet with the other elements of our own social system, monarchy, the Church, and the communities or free cities. We shall feel pre-assured that these were not destined to fall under this feudal form, to which they adapted themselves while struggling against it; and that we may look forward to the hour when victory will declare itself for them in their turn.

LECTURE IV.

THE FEUDAL SYSTEM.

I HAVE thus far endeavored to give you a view of the state of Europe upon the fall of the Roman empire; of its state in the first period of modern history—in the period of barbarism. We have seen that at the end of the period, toward the beginning of the tenth century, the first principle, the first system, which took possession of European society, was the feudal system—that out of the very bosom of barbarism sprung feudalism. The investigation of this system will be the subject of the present lecture.

I need scarcely remind you that it is not the history of events, properly so called, that we propose to consider. I shall not here recount the destinies of the feudal system. The subject which engages our attention is the history of civilization; it is that general, hidden fact, which we have to seek for, out of all the exterior facts in which its existence is contained.

Thus the events, the social crisises, the various states through which society has passed, will in no way interest us, except so far as they are connected with the growth of civilization; we have only to learn from them how they have retarded or forwarded this great work; what they have given it, and what they have withheld from it. It is only in this point of view that we shall consider the feudal system.

In the first of these lectures we settled what civilization was; we endeavored to discover its elements; we saw that it consisted, on one side, in the development of man himself, of the individual, of humanity; on the other, of his outward or social condition. When then we come to any event, to any system, to any general condition of society, we have this twofold question to put to it: What has it done for or against the development of man—for or against the development of society? It will, however, be at once seen that, in the investigation we have undertaken, it will be impossible for us not to come in contact with some of the grandest questions in moral philosophy. When we would, for example, know in what an event, a system, has contributed to the progress of man and of society, it is necessary that we should know what is the *true* development of society and of man; and be enabled to detect those developments which are deceitful, illegitimate—which pervert instead of meliorate—which cause them to retrograde instead of to advance. We shall not attempt to elude this task. By so doing we should mutilate and weaken our ideas, as well as the facts themselves. Besides, the present state of the world, the spirit of the age, compels us at once frankly to welcome this inevitable alliance of philosophy and history.

This indeed forms a striking, perhaps the essential, characteristic of the present times. We are now compelled to consider—science and reality—theory and practice—right and fact—and to make them move side by side. Down to the present time these two powers have lived apart. The world has been accustomed to see theory and practice following two different routes, unknown to each other, or at least never meeting. When doctrines, when general ideas, have wished to intermeddle in affairs, to influence the world, it has only been able to effect this under the appearance and by the aid of fanaticism. Up to the present time the government of human societies, the direction of their affairs, have been divided between two sorts of influences; on one side theorists, men who would rule all according to abstract notions—enthusiasts; on the other, men ignorant of all rational principle—experimentalists, whose only guide is expediency. This state of things is now over. The world will no longer agitate for the sake of some abstract principle, some fanciful theory—some Utopian government which can only exist in the imagination of an enthusiast; nor will it put up with practical abuses and oppressions, however favored by prescription and expediency, where they are opposed to the just principles and the legitimate end of government. To ensure respect, to obtain confidence, governing powers must now unite theory and practice; they must know and acknowledge the influence of both. They must regard as well principles as facts; must respect both truth and necessity—must shun, on one hand, the blind pride of the fanatic theorist, and, on the other, the no less blind pride of the libertine practician. To this better state of things we have been brought by the progress of the human mind and the progress of society. On one side the human mind is so elevated and enlarged that it is able to view at once, as a whole, the subject or fact which comes under its notice, with all the various circumstances and principles which affect it—these it calculates and combines—it so opposes, mixes, and arranges them—that while the everlasting principle is placed boldly and prominently forward so as not to be mistaken, care is taken that it shall not be endangered, that its progress shall not be retarded by a negligent or rash estimate of the circumstances which oppose it. On the other side, social systems are so improved as no longer to shrink from the light of truth; so improved, that facts may be brought to the test of science—practice may be placed by the side of theory, and, notwithstanding its many imperfections, the comparison will excite in us neither discouragement nor disgust.

I shall give way, then, freely to this natural tendency—to this spirit of the age, by passing continually from the investigation of circumstances to the investigation of ideas —from an exposition of facts to the consideration of doctrines. Perhaps there is, in the present disposition of the public, another reason in favor of this method. For some time past there has existed among us a decided taste, a sort of predilection for facts, for looking at things in a practical point of view. We have been so much a prey to the despotism of abstract ideas, of theories—they have, in some respects, cost us so dear, that we now regard them with a degree of distrust. We like better to refer to facts, to particular circumstances, and to judge and act accordingly. Let us not complain of this. It is a new advance—it is a grand step in knowledge, and toward the empire of truth; provided, however, we do not suffer ourselves to be carried too far by this disposition—provided that we do not forget that truth alone has a right to reign in the world; that facts have no merit but in proportion as they bear its stamp, and assimilate themselves more and more to its image; that all true grandeur proceeds from mind; that all expansion belongs to it. The civilization of France possesses this peculiar character; it has never been wanting in intellectual grandeur. It has always been rich in ideas. The power of mind has been great in French society—greater, perhaps, than anywhere else. It must not lose this happy privilege—it must not fall into that lower, that somewhat material condition which prevails in other societies. Intelligence, theories, must still maintain in France the same rank which they have hitherto occupied.

I shall not then attempt to shun these general and philosophical questions. I will not go out of my way to seek them, but when circumstances bring them, naturally before me, I shall attack them without hesitation or embarrassment. This will be the case more than once in considering the feudal system as connected with the history of European civilization.

A great proof that in the tenth century the feudal system was necessary, and the only social system practicable, is the universality of its adoption. Wherever barbarism ceased, feudalism became general. This at first struck men as the triumph of chaos. All unity, all general civilization seemed gone; society on all sides seemed dismembered; a multitude of petty, obscure, isolated, incoherent societies arose. This appeared, to those who lived and saw it, universal anarchy —the dissolution of all things. Consult the poets and historians of the day: they all believed that the end of the world was at hand. Yet this was, in truth, a new and real social system which was forming: feudal society was so necessary, so inevitable, so altogether the only consequnece that could flow from the previous state of things, that all entered into it, all adopted its form. Even elements the most foreign to this system, the Church, the free communities, royalty, all were constrained to accommodate themselves to it. Churches became sovereigns and vassals; cities became lords and vassals; royalty was hidden under the feudal suzerain. All things were given in fief, not only estates, but rights and privileges: the right to cut wood in the forest, the privilege of fishing. The churches gave their surplice-fees in fief: the revenues of baptism—the fees for churching women. In the same mannner, too, that all the great elements of society were drawn within the feudal enclosure, so even the smallest portions, the most trifling circumstances of common life, became subject to feudalism.

In observing the feudal system thus taking possession of every part of society, one might be apt, at first, to believe that the essential, vital principle of feudalism everywhere prevailed. This would be a grand mistake. Although they put on the feudal form, yet the institutions, the elements of society which were not analogous to the feudal system, did not lose their nature, the principles by which they were distinguished. The feudal church, for example, never ceased for a moment to be animated and governed at bottom by the principles of theocracy, and she never for a moment relaxed her endeavors to gain for this the predominancy. Now she leagued with royalty, now with the pope, and now with the people, to destroy this system, whose livery, for the time, she was compelled to put on. It was the same with royalty and the free cities: in one the principle of monarchy, in the others the principle of democracy, continued fundamentally to prevail: and, notwithstanding their feudal appearance, these various elements of European society constantly labored to deliver themselves from a form so foreign to their nature, and to put on that which corresponded with their true and vital principle.

Though perfectly satisfied, therefore, of the universality of the feudal *form*, we must take care not to conclude on that account, that the feudal *principle* was equally universal. We must be no less cautious not to take our ideas of feudalism indifferently from every object which bears its physiognomy. In order to know and understand this system thoroughly—to unravel and judge of its effects upon modern civilization—we must seek it where the form and spirit dwell together; we must study it in the hierarchy of the laic possessors of fiefs; in the association of the conquerors of the European territory. This was the true residence of the feudal system, and into this we will now endeavor to penetrate.

I said a few words, just now, on the importance of questions of a moral nature; and on the danger and inconvenience of passing them by without proper attention. A matter of a totally opposite character arises here, and demands our consideration; it is one which has been, in general, too much neglected. I allude to the physical condition of society; to the changes which take place in the life and manners of a people in consequence of some new event, some revolution, some new state into which it may be thrown. These changes have not always been sufficiently attended to. The modification which these great crisises in the history of the world have wrought in the material existence of mankind—in the physical conditions of the relation of men to one another—have not been investigated with so much advantage as they might have been. These modifications have more influence upon the general body of society than is imagined. Every one knows how much has been said upon the influence of climate, and of the importance which Montesquieu attached to it. Now if we regard only the direct influence of climate upon man, perhaps it has not been so extensive as is generally supposed; it is, to say the least, vague and difficult to appreciate; but the indirect influence of climate, that, for example, which arises from the circumstance that in a hot country man lives in the open air, while in a cold one he lives shut up in his habitation—that he lives here upon one kind of food, and there upon another, are facts of extreme importance; inasmuch as a simple change in physical life may have a powerful effect upon the course of civilization. Every great revolution leads to modifications of this nature in the social system, and consequently claims our consideration.

The establishment of the feudal system wrought a change of this kind, which had a powerful and striking influence upon European civilization. It changed the distribution of the population. Hitherto the lords of the territory, the conquering population, had lived united in masses more or less numerous, either settled in cities, or moving about the country in bands; but by the operation of the feudal system these men were brought to live isolated, each in his dwelling, at long distances apart. You will instantly perceive the influence which this change must have exercised upon the character and progress of civilization. The social preponderance—the government of society, passed at once from cities to the country; the baronial courts of the great landed proprietors took the place of the great national assemblies—the public body was lost in the thousand little sovereignties into which every kingdom was split. This was the first consequence—a consequence purely physical, of the triumph of the feudal system. The more closely we examine this circumstance, the more clearly and forcibly will its effects present themselves to our notice.

Let us now examine this society in itself, and trace out its influence upon the progress of civilization. We will take feudalism, in the first place, in its most simple state, in its primitive fundamental form. We will visit a possessor of a fief in his lonely domain; we will see the course of life which he leads there, and the little society by which he is surrounded.

Having fixed upon an elevated solitary spot, strong by nature, and which he takes care to render secure, the lordly proprietor of the domain builds his castle. Here he settles himself, with his wife and children, and perhaps some few freemen, who, not having obtained fiefs, not having themselves become proprietors, have attached themselves to his fortunes, and continued to live with him and form a part of his household. These are the inhabitants of the interior of the castle. At the foot of the hill on which this castle stands we find huddled together a little population of peasants, of serfs, who cultivate the lands of the possessor of the fief. In the midst of this group of cottages religion soon planted a church and a priest. A priest, in these early days of feudalism, was generally the chaplain of the baron, and the curate of the village, two offices which by and by became separated, and the village had its pastor dwelling by the side of his church.

Such is the first form, the elementary principle, of feudal society. We will now examine this simple form, in order to put to it the twofold question we have to ask of every fact, namely, what it has done toward the progress—first, of man, himself; secondly, of society?

It is with peculiar propriety that we put this twofold question to the little society I have just described, and that we should attach importance to its answers, forasmuch as this society is the type, the faithful picture, of feudal society in the aggregate; the baron, the people of his domain, and the priest, compose, whether upon a large or smaller scale, the feudal system when separated from monarchy and cities, two distinct and foreign elements.

The first circumstance which strikes us in looking at this little community, is the great importance with which the possessor of the fief must have been regarded, not only by himself, but by all around him. A feeling of personal consequence, of individual liberty, was a prevailing feature in the character of the barbarians. The feeling here, however, was of a different nature; it was no longer simply the liberty of the man, of the warrior, it was the importance of the proprietor, of the head of the family, of the master. His situation, with regard to all around him, would naturally beget in him an idea of superiority—a superiority of a peculiar nature, and very different from that we meet with in other systems of civilization. Look, for example, at the Roman patrician, who was placed in one of the highest aristocratic situations of the ancient world. Like the feudal lord, he was head of the family, superior, master; and besides this, he was a religious magistrate, high priest over his household. But mark the difference: his importance as a religious magistrate is derived from without. It is not an importance strictly personal, attached to the individual: he receives it from on high; he is the delegate of divinity, the interpreter of religious faith. The Roman patrician, moreover, was the member of a corporation which lived united in the same place—a member of the senate—again, an importance which he derived from without from his corporation. The greatness of these ancient aristocrats, associated to a religious and political character, belonged to the situation, to the corporation in general, rather than to the individual. That of the proprietor of a fief belonged to himself alone; he held nothing of any one; all his rights, all his power, centred in himself. He is no religious magistrate; he forms no part of a senate; it is in the individual, in his own person, that all his importance resides—all that he is, he is of himself, in his own name alone. What a vast influence must a situation like this have exercised over him who enjoyed it! What haughtiness, what pride, must it have engendered! Above him, no superior of whom he was but the representative and interpreter; near him no equals; no general and powerful law to restrain him—no exterior force to control him; his will suffered no check but from the limits of his power, and the presence of danger. Such seems to me the moral effect that would naturally be produced upon the character or disposition of man, by the situation in which he was placed under the feudal system.

I shall proced to a second consequence equally important, though too little noticed; I mean the peculiar character of the feudal family.

Let us consider for a moment the various family systems. Let us look, in the first place, at the patriarchal family, of which so beautiful a picture is given us in the Bible, and in numerous Oriental treatises. We find it composed of a great number of individuals—it was a tribe. The chief, the patriarch, in this case, lives in common with his children, with his neighbors, with the various generations assembled around him—all his relations or his servants. He not only lives with them, he has the same interests, the same occupations, he leads the same life. This was the situation of Abraham, and of the patriarchs; and is still that of the Bedouin Arabs, who, from generation to generation, continue to follow the same patriarchal mode of life.

Let us look next at the *clan*—another family system, which now scarcely exists, except in Scotland and Ireland, but through which probably the greater part of the European world has passed. This is no longer the patriarchal family. A great difference is found here between the chief and the rest of the community; he leads not the same life; the greater part are employed in husbandry, and in supplying his wants, while the chief himself lives in idleness or war. Still they all descend from the same stock; they all bear the same name; and their common parentage, their ancient traditions, the same remembrances, and the same associations, create a moral tie, a sort of equality, between the members of the clan.

These are the two principal forms of family society as represented by history. Does either of them, let me ask you, resemble the feudal family? Certainly not. At the first glance, there may, indeed, seem some similarity between the feudal family and the clan; but the difference is marked and striking. The population which surrounds the possessor of the fief is quite foreign to him; it bears not his name. They are unconnected by relationship, or by any historical or moral tie. The same holds with respect to the patriarchal family. The feudal proprietor neither leads the same life, nor follows the same occupations as those who live around him; he is engaged in arms, or lives in idleness: the others are laborers. The feudal family is not numerous—it forms no tribe—it is confined to a single family properly so called; to the wife and children, who live separated from the rest of the people in the interior of the castle. The peasantry and serfs form no part of it; they are of another origin, and immeasurably beneath it. Five or six individuals, at a vast height above them, and at the same time foreigners, make up the feudal family. Is it not evident that the peculiarity of its situation must have given to this family a peculiar character? Confined, concentrated, called upon continually to defend itself; mistrusting, or at least shutting itself up from the rest of the world, even from its servants, in-door life, domestic manners must naturally have acquired a great preponderance. We cannot keep out of sight, that the grosser passions of the chief, the constantly passing his time in warfare or hunting, opposed a considerable obstacle to the formation of a strictly domestic society. But its progress, though slow, was certain. The chief, however violent and brutal his out-door exercises, must habitually return into the bosom of his family. He there finds his wife and children, and scarcely any but them; they alone are his constant companions; they alone divide his sorrows and soften his joys; they alone are interested in all that concerns him. It could not but happen in such circumstances, that domestic life must have acquired a vast influence; nor is there any lack of proofs that it did so. Was it not in the bosom of the feudal family that the importance of women, that the value of the wife and mother, at last made itself known? In none of the ancient communities, not merely speaking of those in which the spirit of family never existed, but in those in which it existed most powerfully—say, for example, in the patriarchal system—in none of these did women ever attain to anything like the place which they acquired in Europe under the feudal system. It is to the progress, to the preponderance of domestic manners in the feudal halls and castles, that they owe this change, this improvement in their condition. The cause of this has been sought for in the peculiar manners of the ancient Germans; in a national respect which they are said to have borne, in the midst of their forests, to the female sex. Upon a single phrase of Tacitus, Germanic patriotism has founded a high degree of superiority—of primitive and ineffable purity of manners—in the relations between the two sexes among the Germans. Pure chimeras! Phrases like this of Tacitus—sentiments and customs analogous to those of the Germans of old, are found in the narratives of a host of writers, who have seen, or inquired into, the manners of savage and barbarous tribes. There is nothing primitive, nothing peculiar to a certain race in this matter. It was in the effects of a very decided social situation—it was in the increase and preponderance of domestic manners, that the importance of the female sex in Europe had its rise, and the preponderance of domestic manners in Europe very early became an essential characteristic in the feudal system.

A second circumstance, a fresh proof of the influence of domestic life, forms a striking feature in the picture of a feudal family. I mean the principle of inheritance—the spirit of perpetuity which so strongly predominates in its character. This spirit of inheritance is a natural off-shoot of the spirit of family, but it nowhere took such deep root as in the feudal system, where it was nourished by the nature of the property with which the family was, as it were, incorporated. The fief differed from other possessions in this, that it constantly required a chief, or owner, who could defend it, manage it, discharge the obligations by which it was held, and thus maintain its rank in the general association of the great proprietors of the kingdom. There thus became a kind of identification of the possessor of the fief with the fief itself, and with all its future possessors.

This circumstance powerfully tended to strengthen and knit together the ties of family, already so strong by the nature of the feudal system itself,

Quitting the baronial dwellling, let us now descend to the little population that surrounds it. Everything here wears a different aspect. The disposition of man is so kindly and good, that it is impossible for a number of individuals to be placed for any length of time in a social situation without giving birth to a certain moral tie between them: sentiments of protection, of benevolence, of affection, spring up naturally. Thus it happened in the feudal system. There can be no doubt, but that after a certain time, kind and friendly feelings would grow up between the feudal lord and his serfs. This, however, took place in spite of their relative situation, and by no means through its influence. Considered in itself, this situation was radically vicious. There was nothing morally common between the holder of the fief and his serfs. They formed part of his estate; they were his property; and under this word property are comprised, not only all the rights which we delegate to the public magistrate to exercise in the name of the state, but likewise all those which we possess over private property: the right of making laws, of levying taxes, of inflicting punishment, as well as that of disposing of them—or selling them. There existed not, in fact, between the lord of the domain and its cultivators, so far as we consider the latter as men, either rights, guarantee, or society.

From this I believe has risen that almost universal, invincible hatred which country people have at all times borne to the feudal system, to every remnant of it—to its very name. We are not without examples of men having submitted to the heavy yoke of despotism, of their having become accustomed to it, nay more, of their having freely accepted it. Religious despotism, monarchical despotism, have more than once obtained the sanction, almost the love, of the population which they governed. But feudal despotism has always been repulsed, always hateful. It tyrannized over the destinies of men, without ruling in their hearts. Perhaps this may be partly accounted for by the fact, that, in religious and monarchical despotism, authority is always exercised by virtue of some belief or opinion common to both ruler and subjects; he is the representative, the minister, of another power superior to all human powers. He speaks or acts in the name of Divinity or of a common feeling, and not in the name of man himself, of man alone. Feudal despotism differed from this; it was the authority of man over man; the domination of the personal, capricious will of an individual. This perhaps is the only tyranny to which man, much to his honor, never will submit. Wherever in a ruler, or master, he sees but the individual man—the moment that the authority which presses upon him is no more than an individual, a human will, one like his own, he feels mortified and indignant, and struggles against the yoke which he is compelled to bear. Such was the true, the distinctive character of the feudal power, and such was the origin of the hatred which it has never ceased to inspire.

The religious element which was associated with the feudal power was but little calculated to alleviate its yoke. I do not see how the influence of the priest could be very great in the society which I have just described, or that he could have much success in legitimizing the connexion between the enslaved and the lordly proprietor. The Church has exercised a very powerful influence in the civilization of Europe; but then it has been by proceeding in a general manner—by changing the general dispositions of mankind. When we enter intimately into the little feudal society, properly so called, we find the influence of the priest between the baron and his serfs to have been very slight. It most frequently happened that he was as rude and nearly as much under control as the serf himself; and therefore not very well fitted, either by his position or talents, to enter into a contest with the lordly baron. We must, to be sure, naturally suppose, that, called upon as he was by his office to administer and to keep alive among these poor people the great moral truths of Christianity, he became endeared and useful to them in this respect; he consoled and instructed them; but I believe he had but little power to soften their hard condition.

Having examined the feudal system in its rudest, its simplest form; having placed before you the principal consequences which flowed from it, as respects the possessor of the fief himself, as respects his family, and as respects the population gathered about him; let us now quit this narrow precinct. The population of the fief was not the only one in the land: there were other societies more or less like his own of which he was a member—with which he was connected. What, then, let us ask, was the influence which this general society to which he belonged might be expected to exercise upon civilization?

One short observation before we reply: both the possessor of the fief and the priest, it is true, formed part of a general society; in the distance they had numerous and frequent connexions; not so the cultivators—the serfs. Every time that, in speaking of the population of the country at this period, we make use of some general term, which seems to convey the idea of one single and same society—such for example as the word people—we speak without truth. For this population there was no general society—its existence was purely local. Beyond the estate in which they dwelt, the serfs had no relations whatever—no connexion either with persons, things, or government. For them there existed no common destiny, no common country—they formed not a nation. When we speak of the feudal association as a whole, it is only the great proprietors that are alluded to.

Let us now see what the relations of the little feudal scoiety were with the general society to which it held, and what consequences these relations may be expected to have led to in the progress of civilization.

We all know what the ties were which bound together the posesssors of fiefs; what conditions were attached to their possessions; what were the obligations of service on one part, and of protection on the other. I shall not enter into a detail of these obligations; it is enough for the present purpose that you have a general idea of them. This system, however, seemed naturally to pour into the mind of every possessor of a fief a certain number of ideas and moral sentiments—ideas of duty, sentiments of affection. That the principles of fidelity, devotedness, loaylty, became developed, and maintained by the relations in which the possessors of fiefs stood toward one another, is evident. The fact speaks for itself.

The attempt was made to change these obligations, these duties, these sentiments, and so on, into laws and institutions. It is well known that feudalism wished legally to settle what services the possessor of a fief owed to his sovereign; what services he had a right to expect from him in return; in what cases the vassal might be called upon to furnish military or pecuniary aid to his lord; in what way the lord might obtain the services of his vassals, in those affairs, in which they were not bound to yield them by the mere possession of their fiefs. The attempt was made to place all these rights under the protection of institutions founded to ensure their respect. Thus the baronial jurisdictions were erected to administer justice between the possessors of fiefs, upon complaints duly laid before their common suzerain. Thus every baron of any consideration collected his vassals in parliament, to debate in common the affairs which required their consent or concurrence. There was, in short, a combination of political, judicial, and military means, which show the attempt to organize the feudal system—to convert the relations between the possessors of fiefs into laws and institutions.

But these laws, these institutions, had no stability—no guarantee.

If it should be asked what is a political guarantee, I am compelled to look back to its fundamental character, and to state that this is the constant existence, in the bosom of society, of a will, of an authority disposed and in a condition to impose a law upon the wills and powers of private individuals—to enforce their obedience to the common rule, to make them respect the general law.

There are only two systems of political guarantees possible: there must be either a will, a particular power, so superior to the others that none of them can resist it, but are obliged to yield to its authority whenever it is interposed; or, on the other, a public will, the result of the concurrence —of the development of the wills of individuals, and which likewise is in a condition, when once it has expressed itself, to make itself obeyed and respected by all.

These are the only two systems of political guarantees possible; the despotism of one alone, or of a body; or free government. If we examine the various systems, we shall find that they may all be brought under one of these two.

Well, neither of these existed, or could exist, under the feudal system.

Without doubt the possessors of fiefs were not all equal among themselves. There were some much more powerful than others; and very many sufficiently powerful to oppress the weaker. But there was none, from the king, the first of proprietors, downward, who was in a condition to impose law upon all the others; in a condition to make himself obeyed. Call to mind that none of the permanent means of power and influence at this time existed—no standing army —no regular taxes—no fixed tribunals. The social authorities—the institutions, had, in a manner, to be new formed every time they were wanted. A tribunal had to be formed for every trial—an army to be formed for every war—a revenue to be formed every time that money was needed. All was occasional—accidental—special; there was no central, permanent, independent means of government. It is evident that in such a system no individual had the power to enforce his will upon others; to compel all to respect and obey the general law.

On the other hand, resistance was easy, in proportion as repression was difficult. Shut up in his castle, with but a small number of enemies to cope with, and aware that other vassals in a like situation were ready to join and assist him, the possessor of a fief found but little difficulty in defending himself.

It must then, I think, be confessed, that the first system of political guarantees—namely, that which would make all responsible to the strongest—has been shown to be impossible under the feudal system.

The other system—that of free government, of a public power, a public authority—was just as impracticable. The reason is simple enough. When we speak now of a public power, of what we call the rights of sovereignty—that is, the right of making laws, of imposing taxes, of inflicting punishment, we know, we bear in mind, that these rights belong to nobody; that no one has, on his own account, the right to punish others, or to impose any burden or law upon them. These are rights which belong only to the great body of society, which are exercised only in its name; they are emanations from the people, and held in trust for their benefit. Thus it happens that when an individual is brought before an authority invested with these rights, the sentiment that predominates in his mind, though perhaps he himself may be unconscious of it, is, that he is in the presence of a public legitimate authority, invested with the power to command him, an authority which, beforehand, he has tacitly acknowledged. This was by no means the case under the feudal system. The possessor of a fief, within his domain, was invested with all the rights and privileges of sovereignty; he inherited them with the territory; they were a matter of private property. What are now called public rights were then private rights; what are now called public authorities were then private authorities. When the possessor of a fief, after having exercised sovereign power in his own name, as proprietor over all the population which lived around him, attended an assembly, attended a parliament held by his sovereign—a parliament not in general very numerous, and composed of men of the same grade, or nearly so, as himself —he did not carry with him any notion of a public authority. This idea was in direct contradiction to all about him—to all his notions, to all that he had done within his own domains. All he saw in these assemblies were men invested with the same rights as himself, in the same situation as himself, acting as he had done by virtue of their own personal title. Nothing led or compelled him to see or acknowledge in the very highest portion of the government, or in the institutions which we call public, that character of superiority or generality which seems to us bound up with the notion of political power. Hence, if he was dissatisfied with its decision, he refused to concur in it, and perhaps called in force to resist it.

Force, indeed, was the true and usual guarantee of right under the feudal system, if force can be called a guarantee. Every law continualy had recourse to force to make itself respected or acknowedged. No institution succeeded under it. This was so perfectly felt that institutions were scarcely ever applied to. If the agency of the baronial courts or parliaments of vassals had been of any importance, we should find them more generally employed than, from history, they appear to have been. Their rarity proves their insignificance.

This is not astonishing. There is another reason for it more profound and decisive than any I have yet adduced.

Of all the systems of government and political guarantee, it may be asserted, without fear of contradiction, that the most difficult to establish and render effectual is the federative system; a system which consists in leaving in each place or province, in every separate society, all that portion of government which can abide there, and in taking from it only so much of it as is indispensable to a general society, in order to carry it to the centre of this larger society, and there to imbody it under the form of a central government. This federative system, theoretically the most simple, is found in practice the most complex; for in order to reconcile the degree of independence, of local liberty, which is permitted to remain, with the degree of general order, of general submission, which in certain cases it supposes and exacts, evidently requires a very advanced state of civilization—requires, indeed, that the will of man, that individual liberty, should concur in the establishment and maintenance of the system much more than in any other, because it possesses less than any other the means of coercion.

The federative system, then, is one which evidently requires the greatest maturity of reason, of morality of civilization in the society to which it is applied. Yet we find that this was the kind of government which the feudal system attempted to establish: for feudalism, as a whole, was truly a confederation. It rested upon the same principles, for example, as those on which is based, in the present day, the federative system of the United States of America. It affected to leave in the hands of each great proprietor all that portion of the government, of sovereignty, which could be exercised there, and to carry to the suzerain, or to the general assembly of barons, the least possible portion of power, and only this in cases of absolute necessity. You will easily conceive the impossibility of establishing a system like this in a world of ignorance, of brute passions, or, in a word, where the moral condition of man was so imperfect as under the feudal system. The very nature of such a government was in opposition to the notions, the habits and manners of the very man to whom it was to be applied. How then can we be astonished at the bad success of this attempt at organization?

We have now considered the feudal system, first, in its most simple element, in its fundamental principle; and then in its collective form, as a whole: we have examined it under these two points of view, in order to see what it did and what it might have been expected to do; what has been its influence on the progress of civilization. These investigations, I think, bring us to this twofold conclusion:—

1. Feudalism seems to have exercised a great, and, upon the whole, a salutary influence upon the intellectual development of individuals. It gave birth to elevated ideas and feelings in the mind, to moral wants, to grand developments of character and passion.

2. With regard to society, it was incapable of establishing either legal order or political guarantee. In the wretched

state to which society had been reduced by barbarism, in which it was incapable of a more regular or enlarged form, the feudal system seemed indispensable as a step toward re-association; still this system, in itself radically vicious, could neither regulate nor enlarge society. The only political right which the feudal system was capable of exercising in European society, was the right of resistance: I will not say legal resistance, for there can be no question of legal resistance in a society so little advanced. The progress of society consists pre-eminently in substituting, on one hand, public authority for private will; and, on the other, legal resistance for individual resistance. This is the great end, the chief perfection, of social order; a large field is left to personal liberty, but when personal liberty offends, when it becomes necessary to call it to account, our only appeal is to public reason; public reason is placed in the judge's chair to pass sentence on the charge which is preferred against individual liberty. Such is the system of legal order and of legal resistance. You will easily perceive, that there was nothing bearing any resemblance to this in the feudal system. The right of resistance, which was maintained and practised in this system, was the right of personal resistance; a terrible and anti-social right, inasmuch as its only appeal is to brute force—to war—which is the destruction of society itself; a right, however, which ought never to be entirely erased from the mind of man, because by its abolition he puts on the fetters of servitude. The notion of the right of resistance had been banished from the Roman community, by the general disgrace and infamy into which it had fallen, and it could not be regenerated from its ruins. It could not, in my opinion, have sprung more naturally from the principles of Christian society. It is to the feudal system that we are indebted for its re-introduction among us. The glory of civilization is to render this principle for ever inactive and useless; the glory of the feudal system is its having constantly professed and defended it.

Such, if I am not widely mistaken, is the result of our investigation of the feudal community, considered in itself, in its general principles, and independently of its historical progress. If we now turn to facts, to history, we shall find it to have fallen out, just as might have been expected, that the feudal system accomplished its task; that its destiny has been conformable to its nature. Events may be adduced in proof of all the conjectures, of all the inductions, which I have drawn from the nature and essential character of this system.

Take a glance, for example, at the general history of feudalism, from the tenth to the thirteenth centuries, and say, is it not impossible to deny that it exercised a vast and salutary influence upon the progress of individual man—upon the development of his sentiments, his disposition, and his ideas? Where can we open the history of this period, without discovering a crowd of noble sentiments, of splendid achievements, of beautiful developments of humanity, evidently generated in the bosom of feudal life. Chivalry, which in reality bears scarcely the least resemblance to feudalism, was nevertheless its offspring. It was feudalism which gave birth to that romantic thirst and fondness for all that is noble, generous, and faithful—for that sentiment of honor, which still raises its voice in favor of the system by which it was nursed.

But turn to another side. Here we see that the first sparks of European imagination, that the first attempts of poetry, of literature, that the first intellectual gratifications which Europe tasted in emerging from barbarism, sprung up under the protection, under the wings, of feudalism. It was in the baronial hall that they were born, and cherished, and protected. It is to the feudal times that we trace back the earliest literary monuments of England, France, and Germany, the earliest intellectual enjoyments of modern Europe.

As a set-off to this, if we question history respecting the influence of feudalism upon the social system, its reply is, though still in accordance with our conjectures, that the feudal system has everywhere opposed not only the establishment of general order, but at the same time the extension of general liberty. Under whatever point of view we consider the progress of society, the feudal system always appears as an obstacle in its way. Hence, from the earliest existence of feudalism, the two powers which have been the prime movers in the progress of order and liberty—monarchical power on the one hand, and popular power on the other—that is to say, the king and the people—have both attacked it, and struggled against it continually. What few attempts were made at different periods to regulate it, to impart to it somewhat of a legal, a general character—as was done in England, by William the Conqueror and his sons; in

France, by St. Louis; and by several of the German emperors—all these endeavors, all these attempts failed. The very nature itself of feudality is opposed to order and legality. In the last century, some writers of talent attempted to dress out feudalism as a social system; they endeavored to make it appear a legitimate, well-ordered, progressive state of society, and represented it as a golden age. Ask them, however, where it existed: summon them to assign it a locality, and a time, and they will be found wanting. It is a Utopia without date, a drama, for which we find, in the past, neither theatre nor actors. The cause of this error is noways difficult to discover; and it accounts as well for the error of the opposite class, who cannot pronounce the name of feudalism without coupling to it an absolute anathema. Both these parties have looked at it, as the two knights did at the statue of Janus, only on one side. They have not considered the two different points of view from which feudalism may be surveyed. They do not distinguish, on one hand, its influence upon the progress of the individual man, upon his felings, his faculties, his disposition and passions; nor, on the other, its influence upon the social condition. One party could not imagine that a social system in which were to be found so many noble sentiments, so many virtues, in which were seen sprouting forth the earliest buds of literature and science; in which manners became not only more refined, but attained a certain elevation and grandeur; in such a system they could not imagine that the evil was so great or so fatal as it was made to appear. The other party, seeing but the misery which feudalism inflicted on the great body of the people—the obstacles which it opposed to the establishment of order and liberty—would not believe that it could produce noble characters, great virtues, or any improvement whatsoever. Both these parties have misunderstood the twofold principle of civilization: they have not been aware that it consists of two movements, one of which for a time may advance independently of the other; although after a lapse of centuries, and perhaps a long series of events, they must at last reciprocally recall and bring forward each other.

To conclude, feudalism, in its character and influence, was just what its nature would lead us to expect. Individualism, the energy of personal existence, was the prevailing principle among the vanquishers of the Roman world; and the development of the individual man, of his mind, and faculties, might above all be expected to result from the social system, founded by them and for them. That which man himself carries into a social system, his intellectual moral disposition at the time he enters it, has a powerful influence upon the situation in which he establishes himself—upon all around him. This situation in its turn reacts upon his dispositions, strengthens and improves them. The individual prevailed in German society; and the influence of the feudal system, the offspring of German society, displayed itself in the improvement and advance of the individual. We shall find the same fact to recur in the other elements of our civilization: they all hold faithful to their original principle; they have advanced and pushed the world in that same road by which they first entered. The subject of the next lecture—the history of the Church, and its influence upon European civilization, from the fifth to the twelfth century—will furnish us with a new and striking example of this fact.

LECTURE V.

THE CHURCH.

HAVING investigated the nature and influence of the feudal system, I shall take the Christian Church, from the fifth to the twelfth century, as the subject of the present lecture. I say the *Christian Church*, because, as I have observed once before, it is not about Christianity itself, Christianity as a religious system, that I shall occupy your attention, but the Church as an ecclesiastical society—the Christian hierarchy.

This society was almost completely organized before the close of the fifth century. Not that it has not undergone many and important changes since that period, but from this time the Church, considered as a corporation, as the government of the Christian world, may be said to have attained a complete and independent existence.

A single glance will be sufficient to convince us that there existed, in the fifth century, an immense difference between the state of the Church and that of the other elements of European civilization. You will remember that I have pointed out, as primary elements of our civilization, the municipal system, the feudal system, monarchy, and the Church. The municipal system, in the fifth century, was no more than a fragment of the Roman empire, a shadow without life, or definite form. The feudal system was still a chaos. Monarchy existed only in name. All the *civil* elements of modern society were either in their decline or infancy. The Church alone possessed youth and vigor; she alone possessed at the same time a definite form, with activity and strength; she alone possessed at once movement and order, energy and system, that is to say, the two greatest means of influence. Is it not, let me ask you, by mental vigor, by intellectual movement on one side, and by order and discipline on the other, that all institutions acquire their power and influence over society? The Church, moreover, awakened attention to, and agitated all the great questions which interest man; she busied herself with all the great problems of his nature, with all he had to hope or fear for futurity. Hence her influence upon modern civilization has been so powerful—more powerful, perhaps, than its most violent adversaries, or its most zealous defenders, have supposed. They, eager to advance or abuse her, have only regarded the Church in a contentious point of view; and with that contrasted spirit which controversy engenders, how could they do her justice, or grasp the full scope of her sway?

To us, the Church, in the fifth century, appears as an organized and independent society, interposed between the masters of the world, the sovereigns, the possessors of temporal power, and the people, serving as a connecting link, between them, and exercising its influence over all.

To know and completely understand its agency, then, we must consider it from three different points of view: we must consider it first in itself—we must see what it really was, what was its internal constitution, what the principles which there bore sway, what its nature. We must next consider it in its relations with temporal rulers—kings, lords, and others; and, finally, in its relations with the people. And when by this threefold investigation we have formed a complete picture of the Church, of its principles, its situation, and the influence which it exercised, we will verify this picture by history; we will see whether facts, whether what we properly call events, from the fifth to the twelfth century, agree with the conclusions which our threefold examination of the Church, of its own nature, of its relations with the masters of the world, and with the people, had previously led us to come to respecting it.

Let us first consider the Church in itself, its internal condition, its own nature.

The first, and perhaps the most important fact that demands our attention here, i its existence; the existence of a government of religion, of a priesthood, of an ecclesiastical corporation.

In the opinion of many enlightened persons, the very notion of a religious corporation, of a priesthood, of a government of religion, is absurd. They believe that a religion, whose object is the establishment of a clerical body, of a priesthood legally constituted in short, of a government of religion, must exercise, upon the whole, an influence more dangerous than useful. In their opinion religion is a matter purely individual betwixt man and God; and that whenever religion loses this character, whenever an exterior authority interferes between the individual and the object of his religious belief, that is, between him and God, religion is corrupted, and society in danger.

It will not do to pass by this question without taking a deeper view of it. In order to know what has been the influence of the Christian Church, we must know what ought to be, from the nature of the institution itself, the influence of a church, the influence of a priesthood. To judge of this influence we must inquire more especially whether religion is, in fact, purely individual; whether it excites and gives birth to nothing beyond this intimate relation between each individual and God; or whether it does not, in fact, necessarily become a source of new relations between man and man, and so necessarily lead to the formation of a religious society, and from that to a government of this society.

If we reduce religion to what is properly called religious feeling—to that feeling which, though very real, is somewhat vague, somewhat uncertain in its object, and which we can scarcely characterize but by naming it—to that feeling which addresses itself at one time to exterior nature, at another to the inmost recesses of the soul; to-day to the imagination, to-morrow to the mysteries of the future; which wanders everywhere, and settles nowhere; which, in a word, exhausts both the world of matter and of fancy in search of a resting-place, and yet finds none—if we reduce religion to this feeling; then, it would seem, it may remain purely individual. Such a feeling may give rise to a passing association; it may, it will indeed, find a pleasure in sympathy; it will feed upon it, it will be strengthened by it; but its fluctuating and doubtful character will prevent its becoming the principle of permanent and extensive association; will prevent it from accommodating itself to any system of precepts, of discipline, of forms; will prevent it, in a word, from giving birth to a society, to a religious government.

But either I have strangely deceived myself, or this religious feeling does not comprehend the whole religious nature of man. Religion, in my opinion, is quite another thing, and infinitely more comprehensive than this.

Joined to the destinies and nature of man, there are a number of problems whose solution we cannot work out in the present life; these, though connected with an order of things strange and foreign to the world around us, and apparently beyond the reach of human faculties, do not the less invincibly torment the soul of man, part of whose nature it seems to be, anxiously to desire and struggle for the clearing up of the mystery in which they are involved. The solution of these problems—the creeds and dogmas which contain it, or at least are supposed to contain it—such is the first object, the first source, of religion.

Another road brings us to the same point. To those among us who have made some progress in the study of moral philosophy, it is now, I presume, become sufficiently evident, that morality may exist independently of religious ideas; that the distinction between moral good and moral evil, the obligation to avoid evil and to cleave to that which is good, are laws as much acknowledged by man, in his proper nature, as the laws of logic; and which spring as much from a principle within him, as in his actual life they find their application. But granting these truths to be proved, yielding up to morality its independence, a question naturally arises in the human mind: whence cometh morality, whither doth it lead? This obligation to do good, which exists of itself, is it a fact standing by itself, without author, without aim? Doth it not conceal, or rather doth it not reveal to man, an origin, a destiny, reaching beyond this world? By this question, which arises spontaneously and inevitably, morality, in its turn, leads man to the porch of religion, and opens to him a sphere from which he has not borrowed it.

Thus on one side the problems of our nature, on the other the necessity of seeking a sanction, an origin, an aim, for morality, open to us fruitful and certain sources of religion. Thus it presents itself before under many other aspects besides that of a simple feeling such as I have described. It presents itself as an assemblage:

First, of doctrines called into existence by the problems which man finds in himself.

Secondly, of precepts which correspond with these doctrines, and give to natural morality a signification and sanction.

Thirdly, and lastly, of promises which addresses themselves to the hopes of humanity respecting futurity.

This is truly what constitutes religion. This is really what it is at bottom, and not a mere form of sensibility, a sally of the imagination, a species of poetry.

Religion thus brought back to its true element, to its essence, no longer appears as an affair purely individual, but as a powerful and fruitful principle of association. Would you regard it as a system of opinions, of dogmas? The answer is, truth belongs to no one; it is universal, absolute; all men are prone to seek it, to profess it in common. Would you rest upon the precepts which are associated with the doctrines? The reply is, law obligatory upon one is obligatory upon all—man is bound to promulgate it, to bring all under its authority. It is the same with respect to the promises which religion makes as the rewards of obedience to its faith and its precepts; it is necessary they should be spread, and that these fruits of religion should be offered to all. From the essential elements of religion then is seen to spring up a religious society; and it springs from them so infallibly, that the word which expresses the social feeling with the greatest energy, which expresses our invincible desire to propagate ideas, to extend society, is proselytism —a term particularly applied to religious creeds, to which it seems almost exclusively consecrated.

A religious society once formed—when a certain number of men are joined together by the same religious opinions and belief, yield obedience to the same law of religious precepts, and are inspired with the same religious hopes, they need a government. No society can exist a week, no, not even an hour, without a government. At the very instant in which a society is formed, by the very act of its formation it calls forth a government, which proclaims the commom truth that holds them together, which promulgates and maintains the precepts that this truth may be expected to bring forth. That a religious society, like all others, requires a controlling power, a government, is implied in the very fact that a society exists.

And not only is a government necessary, but it naturally arises of itself. I cannot spare much time to show how governments rise and become established in society in general. I shall only remark, that when matters are left to take their natural course, when no exterior force is applied to drive them from their usual route, power will fall into the hands of the most capable, of the most worthy, into the hands of those who will lead society on its way. Are there thoughts of a military expedition? the bravest will have the command. Is society anxious about some discovery, some learned enterprise? the most skillful will be sought for. The same will take place in all other matters. Let but the common order of things be observed, let the natural inequality of men freely display itself, and each will find the station that he is best fitted to fill. So as regards religion, men will be found no more equal in talents, in abilities, and in power, than they are in other matters: this man has a more striking method than others in proclaiming the doctrines of religion and making converts; another has more power in enforcing religious precepts; a third may excel in exciting religious hopes and emotions, and keeping the soul in a devout and holy frame. The same inequality of faculties and of influence, which gives rise to power in civil society, will be found to exist in religious, society. Missionaries, like generals, go forth to conquer. So that while, on the one hand, religious government naturally flows from the nature of a religious society, it as naturally develops itself, on the other, by the simple effect of human faculties, and their unequal distribtion.

That the moment that religion takes possession of a man a religious society begins to be formed; and the moment this religious society appears to give birth to a government.

A grave objection, however, here presents itself: in this case there is nothing to command, nothing to impose; no kind of force can here be legitimate. There is no place for government, because here the most perfect liberty ought to prevail.

Be it so. But is it not forming a gross and degrading idea of government to suppose that it resides *only*, to suppose that it resides *chiefly*, in the force which it exercises to make itself obeyed, in its coercive element?

Let us quit religion for a moment, and turn to civil governments. Trace with me, I beseech you, the simple march of circumstances. Society exists. Something is to be done, no matter what, in its name and for its interest; a law has to be executed, some measure to be adopted, a judgment to be pronounced. Now, certainly, there is a proper method of supplying these social wants; there is a proper law to make, a proper measure to adopt, a proper judgment to pronounce. Whatever may be the matter in hand, whatever may be the interest in question, there is, upon every occasion, a truth which must be discovered, and which ought to decide the matter, and govern the conduct to be adopted.

The first business of government is to seek this truth, is to discover what is just, reasonable, and suitable to society. When this is found, it is proclaimed: the next business is to introduce it to the public mind; to get it approved by the men upon whom it is to act; to persuade them that it is reasonable. In all this is there anything coercive? Not at all. Suppose now that the truth which ought to decide upon the affair, no matter what; suppose, I say, that the truth being found and proclaimed, all understandings should be at once convinced; all wills at once determined; that all should acknowledge that the government was right, and obey it spontaneously. There is nothing yet of compulsion, no occasion for the employment of force. Does it follow then that a government does not exist? Is there nothing of government in all this? To be sure there is, and it has accomplished its task. Compulsion appears not till the resistance of individuals calls for it—till the idea, the decision which authority has adopted, fails to obtain the approbation or the voluntary submission of all. Then government employs force to make itself obeyed. This is a necessary *consequence* of human imperfection; an imperfection which resides as well in power as in society. There is no way of entirely avoiding this; civil governments will always be obliged to have recourse, to a certain degree, to compulsion. Still it is evident they are not made up of compulsion, because, whenever they can, they are glad to do without it, to the great blessing of all; and their highest point of perfection is to be able to discard it, and to trust to means purely moral, to their influence upon the understanding: so that, in proportion as government can dispense with compulsion and force, the more faithful it is to its true nature, and the better it fulfils the purpose for which it is sent. This is not to shrink, this is not to give way, as people commonly cry out; it is merely acting in a different manner, in a manner much more general and powerful. Those governments which employ the most compulsion perform much less than those which scarcely ever have recourse to it. Government, by addressing itself to the understanding, by engaging the freewill of its subjects, by acting by means purely intellectual, instead of contracting, expands and elevates itself; it is then that it accomplishes most, and attains to the grandest objects. On the contrary, it is when government is obliged to be constantly employing its physical arm that it becomes weak and restrained—that it does little, and does that little badly.

The essence of government then by no means resides in compulsion, in the exercise of brute force; it consists more especially of a system of means and powers, conceived for the purpose of discovering upon all occasions what is best to be done; for the purpose of discovering the truth which by right ought to govern society, for the purpose of persuading all men to acknowledge this truth, to adopt and respect it willingly and freely. Thus I think I have shown that the necessity for, and the existence of a government, are very conceivable, even though there should be no room for compulsion, even though it should be absolutely forbidden.

This is exactly the case in the government of religious society. There is no doubt but compulsion is here strictly forbidden; there can be no doubt, as its only territory is the conscience of man, but that every species of force must be illegal, whatever may be the end designed. But government does not exist the less on this account. It still has to perform all the duties which we have just now enumerated. It is incumbent upon it to seek out the religious doctrines which resolve the problems of human destiny; or, if a general system of faith beforehand exists, in which these problems are already resolved, it will be its duty to discover and set forth its consequences in each particular case. It will be its duty to promulgate and maintain the precepts with correspond to its doctrines. It will be its duty to preach them, to teach them, and, if society wanders from them, to bring it back again to the right path. No compulsion; but the investigation, the preaching, the teaching of religious truths; the administering to religious wants; admonishing; censuring; this is the task which religious government has to perform. Suppress all force and coercion as much as you desire, still you will see all the essential questions connected with the organization of a government present themselves before you, and demand a solution. The question, for example, whether a body of religious magistrates is necessary, or whether it is possible to trust to the religious inspiration of individuals? This question, which is a subject of debate between most religious societies and that of the Quakers, will always exist, it must always remain a matter of discussion. Again, granting a body of religious magistrates to be necessary, the question arises whether a system of equality is to be preferred, or an hierarchal constitution—a graduated series of powers? This question will not cease because you take from the ecclesiastical magistrates, whatever they may be, all means of compulsion. Instead then of dissolving religious society in order to have the right to destroy religious government, it must be acknowledged that religious society forms itself naturally, that religious government flows no less naturally from religious society, and that the problem to be solved is on what conditions this government ought to exist, on what it is based, what are its principles, what the conditions of its legitimacy? This is the investigation which the existence of religious governments as of all others, compels us to undertake.

The conditions of legitimacy are the same in the government of a religious society as in all others. They may be reduced to two: the first is, that authority should be placed and constantly remain, as effectually at least as the imperfection of all human affairs will permit, in the hands of the best, the most capable; so that the legitimate superiority, which lies scattered in various parts of society, may be thereby drawn out, collected, and delegated to discover the social law—to exercise its authority. The second is, that the authority thus legitimately constituted should respect the legitimate liberties of those over whom it is called to govern. A good system for the formation and organization of authority, a good system of securities for liberty, are the two conditions in which the goodness of government in general resides, whether civil or religious. And it is by this standard that all governments should be judged.

Instead, then, of reproaching the Church, the government of the Christian world, with its existence, let us examine how it was constituted, and see whether its principles correspond with the two essential conditions of all good government.

Let us examine the Church in this twofold point of view.

In the first place, with regard to the formation and transmission of authority in the Church, there is a word, which has often been made use of, which I wish to get rid of altogether. I mean the word *caste*. This word has been too frequently applied to the Christian clergy, but its application to that body is both improper and unjust. The idea of hereditary right is inherent to the idea of caste. In every part of the world, in every country in which the system of *caste* has prevailed—in Egypt, in India—from the earliest time to the present day—you will find that castes have been everywhere essentially hereditary: they are, in fact, the transmission of the same rank and condition, of the same power, from father to son. Now where there is no inheritance there is no caste, but a corporation. The *esprit de corps*, or that certain degree of love and interest which every individual of an order feels toward it as a whole, as well as toward all its members, has its inconveniences, but differs very essentially from the spirit of caste. The celibacy of the clergy of itself renders the application of this term to the Christian Church altogether improper.

The important consequences of this distinction cannot have escaped you. To the system of castes, to the circumstance of inheritance, certain peculiar privileges are necessarily attached; the very definition of caste implies this. Where the same functions, the same powers become hereditary in the same families, it is evident that they possess peculiar privileges, which none can acquire independently of birth. This is indeed exactly what has taken place wherever the religious government has fallen into the hands of a caste; it has become a matter of privilege; all were shut out from it but those who belonged to the families of the caste. Now nothing like this is to be found in the Christian Church. Not only is the Church entirely free from this fault, but she has constantly maintained the principle, that all men, whatever their origin, are equally privileged to enter her ranks, to fill her highest offices, to enjoy her proudest dignities. The ecclesiastical career, particularly from the fifth to the twelfth century, was open to all. The Church was recruited from all ranks of society, from the lower as well as the higher—indeed, most frequently from the lower. When all around her fell under the tyranny of privilege, she alone maintained the principle of equality, of competition and emulation; she alone called the superior of all classes to the possession of power. This is the first great consequence which naturally flowed from the fact that the Church was a corporation and not a caste.

I will show you a second. It is the inherent nature of all castes to possess a degree of immobility. This assertion requires no proof. Turn over the pages of history, and you will find that wherever the tyranny of castes has predominated, society, whether religious or political, has universally become sluggish and torpid. A dread of improvement was certainly introduced at a certain epoch, and up to a certain point, into the Christian Church. But whatever regret this may cost us, it cannot be said that this feeling ever generally prevailed. It cannot be said that the Christian Church ever remained inactive and stationary. For a long course of centuries she was always in motion; at one time pushed forward by her opponents without, at others driven on by an inward impulse—by the want of reform, or of interior development. The Church, indeed, taken as a whole, has been constantly changing—constantly advancing—her history is diversified and progressive. Can it be doubted that she was indebted for this to the admission of all classes to the priestly offices, to the continual filling up of her ranks, upon a principle of equality, by which a stream of young and vigorous blood was ever flowing into her veins, keeping her unceasingly active and stirring, and defending her from the reproach of apathy and immobility which might otherwise have triumphed over her?

But how did the Church, in admitting all classes to power, satisfy herself that they had the right to be so admitted? How did she discover and proceed in taking from the bosom of society, the legitimate superiorities who should have a share in her government? In the Church two principles were in full vigor: *first*, the election of the inferior by the superior, which, in fact, was nothing more than choice or nomination; *secondly*, the election of the superior by the subordinates, or election properly so called, and such as we conceive to be election in the present day.

The ordination of priests, for example, the power of raising a man to the priestly office, rested solely with the superior. He alone made choice of the candidate for holy orders. The case was the same in the collation to certain ecclesiastical benefices, such as those attached to feudal grants, and some others; it was the superior, whether king, pope, or lord, who nominated to the bench. In other cases the true principle of election prevailed. The bishops had been, for a long time, and were still, often, in the period under consideration, elected by the inferior clergy; even the people sometimes took part in them. In monasteries the abbot was elected by the monks. At Rome, the pope was elected by the college of cardinals; and, at an earlier date, even all the Roman clergy had a voice in his election. You may here clearly observe, then, the two principles, the choice of the inferior by the superior, and the election of the superior by the subordinates; which were admitted and acted upon in the Church, particularly at the period which now engages our attention. It was by one of these two means that men were appointed to the various offices in the Church, or obtained any portion of ecclesiastical authority.

These two principles were not only in operation at the same time, but being altogether opposite in their nature, a constant struggle prevailed between them. After a strife for centuries, after many vicissitudes, the nomination of the inferior by the superior gained the day in the Christian Church. Yet, from the fifth to the twelfth century, the opposite principle, the election of the superior by the subordinates, continued generally to prevail.

We must not be astonished at the co-existence of these two opposite principles. If we look at society in general, at the common course of affairs, at the manner in which authority is there transmitted, we shall find that this transmission is sometimes effected by one of these modes, and sometimes the other. The Church did not invent them, she found them in the providential government of human things, and borrowed them from it. There is somewhat of truth, of utility, in both. Their combination would often prove the best mode of discovering legitimate power. It is a great misfortune, in my opinion, that only one of them, the choice of the inferior by the superior, should have been victorious in the Church. The second, however, was never entirely banished, but under various names, with more or less success, has re-appeared in every epoch, with at least sufficient force to protest against, and interrupt, prescription.

The Christian Church, at the period of which we are speaking, derived an immense force from its respect for equality and the various kinds of legitimate superiority. It was the most popular society of the time—the most accessible: it alone opened its arms to all the talents, to all the ambitiously noble of our race. To this, above all, it owed its greatness, at least certainly much more than to its riches, and the illegitimate means which it but too often employed.

With regard to the second condition of a good government, namely, a respect for liberty, that of the Church leaves much to be desired.

Two bad principles here met together. One avowed, forming part and parcel, as it were, of the doctrines of the Church; the other, in no way a legitimate consequence of her doctrines, was introduced into her bosom by human weakness.

The first was a denial of the rights of individual reason

—the claim of transmitting points of faith from the highest authority, downward, throughout the whole religious body, without allowing to any one the right of examining them for himself. But it was more easy to lay this down as a principle than to carrry it out in practice; and the reason is obvious, for a conviction cannot enter into the human mind unless the human mind first opens the door to it; it cannot enter by force. In whatever way it may present itself, whatever name it may invoke, reason looks to it, and if it forces an entrance, it is because reason is satisfied. Thus individual reason has always continued to exist, and under whatever name it may have been disguised, has always considered and reflected upon the ideas which have been attempted to be forced upon it. Still, however, it must be admitted but as too true, that reason often becomes impaired; that she loses her power, becomes mutilated and contracted—that she may be brought not only to make a sorry use of her faculties, but to make a more limited use of them than she ought to do. So far indeed the bad principle which crept into the Church took effect, but with regard to the practical and complete operation of this principle, it never took place—it was impossible it ever should.

The second vicious principle was the right of compulsion assumed by the Romish Church; a right, however, contrary to the very nature and spirit of religious society, to the origin of the Church itself, and to its primitive maxims. A right, too, disputed by some of the most illustrious fathers of the Church—by St. Ambrose, St. Hilary, St. Martin—but whch, nevertheless, prevailed and became an important feature in its history. The right it assumed of forcing belief, if these two words can stand together, or of punishing faith physically, of persecuting heresy, that is to say, a contempt for the legitimate liberty of human thought, was an error which found its way into the Romish Church before the beginning of the fifth century, and has in the end cost her very dear.

If then we consider the state of the Church with regard to the liberty of its members, we must confess that its principles in this respect were less legitimate, less salutary, than those which presided at the rise and formation of ecclesiastical power. It must not, however, be supposed, that a bad principle radically vitiates an institution; nor even that it does it all the mischief of which it is pregnant. Nothing tortures history more than logic. No sooner does the human mind seize upon an idea, than it draws from it all its possible consequences; makes it produce, in imagination, all that it would in reality be capable of producing, and then figures it down in history with all the extravagant additions which itself has conjured up. This. however, is nothing like the truth. Events are not so prompt in their consequences, as the human mind in its deductions. There is in all things a mixture of good and evil, so profound, so inseparable. that, in whatever part you penetrate, if even you descend to the lowest elements of society, or into the soul itself, you will there find these two principles dwelling together, developing themselves side by side, perpetually struggling and quarrelling with each other. but neither of them ever obtaining a complete victory, or absolutely destroying its fellow. Human nature never reaches to the extreme either of good or evil. It passes, without ceasing, from one to the other; it recovers itself at the moment when it seems lost forever It slips and loses ground at the moment when it seems to have assumed the firmest position.

We again discover here that character of discordance, of diversity. of strife, to which I formerly called your attention, as the fundamental character of European civilization. Besides this, there is another general fact which characterizes the government of the Church, which we must not pass over without notice. In the present day, when the idea of government presents itself to our mind, we know, of whatever kind it may be, that it will scarcely pretend to any authority beyond the outward actions of men, beyond the civil relations between man and man. Governments do not profess to carry their rule further than this. With regard to human thought, to the human conscience, to the intellectual powers of man: with regard to individual opinions, to private morals—with these they do not interfere: this would be to invade the domain of liberty.

The Christian Church did, and was bent upon doing, exactly the contrary. What she undertook to govern was the human thought, human liberty, private morals, individual opinions. She did not draw up a code like ours, which took account only of those crimes that are at the same time offensive to morals and dangerous to society, punishing them only when, and because, they bore this twofold character; but prepared a catalogue of all those actions, criminal more particularly in a moral point of view, and punished them all under the name of sins. Her aim was their entire suppression. In a word, the government of the Church did not, like our modern governments, direct her attention to the outward man, or to the purely civil relations of men among themselves; she addressed herself to the inward man, to the thought, to the conscience; in fact, to that which of all things is most hidden and secure, most free, and which spurns the least restraint. The Church, then, by the very nature of its undertaking, combined with the nature of some of the principles upon which its government was founded, stood in great peril of falling into tyranny; of an illegitimate employment of force. In the meantime, this force was encountered by a resistance within the Church itself, which it could never overcome. Human thought and liberty, however fettered, however confined for room and space in which to exercise their faculties, oppose with so much energy every attempt to enslave them, that their reaction makes even despotism itself to yield, and give up something every moment. This took place in the very bosom of the Christian Church. We have seen heresy proscribed—the right of free inquiry condemned; a contempt shown for individual reason, the principle of the imperative transmission of doctrines by human authority established. And yet where can we find a society in which individual reason more boldly developed itself than in the Church? What are sects and heresies, if not the fruit of individual opinions? These sects, these heresies, all these oppositions which arose in the Christian Church, are the most decisive proof of the life and moral activity which reigned within her: a life stormy, painful, sown with perils, with errors and crimes—yet splendid and mighty, and which has given place to the noblest developments of intelligence and mind. But leaving the opposition, and looking to the ecclesiastical government itself—how does the case stand here? You will find it constituted, you will find it acting, in a manner quite opposite to what you would expect from some of its principles. It denies the right of inquiry, it wishes to deprive individual reason of its liberty; yet it appeals to reason incessantly; practical liberty actually predominates in its affairs. What are its institutions, its means of action? Provincial councils, national councils, general councils; a perpetual correspondence, a perpetual publication of letters, of admonitions, of writings. No government ever went so far in discussions and open deliberations. One might fancy one's self in the midst of the philosophical schools of Greece. But it was not here a mere discussion, it was not a simple search after truth that here occupied the attention; it was questions of authority, of measures to be taken, of decrees to be drawn up, in short, the business of a government. Such indeed was the energy of intellectual life in the bosom of this government, that it became its predominant, universal character; to this all others gave way; and that which shone forth from all its parts, was the exercise of reason and liberty.

I am far, notwithstanding all this, from believing that the vicious principles, which I have endeavored to explain, and which, in my opinion, existed in the Christian Church, existed there without producing any effect. In the period now under review, they already bore very bitter fruits; at a later period they bore others still more bitter; still they did not produce all the evils which might have been expected, they did not choke the good which sprang up in the same soil. Such was the Church considered in itself, in its interior, in its own nature.

Let us now consider it in its relations with sovereigns, with the holders of temporal authority. This is the second point of view in which I have promised to consider it.

When at the fall of the western empire, when, instead of the ancient Roman government, under which the Church had been born, under which she had grown up, with which she had common habits and old connexions, she found herself surrounded by barbarian kings, by barbarian chieftains, wandering from place to place, or shut up in their castles, with whom she had nothing in common, between whom and her there was as yet no tie—neither traditions, nor creeds, nor feelings; her danger appeared great, and her fears were equally so.

One only idea became predominant in the Church; it was to take possession of these new-comers—to convert them. The relations of the Church with the barbarians had, at first, scarcely any other aim.

To gain these barbarians, the most effective means seemed to be to dazzle their senses and work upon their imagination. Thus it came to pass that the number, pomp, and variety of religious ceremonies were at this epoch wonderfully increased. The ancient chronicles particularly show, that it was principally in this way that the Church worked upon the barbarians. She converted them by grand spectacles.

But even when they had become settled and converted, even after the growth of some common ties between them, the danger of the Church was not over. The brutality, the unthinking, the unreflecting character of the barbarians were so great, that the new faith, the new feelings with which they had been inspired, exercised but a very slight empire over them. When every part of society fell a prey to violence, the Church could scarcely hope altogether to escape. To save herself she announced a principle, which had already been set up, though but very vaguely, under the empire; the separation of spiritual and temporal power, and their mutual independence. It was by the aid of this principle that the Church dwelt freely by the side of the barbarians; she maintained that force had no authority over religious belief, hopes, or promises, and that the spiritual and temporal worlds are completely distinct.

You cannot fail to see at once the beneficial consequences which have resulted from this principle. Independently of the temporary service it was of to the Church, it has had the inestimable effect of founding in justice the separation of the two authorities, of preventing one from controlling the other. In addition to this, the Church, by asserting the independence of the intellectual world, in its collective form, prepared the independence of the intellectual world in individuals—the independence of thought. The Church declared that the system of religious belief could not be brought under the yoke of force, and each individual has been led to hold the same language for himself. The principle of free inquiry, the liberty of individual thought, is exactly the same as that of the independence of the spiritual authority in general, with regard to temporal power.

The desire for liberty, unfortunately, is but a step from the desire for power. The Church soon passed from one to the other. When she had established her independence, it was in accordance with the natural course of ambition that she should attempt to raise her spiritual authority above temporal authority. We must not, however, suppose that this claim had any other origin than the weaknesses of humanity; some of these are very profound, and it is of importance that they should be known.

When liberty prevails in the intellectual world, when the thoughts and consciences of men are not enthralled by a power which calls in question their right of deliberating, of deciding, and employs its authority against them; when there is no visible constituted spiritual government laying claim to the right of dictating opinions; in such circumstances, the idea of the domination of the spiritual order over the temporal could scarcely spring up. Such is very nearly the present state of the world. But when there exists, as there did in the tenth century, a government of the spiritual order; when the human thought and conscience are subject to certain laws, to certain institutions, to certain authorities, which have arrogated to themselves the right to govern, to constrain them; in short, when spiritual authority is established, when it has effectively taken possession, in the name of right and power, of the human reason and conscience, it is natural that it should go on to assume a domination over the temporal order; that it should argue: "What! have I a right, have I an authority over that which is most elevated, most independent in man—over his thoughts, over his interior will, over his conscience; and have I not a right over his exterior, his temporal and material interests? Am I the interpreter of divine justice and truth, and yet not able to regulate the affairs of this world according to justice and truth?"

The force of this reasoning shows that the spiritual order had a natural tendency to encroach on the temporal. This tendency was increased by the fact, that the spiritual order, at this time, comprised all the intelligence of the age, every possible development of the human mind. There was but one science, *theology;* but one spiritual order, the theological: all the other sciences, rhetoric, arithmetic, and even music, centred in theology.

The spiritual power, finding itself thus in possession of all the intelligence of the age, at the head of all intellectual activity, was naturally enough led to arrogate to itself the general government of the world.

A second cause, which very much favored its views, was the dreadful state of the temporal order, the violence and inquity which prevailed in all temporal governments.

For some centuries past men might speak, with a degree of confidence, of temporal power; but temporal power, at the epoch of which we are speaking, was mere brutal force, a system of rapine and violence. The Church, however imperfect might be her notions of morality and justice, was infinitely superior to a temporal government such as this; and the cry of the people continually urged her to take its place.

When a pope or bishop proclaimed that a sovereign had lost his rights, that his subjects were released from their oath of fidelity, this interference, though undoubtedly liable to the greatest abuses, was often, in the particular case to which it was directed, just and salutary. It generally holds, indeed, that where liberty is wanting, religion, in a great measure, supplies its place. In the tenth century, the oppressed nations were not in a state to protect themselves, to defend their rights against civil violence—religion, in the name of Heaven, placed itself between them. This is one of the causes which most contributed to the success of the usurpations of the Church.

There is a third cause, which, in my opinion, has not been sufficiently noticed. This is the manifold character and situation of the leaders of the Church; the variety of aspects under which they appeared in society. On one side they were prelates, members of the ecclesiastical order, a portion of the spiritual power, and as such independent; on the other, they were vassals, and by this title formed one of the links of civil feudalism. But this was not all: besides being vassals, they were also subjects. Something similar to the ancient relations in which the bishops and clergy had stood toward the Roman emperors now existed between the clergy and the barbarian sovereigns. A series of causes, which it would be tedious to detail, had brought the bishops to look upon the barbarian kings, to a certain degree, as the successors of the Roman emperors, and to attribute to them the same rights. The heads of the clergy then had a threefold character: first, they were ecclesiastics, and as such held to the performance of certain duties; secondly, they were feudal vassals, with the rights and obligations of such; thirdly, they were mere subjects, and as such bound to render obedience to an absolute sovereign. Observe the necessary consequences of this. The temporal sovereigns, no whit less covetous, no whit less ambitious than the bishops, frequently made use of their temporal power, as superiors or sovereigns, to attack the independence of the Church, to usurp the right of collating to benefices, of nominating to bishoprics, and so on. On the other side, the bishops often sheltered themselves under their spiritual independence to refuse the performance of their obligations as vassals and subjects; so that on both sides there was an inevitable tendency to trespass on the rights of the other: on the side of the sovereigns, to destroy spiritual independence; on the side of the heads of the Church, to make their spiritual independence the means of universal dominion.

This result showed itself sufficiently plain in events well known to you all; in the quarrel respecting investitures; in the struggle between the Holy See and the empire. The threefold character of the heads of the Church, and the difficulty of preventing them from trespassing on one another, was the real cause of the uncertainty and strife of all its pretensions.

Finally, the Church had a third connexion with the sovereigns, and it was to her the most disastrous and fatal. She laid claim to the right of coercion, to the right of restraining and punishing heresy. But she had no means by which to do this; she had no physical force at her disposal: when she had condemned the heretic, she was without the power to carry her sentence into execution. What was the consequence? She called to her aid the secular arm; she had to borrow the power of the civil authority as the means of compulsion. To what a wretched shift was she thus driven by the adoption of the wicked and detestable principles of coercion and persecution!

I must stop here. There is not sufficient time for us to finish our investigation of the Church. We have still to consider its relation with the people, the principles which prevailed in its intercourse with them, and what consequences resulted from its bearing upon civilization in general. I shall afterward endeavor to confirm by history, by facts, by what befell the Church from the fifth to the twelfth century, the inductions which we have drawn from the nature of her institutions and principles.

LECTURE VI.

THE CHURCH.

IN the present lecture we shall conclude our inquiries respecting the state of the Church. In the last, I stated that I should place it before you in three principal points of view: first, in itself—in its interior constitution and nature, as a distinct and independent society; secondly, in its relations with sovereigns, with temporal power; thirdly, in its relations with the people. Having then been able to accomplish no more than the first two parts of my task, it remains for me to-day to place before you the Church in its relations with the people. I shall endeavor, after I have done this, to sum up this threefold examination, and to give a general judgment respecting the influence of the Church from the fifth to the twelfth century; finally, I shall close this part of my subject by verifying my statements by an appeal to facts, by an examination of the history of the Church during this period.

You will easily understand that, in speaking of the relations of the Church with the people, I shall be obliged to confine myself to very general views. It is impossible that I should enter into a detail of the practices of the Church, or recount the daily intercourse of the clergy with their charge. It is the prevailing principles, and the great effects of the system and conduct of the Church toward the body of Christians, that I shall endeavor to bring before you.

A striking feature, and, I am bound to say, a radical vice in the relations of the Church with the people, was the separation of the governors and the governed, which left the governed without any influence upon their government, which established the independence of the clergy with respect to the general body of Christians.

It would seem as if this evil was called forth by the state of man and society, for it was introduced into the Christian Church at a very early period. The separation of the clergy and the people was not altogether perfected at the time of which we are speaking; there were certain occasions—the election of bishops, for example—upon which the people, at least sometimes, took part in Church government. This interference, however, became weaker and weaker, as well as more rare; even in the second century it had begun rapidly and visibly to decline. Indeed, the tendency of the Church to detach itself from the rest of society, the establishment of the independence of the clergy, forms, to a great extent, the history of the Church from its very cradle.

It is impossible to disguise the fact, that from this circumstance sprang the greater number of abuses, which, from this period, cost the Church so dear; as well as many others which entered into her system in after-times. We must not, however, impute all its faults to this principle, nor must we regard this tendency to isolation as peculiar to the Christian clergy. There is in the very nature of religious society a powerful inclination to elevate the governors above the governed; to regard them as something distinct, something divine. This is the effect of the mission with which they are charged; of the character in which they appear before the people. This effect, however, is more hurtful in a religious society than in any other. For with what do they pretend to interfere? With the reason and conscience and future destiny of man: that this to say, with that which is the closest locked up; with that which is most strictly individual, with that which is most free. We can imagine how, up to a certain point, a man, whatever ill may result from it, may give up the direction of his temporal affairs to an outward authority. We can conceive a nation of that philosopher who, when one told him that his house was on fire, said, "Go and tell my wife; I never meddle with household affairs." But when our conscience, our thoughts, our intellectual existence are at stake—to give up the government of one's self, to deliver over one's very soul to the authority of a stranger, is, indeed, a moral suicide: is, indeed, a thousand times worse than bodily servitude—than to become a mere appurtenance of the soil.

Such, nevertheless, was the evil which, without ever, as I shall presently show, completely prevailing, invaded more and more the Christian Church in its relations with the people. We have already seen, that even in the bosom of the Church itself, the lower orders of the clergy had no guarantee for their liberty; it was much worse, out of the Church, for the laity. Among churchmen there was at least discussion, deliberation, the display of individual faculties; the struggle, itself, supplied in some measure the place of liberty. There was nothing, however, like this between the clergy and the people. The laity had no further share in the government of the Church than as simple lookers-on. Thus we see quickly shoot up and thrive, the idea that theology, that religious questions and affairs, were the privileged territory of the clergy; that the clergy alone had the right, not only to decide upon all matters respecting it, but likewise that they alone had the right to study it, and that the laity ought not to intermeddle with it. At the period of which we are now speaking, this theory had fully established its authority, and it has required ages, and revolutions full of terror, to overcome it; to restore to the public the right of debating religious questions, and inquiring into their truths.

In principle, then, as well as in fact, the legal separation of the clergy and the laity was nearly completed before the twelfth century.

It must not, however, be understood, that the Christian world had no influence upon its government during this period. Of legal interference it was destitute, but not of influence. It is, indeed, almost impossible that such should be the case under any kind of government, and more particularly so of one founded upon the common opinions and belief of the governing and governed. For, wherever this community of ideas springs up and expands, wherever the same intellectual movement carries onward for government and the people, there necessarily becomes formed between them a tie, which no vice in their organization can ever altogether break. To make you clearly understand what I mean, I will give you an example, familiar to us all, taken from the political world. At no period in the history of France had the French nation less power of a legal nature, I mean by way of institutions, of interfering in the government, than in the seventeenth and eighteenth centuries, during the reigns of Louis XIV. and XV. All the direct and official means by which the people could exercise any authority had been cut off and suppressed. Yet there cannot be a doubt but that the public, the country, exercised, at this time, more influence upon the government than at any other, more, for example, than when the states-general had been frequently convoked; than when the parliaments intermeddled to a considerable extent in politics, than when the people had a much greater legal participation in the government.

It must have been observed by all that there exists a power which no law can comprise or suppress, and which, in times of need, goes even further than institutions. Call it the spirit of the age, public intelligence, opinion, or what you will, you cannot doubt its existence. In France, during the seventeenth and eighteenth centuries, this public opinion was more powerful than at any other epoch; and, though it was deprived of the legal means of acting upon the government, yet it acted indirectly, by the force of ideas common to the governing and the governed, by the absolute necessity under which the governing found themselves of attending to the opinions of the governed. What took place in the Church from the fifth to the twelfth century was very similar to this. The body of the Christian world, it is true, had no legal means of expressing its desires; but there was a great advancement of mind in religious matters: this movement bore along clergy and laity together, and in this way the people acted upon the Church.

It is of the greatest importance that these indirect influences should be kept in view in the study of history. They are much more efficacious, and often more salutary, than we take them to be. It is very natural that men should wish their influence to be prompt and apparent; that they should covet the credit of promoting success, of establishing power, of procuring triumph. But this is not always either possible or useful. There are times and situations when the indirect, unperceived influence is more beneficial, more practicable. Let me borrow another illustration from politics. We know that the English parliament more than once, and particularly in 1641, demanded, as many other popular assemblies have done in such cases, the power to nominate the ministers and great officers of the crown. The immense direct force which by this means it would exercise upon the government was regarded as a precious guarantee. But how has it turned out? Why, in the few cases in which it has been permitted to possess this power, the result has been always unfavorable. The choice has been badly concerted; affairs badly conducted. But what is the case in the present day? Is it not the influence of the two houses of parliament which determines the choice of ministers, and the nomination to all the great offices of state? And, though this influence be indirect and general, it is found to work better than the direct interference of parliament, which has always terminated badly.

There is one reason why this should be so, which I must beg leave to lay before you, at the expense of a few minutes of your time. The direct action upon government supposes those to whom it is confided possessed of superior talents—of superior information, understanding, and prudence. As they go to the object at once, and *per saltem* as it were, they must be sure not to miss their mark. Indirect influences, on the contrary, pursuing a tortuous course—only arriving at their object through numerous difficulties—become rectified and adapted to their end by the very obstacles they have to encounter. Before they can succeed, they must undergo discussion, be combated and controlled; their triumph is slow, conditional, and partial. It is on this account that where society is not sufficiently advanced to make it prudent to place immediate power in the hands of the people, these indirect influences, though often insufficient, are nevertheless to be preferred. It was by such that the Christian world acted upon its government;—acted, I must allow, very inadequately—by far too little; but still it is something that it acted at all.

There was another thing which strengthened the tie between the clergy and laity. This was the dispersion of the clergy into every part of the social system. In almost all other cases, where a church has been formed independent of the people whom it governed, the body of priests has been composed of men in nearly the same condition of life. I do not mean that the inequalities of rank were not sufficiently great among them, but that the power was lodged in the hands of colleges of priests living in common, and governing the people submitted to their laws from the innermost recess of some sacred temple. The organization of the Christian Church was widely different. From the thatched cottage of the husbandman—from the miserable hut of the serf at the foot of the feudal chateau to the palace of the monarch—there was everywhere a clergyman. This diversity in the situation of the Christian priesthood, their participation in all the varied fortunes of humanity—of common life—was a great bond of union between the laity and clergy; a bond which has been wanting in most other hierarchies invested with power. Besides this, the bishops, the heads of the Christian clergy, were, as we have seen, mixed up with the feudal system: they were, at the same time, members of the civil and of the ecclesiastical governments. This naturally led to similarity of feeling, of interests, of habits, and of manners, in the clergy and laity. There has been a good deal said, and with reason, of military bishops, of priests who led secular lives; but we may be assured that this evil, however great, was not so hurtful as the system which kept priests forever locked up in a temple, altogether separated from common life. Bishops who took a share in the cares, and, up to a certain point, in the disorders of civil life, were of more use in society than those who were altogether strangers to the people, to their wants, their affairs, and their manners. In our system there has been, in this respect, a similarity of fortune, of condition, which, if it have not altogether corrected, has, at least, softened the evil which the separation of the governing and governed must in all cases prove.

Now, having pointed out this separation, having endeavored to determine its extent, let us see how the Christian Church governed—let us see in what way it acted upon the people under its authority.

What did it do, on one hand, for the development of man, for the intellectual progress of the individual?

What did it do, on the other, for the melioration of the social system?

What regard to individual development, I fear the Church, at this epoch, gave herself but little trouble about it. She endeavored to soften the rugged manners of the great, and to render them more kind and just in their conduct toward the weak. She endeavored to inculcate a life of morality among the poor, and to inspire them with higher sentiments and hopes than the lot in which they were cast would give rise to. I believe not, however, that for individual man—for the drawing forth or advancement of his capacities—that the Church did much, especially for the laity, during this period. What she did in this way was confined to the bosom of her own society. For the development of the clergy, for the instruction of the priesthood, she was anxiously alive: to promote this she had her schools, her colleges, and all other institutions which the deplorable state of society would permit. These schools and colleges, it is true, were all theological, and destined for the education of the clergy alone; and though, from the intimacy between the civil and religious orders, they could not but have some influence upon the rest of the world, it was very slow and indirect. It cannot, indeed, be denied but the Church, too, necessarily excited and kept alive a general activity of mind, by the career which she opened to all those whom she judged worthy to enlist into her ranks, but beyond this she did little for the intellectual improvement of the laity.

For the melioration of the social state her labors were greater and more efficacious.

She combated with much perseverance and pretinacity the great vices of the social condition, particularly slavery. It has been frequently asserted that the abolition of slavery in the modern world must be altogether carried to the credit of Christianity. I believe this is going too far: slavery subsisted for a long time in the bosom of Christian society without much notice being taken of it—without any great outcry against it. To effect its abolition required the co-operation of several causes—a great development of new ideas, of new principles of civilization. It cannot, however, be denied that the Church employed its influence to restrain it; the clergy in general, and especially several popes, enforced the manumission of their slaves as a duty incumbent upon laymen, and loudly inveighed against the scandal of keeping Christians in bondage. Again, the greater part of the forms by which slaves were set free, at various epochs, are founded upon religious motives. It is under the impression of some religious feeling—the hopes of the future, the equality of all Christian men, and so on—that the freedom of the slave is granted. These, it must be confessed, are rather convincing proofs of the influence of the Church, and of her desire for the abolition of this evil of evils, this iniquity of iniquities!

The Church did not labor less worthily for the improvement of civil and criminal legislation. We know to what a terrible extent, notwithstanding some few principles of liberty, this was absurd and wretched; we have read of the irrational and superstitious proofs to which the barbarians occasionally had recourse—their trial by battle, their ordeals, their oaths of compurgation—as the only means by which they could discover the truth. To replace these by more rational and legitimate proceedings, the Church earnestly labored, and labored not in vain. I have already spoken of the striking difference between the laws of the Visigoths, mostly promulgated by the councils of Toledo, and the codes of the barbarians. It is impossible to compare them without at once admitting the immense superiority of the notions of the Church in matters of jurisprudence, justice, and legislation—in all relating to the discovery of truth, and a knowledge of human nature. It must certainly be admitted that the greater part of these notions were borrowed from Roman legislation; but it is not less certain that they would have perished if the Church had not preserved and defended them—if she had not labored to spread them abroad. If the question, for example, is respecting the employment of oaths, open the laws of the Visigoths, and see with what prudence it controls their use:—

> Let the judge, in order to come at the truth, first interrogate the witnesses, then examine the papers, and not allow of oaths too easily. The investigation of truth and justice demands, that the documents on both sides should be carefully examined, and that the necessity of the oath, suspended over the head of both parties, should only come unexpectedly. Let the oath only be adopted in causes in which the judge shall be able to discover no written documents, no proof, nor guide to the truth.

In criminal matters, the punishment is proportioned to the offense, according to tolerably correct notions of philosophy, morals, and justice; the efforts of an enlightened legislator struggling against the violence and caprice of barbarian manners. The title of *cæde et morte hominum* gives us a very favorable example of this, when compared with the corresponding laws of the other nations. Among the latter, it is the damage alone which seems to constitute the crime; and the punishment is sought for in the pecuniary preparation which is made in compounding for it; but in the code of the Visigoths the crime is traced to its true and moral principle—the intention of the perpetrator. Various shades of guilt—involuntary homicide, chance-medley homicide, justifiable homicide, unpremeditated homicide, and wilful murder—are distinguished and defined nearly as accurately as in our modern codes; the punishments likewise varying, so as to make a fair approximation to justice. The legislator, indeed, carried the principle of justice still further. He endeavored, if not to abolish, at least to lessen, that difference of legal value, which the other barbarian laws put upon the life of man. The only distinction here made was between the freeman and the slave. With regard to the freeman, the punishment did not vary either according to the perpetrator, or according to the rank of the slain, but only according to the moral guilt of the murderer. With regard to slaves, not daring entirely to deprive masters of the right of life and death, he at least endeavored to restrain it and destroy its brutal character by subjecting it to an open and regular procedure.

The law itself is worthy of attention, and I therefore shall give it at at length:—

"If no one who is culpable, or the accomplice in a crime, ought to go unpunished, how much more reasonable is it that those should be restrained who commit suicide maliciously, or from a slight cause! Thus, as masters in their pride often put their slaves to death without any cause, it is proper to extirpate altogether this license, and to decree that the present law shall be for ever binding upon all. No master or mistress shall have power to put to death any of their slaves, male or female, or any of their dependants, without public judgment. If any slave, or other servant, commits a crime which renders them subject to capital punishment, his master or his accuser shall immediately give information to the judge, or count, or duke, of the place in which the crime has been perpetrated. After the matter has been tried, if the crime is proved, let the criminal receive, either by the judge or by his own master, the sentence of death which he has merited; in such manner, however, that if the judge desires not to put the accused to death, he must draw up against him in writing, a capital sentence, and then it will remain with his master to kill him or grant him his life. But when, indeed, a slave, by a fatal audacity, in resisting his master, shall strike, or attempt to strike him with his arm, with a stone, or by any other means, and the master, in defending himself, kills the slave in his anger, the master shall in nowise be liable to the punishment of homicide. But it will be necessary to prove that the fact has so happened, and that by the testimony or oath of the slaves, male or female, who witnessed it, and also by the oath of the person himself who committed the deed. Whosoever from pure malice shall kill a slave himself, or employ another to do so, without his having been publicly tried, shall be considered infamous, shall be declared incapable of giving evidence, shall be banished for life, and his property given to his nearest heirs."—(*For. Jud.* L. VI., tit. V., 1. 12.)

There is another circumstance connected with the institutions of the Church, which has not, in general, been so much noticed as it deserves. I allude to its penitentiary system, which is the more interesting in the present day, because, so far as the principles and applications of moral law are concerned, it is almost completely in unison with the notions of modern philosophy. If we look closely into the nature of the punishments inflicted by the Church at public penance, which was its principle mode of punishing, we shall find that their object was, above all other things, to excite repentance in the soul of the guilty; in that of the lookers-on, the moral terror of example. But there is another idea which mixes itself up with this—the idea of expiation. I know not, generally speaking, whether it be possible to separate the idea of punishment from that of expiation; and whether there be not in all punishment, independently of the desire to awaken the guilty to repentance, and to deter those from vice who might be, under temptation, a secret and imperious desire to expiate the wrong committed. Putting this question, however, aside, it is sufficiently evident that repentance and example were the objects proposed by the Church in every part of its system of penance. And is not the attainment of these very objects the end of every truly philosophical legislation? Is it not for the sake of these very principles that the most enlightened lawyers have clamored for a reform in the penal legislation of Europe? Open their books —those of Jeremy Bentham for example—and you will be astonished at the numerous resemblances which you will everywhere find between their plans of punishment and those adopted by the Church. We may be quite sure that they have not borrowed them from her; and the Church could scarcely foresee that her example would one day be quoted in support of the system of philosophers not very remarkable for their devotion.

Finally, she endeavored by every means in her power to suppress the frequent recourse which at this period was had to violence and the continual wars to which society was so prone. It is well known what the truce of God was, as well as a number of other similar measures by which the Church hoped to prevent the employment of physical force, and to introduce into the social system more order and gentleness. The facts under this head are so well known, that I shall not go into any detail concerning them.

Having now run over the principal points to which I wished to draw attention respecting the relations of the Church to the people; having now considered it under the three aspects, which I proposed to do, we know it within and without; in its interior constitution, and in its twofold relations with society. It remains for us to deduce from what we have learned by way of inference, by way of conjecture, its general influence upon European civilization. This is almost done to our hands. The simple recital of the facts of the predominant principles of the Church, both reveals and explains its influence: the results have in a manner been brought before us with the causes. If, however, we endeavor to sum them up, we shall be led, I think, to two general conclusions.

The fist is, that the Church has exercised a vast and important influence upon the moral and intellectual order of Europe; upon the notions, sentiments, and manners of society. This fact is evident; the intellectual and moral progress of Europe has been essentially theological. Look at its history from the fifth to the sixteenth century, and you will find throughout that theology has possessed and directed the human mind; every idea is impressed with theology; every question that has been started, whether philosophical, political, or historical, has been considered in a religious point of view. So powerful, indeed, has been the authority of the Church in matters of intellect, that even the mathematical and physical sciences have been obliged to submit to its doctrines. The spirit of theology has been as it were the blood which has circulated in the veins of the European world down to the time of Bacon and Descartes. Bacon in England, and Descartes in France, were the first who carried the human mind out of the pale of theology.

We shall find the same fact hold if we travel through the regions of literature: the habits, the sentiments, the language of theology there show themselves at every step.

This influence, taken altogether, has been salutary. It not only kept up and ministered to the intellectual movement in Europe, but the system of doctrines and precepts, by whose authority it stamped its impress upon that movement, was incalculably superior to any which the ancient world had known.

The influence of the Church, moreover, has given to the development of the human mind, in our modern world, an extent and variety which it never possessed elsewhere. In the east, intelligence was altogether religious: among the Greeks, it was almost exclusively human: there human culture—humanity, properly so called, its nature and destiny—actually disappeared; here it was man alone, his passions, his feelings, his present interests, which occupied the field. In our world the spirit of religion mixes itself with all, but excludes nothing. Human feelings, human interests, occupy a considerable space in every branch of our literature; yet the religious character of man, that portion of his being which connects him with another world, appears at every turn in them all. Could modern intelligence assume a visible shape we should recognize at once, in its mixed character, the finger of man and the finger of God. Thus the two great sources of human development, humanity and religion, have been open at the same time and flowed in plenteous streams. Notwithstanding all the evil, all the abuses, which may have crept into the Church—notwithstanding all the acts of tyranny of which she has been guilty, we must still acknowledge her influence upon the progress and culture of the human intellect to have been beneficial; that she has assisted in its development rather than its compression, in its extension rather than its confinement.

The case is widely different when we look at the Church in a political point of view. By softening the rugged manners and sentiments of the people; by raising her voice against a great number of practical barbarisms, and doing what she could to expel them, there is no doubt but the Church largely contributed to the melioration of the social condition; but with regard to politics, properly so called, with regard to all that concerns the relations between the governing and the governed—between power and liberty—I cannot conceal my opinion, that its influence has been baneful. In this respect the Church has always shown herself as the interpreter and defender of two systems, equally vicious, that is, of theocracy, and of the imperial tyranny of the Roman empire—that is to say, of despotism, both religious and civil. Examine all its institutions, all its laws; peruse its canons, look at its procedure, and you will everywhere find the maxims of theocracy or the empire to predominate. In her weakness, the Church sheltered herself under the absolute power of the Roman emperors; in her strength she laid claim to it herself, under the name of spiritual power. We must not here confine ourselves to a few particular facts. The Church has often, no doubt, set up and defended the rights of the people against the bad government of their rulers; often, indeed, has she approved and excited insurrection; often too has she maintained the rights and interests of the people in the presence of their sovereigns. But when the question of political securities came into debate between power and liberty; when any step was taken to establish a system of permanent institutions, which might effectually protect liberty from the invasions of power in general; the Church always ranged herself on the side of despotism.

This should not astonish us, neither should we be too ready to attribute it to any particular failing in the clergy, or to any particular vice in the Church. There is a more profound and powerful cause.

What is the object of religion? of *any* religion, true or false? It is to govern the human passions, the human will

All religion is a restraint, an authority, a government. It comes in the name of a divine law, to subdue, to mortify human nature. It is then to human liberty that it directly opposes itself. It is human liberty that resists it, and that it wishes to overcome. This is the grand object of religion, its mission, its hope.

But while it is with human liberty that all religions have to contend, while they aspire to reform the will of man, they have no means by which they can act upon him—they have no moral power over him, but through his own will, his liberty. When they make use of exterior means, when they resort to force, to seduction—in short, make use of means opposed to the free consent of man, they treat him as we treat water, wind, or any power entirely physical: they fail in their object; they attain not their end; they do not reach, they cannot govern the will. Before religions can really accomplish their task, it is necessary that they should be accepted by the free-will of man: it is necessary that man should submit, but it must be willingly and freely, and that he still preserves his liberty in the midst of this submission. It is in this that resides the double problem which religions are called upon to resolve.

They have too often mistaken their object. They have regarded liberty as an obstacle, and not as a means; they have forgotten the nature of the power to which they address themselves, and have conducted themselves toward the human soul as they would toward a material force. It is this error that has led them to range themselves on the side of power, on the side of despotism, against human liberty; regarding it as an adversary, they have endeavored to subjugate rather than to protect it. Had religions but fairly considered their means of operation, had they not suffered themselves to be drawn away by a natural but deceitful bias, they would have seen that liberty is a condition, without which man cannot be morally governed; that religion neither has nor ought to have any means of influence not strictly moral: they would have respected the will of man in their attempt to govern it. They have too often forgotten this, and the issue has been that religious power and liberty have suffered together.

1 will not push further this investigation of the general consequences that have followed the influence of the Church upon European civilization. I have summed them up in this double result—a great and salutary influence upon its moral and intellectual condition; an influence rather hurtful

than beneficial to its political condition. We have now to try our assertions by facts, to verify by history what we have as yet only deduced from the nature and situation of ecclesiastical society. Let us now see what was the destiny of the Christian Church from the fifth to the twelfth century, and whether the principles which I have laid down, the results which I have endeavored to draw from them, have really been such as I have represented them.

Let me caution you, however, against supposing that these principles, these results, appeared all at once, and as clearly as they are here set forth by me. We are apt to fall into the great and common error, in looking at the past through centuries of distances, of forgetting moral chronology; we are apt to forget—extraordinary forgetfulness! that history is essentially successive. Take the life of any man —of Oliver Cromwell, of Cardinal Richelieu, of Gustavus Adolphus. He enters upon his career; he pushes forward in life, and rises; great circumstances act upon him; he acts upon great circumstances. He arrives at the end of all things —and then it is we know him. But it is in his whole character; it is as a complete, a finished piece; such in a manner as he is turned out, after a long labor, from the workshop of Providence. Now at his outset he was not what he thus became; he was not completed—not finished at any single moment of his life; he was formed successively. Men are formed morally in the same way as they are physically. They change every day. Their existence is constantly undergoing some modification. The Cromwell of 1650 was not the Cromwell of 1640 It is true, there is always a large stock of individuality; the same man still holds on; but how many ideas, how many sentiments, how many inclinations have changed in him! What a number of things he has lost and acquired! Thus, at whatever moment of his life we may look at a man, he is never such as we see him when his course is finished.

This, nevertheless, is an error into which a great number of historians have fallen. When they have acquired a complete idea of a man, have settled his character, they see him in his same character throughout his whole career. With them, it is the same Cromwell who enters parliament in 1628, and who dies in the palace of White Hall thirty years afterward. Just such mistakes as these we are very apt to fall into with regard to institutions and general influences. I caution you against them. I have laid down in their complete form, as a whole, the principles of the Church, and the consequences which may be deduced from them. Be assured, however, that historically this picture is not true. All it represents has taken place disjointly, successively; has been scattered here and there over space and time. Expect not to find, in the recital of events, a similar completeness or whole, the same prompt and systematic concatenation. One principle will be visible here, another there; all will be incomplete, unequal, dispersed; we must come to modern times, to the end of its career, before we can view it as a whole.

I shall now lay before you the various states through which the Church passed from the fifth to the twelfth century. We may not find, perhaps, the complete demonstration of the statements which I have made, but we shall see enough, I apprehend, to convince us that they are founded in truth.

The first state in which we see the Church in the fifth century, is as the Church imperial—the Church of the Roman empire. Just at the time the empire fell, the Church believed she had attained the summit of her hopes: after a long struggle, she had completely vanquished paganism. Gratian, the last emperor who assumed the pagan dignity of sovereign pontiff, died at the close of the fourth century. The Church believed herself equally victorious in her struggle against heretics, particularly against Arianism, the principal heresy of the time. Theodosius, at the end of the fourth century, put them down by his imperial edicts; and had the double merit of subduing the Arian heresy and abolishing the worship of idols throughout the Roman world. The Church, then, was in possession of the government, and had obtained the victory over her two greatest enemies. It was at this moment that the Roman empire failed her, and she stood in the presence of new pagans, of new heretics—in the presence of the barbarians—of Goths, of Vandals, of Burgundians and Franks. The fall was immense. You may easily imagine that an affectionate attachment for the empire was for a long time preserved in the Romish Church. Hence we see her cherish so fondly all that was left of it—municipal government and absolute power. Hence, when she had succeeded in converting the barbarians, she endeavored to re-establish the empire; she called upon the barbarian kings, she conjured them to become Roman emperors, to assume the privilege of Roman emperors; to enter into the same relations with the Church which had existed between her and the Roman empire. This was the great ject for which the bishops of the fifth and sixth centuries labored. Such was the general state of the Church.

The attempt could not succeed—it was impossible to make a Roman empire, to mould a Roman society out of barbarians. Like the civil world, the Church herself sunk into barbarism. This was her second state. Comparing the writings of the monkish ecclesiastical chroniclers of the eighth century with those of the preceding six, the difference is immense. All remains of Roman civilization had disappeared, even its very language—all became buried in complete barbarism. On one side the rude barbarians, entering into the Church, became bishops and priests; on the other, the bishops, adopting the barbarian life, became, without quitting their bishoprics, chiefs of bands of marauders, and wandered over the country, pillaging and destroying like so many companies of Clovis. Gregory of Tours gives an account of several bishops who thus passed their lives, and among others Salone and Sagitttarius.

Two important facts took place while the Church continued in this state of barbarism.

The first was the separation of the spiritual and temporal powers. Nothing could be more natural than the birth of this principle at this epoch. The Church would have restored the absolute power of the Roman empire that she might partake of it, but she could not; she therefore sought her safety in independence. It became necessary that she should be able in all parts to defend herself by her own power; for she was threatened in every quarter. Every bishop, every priest, saw the rude chiefs in their neighborhood interfering in the affairs of the Church they might procure a slice of its wealth, its territory, its power; and no other means of defense seemed left but to say, "The spiritual order is completely separated from the temporal; you have no right to interfere with it." This principle became, at every point of attack, the defensive armor of the Church against barbarism.

A second important fact which took place at this same period, was the establishment of the monastic orders in the west. It was at the commencement of the sixth century that St. Benedict published the rules of his order for the use of the monks of the west, then few in number, but who from this time prodigiously increased. The monks at this epoch did not yet belong to the clerical body, but were still regarded as a part of the laity. Priests and even bishops were sometimes chosen from among them; but it was not till the close of the fifth and beginning of the sixth century that monks in general were considered as belonging to the clergy, properly so called. Priests and bishops now entered the cloister, thinking by so doing they advanced a step in their religious life, and increased the sanctity of their office. The monastic life thus all at once became exceedingly popular throughout Europe. The monks had a greater power over the imagination of the barbarians than the secular clergy. The simple bishop and priest had in some measure lost their hold upon the minds of barbarians, who were accustomed to see them every day; to maltreat, perhaps to pillage them. It was a more important matter to attack a monastery, a body of holy men congregated in a holy place. Monasteries, therefore, became during this barbarous period an asylum for the Church, as the Chucrh was for the laity. Pious men here took refuge, as others in the east had done before in the Thebias, in order to escape the worldly life and corruption of Constantinople.

These, then, are the two most important facts in the history of the Church, during the period of barbarism. First, the separation of the spiritual and temporal powers; and, secondly, the introduction and establishment of the monastic orders in the west.

Toward the end of this period of barbarism, a fresh attempt was made to raise up a new Roman empire—I allude to the attempt of Charlemagne. The Church and the civil sovereign again contracted a close alliance. The Holy See was full of docility while this lasted, and greatly increased its power. The attempt, however, again failed. The empire of Charlemagne was broken up; but the advantages which the See of Rome derived from its alliance were great and permanent. The popes henceforward were decidedly the chiefs of the Christian world.

Upon the death of Charlemagne, another period of unsettledness and confusion followed. The Church, together with civil society, again fell into a chaos; again with civil scoiety she arose, and with it entered into the frame of the feudal system. This was the third state of the Church. The dissolution of the empire formed by Charlemagne, was followed by nearly the same results in the Church as in civillife; all unity disappeared, all became local, partial, and individual. Now began a struggle, in the situation of the clergy, such as had scarcely ever before been seen: it was the struggle of the feelings and interest of the possessor of the fief, with the feelings and interest of the priest. The chiefs of the clergy were placed in this double situation; the spirit of the priest and of the temporal baron struggled within them for mastery. The ecclesiastical spirit naturally became weakened and divided by this process—it was no longer so powerful, so universal. Individual interest began to prevail. A taste for independence, the habits of the feudal life, loosened the ties of the hierarchy. In this state of things, the Church made an attempt within its own bosom to correct the effects of this general break-up. It endeavored in several parts of its empire, by means of federation, by common assemblies and deliberations, to organize national churches. It is during this period, during the sway of the feudal system, that we meet with the greatest number of councils, convocations, and ecclesiastical assemblies, as well provincial as national. In France especially, this endeavor at unity appeared to be followed up with much spirit. Hincmar, Archbishop of Rheims, may be considered as the representative of this idea. He labored incessantly to organize the French Church; he sought out and employed every means of correspondence and union which he thought likely to introduce into the Feudal Church a little more unity. We find him on one side maintaining the independence of the Church with respect to temporal power, on the other its independence with respect to the Roman See; it was he who, learning that the pope wished to come to France, and threatened to excommunicate the bishops, said, *Si excommunicaturus venerit, excommunicatus abibit.*

But the attempt thus to organize a Feudal Church succeeded no better than the attempt to re-establish the imperial one. There were no means of reproducing any degree of unity among its members; it tended more and more toward dissolution. Each bishop, each prelate, each abbot, isolated himself more and more in his diocese or monastery. Abuses and disorders increased from the same cause. At no time was the crime of simony carried to a greater extent—at no time were ecelcsiastical benefices disposed of in a more arbitrary manner—never were the morals of the clergy more loose and disorderly.

Both the people and the better portion of the clergy were greatly scandalized at this sad state of things; and a desire for reform in the Church soon began to show itself—a desire to find some authority round which it might rally its better principles, and which might impose some wholesome restraints on the others. Several bishops—Claude of Turin, Agobard of Lyons, etc.,—in their respective dioceses attempted this, but in vain; they were not in a condition to accomplish so vast a work. In the whole Church there was only one power that could succeed in this, and that was the Roman See; nor was that power slow in assuming the position which it wished to attain. In the course of the eleventh century, the Church entered upon its fourth state—that of a theocracy supported by monastic institutions.

The person who raised the Holy See to this power, so far as it can be considered the work of an individual, was Gregory VII.

It has been the custom to represent this great pontiff as an enemy to all improvement, as opposed to intellectual development, to the progress of society; as a man whose desire was to keep the world stationary or retrograding. Nothing is farther from the truth. Gregory, like Charlemagne and Peter the Great, was a reformer of the despotic school. The part he played in the Church was very similar to that which Charlemagne and Peter the Great, the one in France and the other in Russia, played among the laity. He wished to reform the Church first, and next civil society by the Church. He wished to introduce into the world more morality, more justice, more order and regularity; he wished to do all this through the Holy See, and to turn all to his own profit.

While Gregory was endeavoring to bring the civil world into subjection to the Church, and the Church to the See of Rome—not, as I have said before, to keep it stationary, or make it retrogade, but with a view to its reform and improvement—an attempt of the same nature, a similar movement, was made within the solitary enclosures of the monasteries. The want of order, of discipline, and of a stricter morality, was severely felt and cried out for with a zeal that would not be said nay. About this time Robert De Moleme established his severe rule at Citeaux; about the same time flourished St. Norbert, and the reform of the canons, the reform of Cluny, and, at last, the great reform of St. Bernard. A general fermentation reigned within the monasteries: the old monks did not like this; in defending themselves, they called these reforms an attack upon their liberty; pleaded the necessity of conforming to the manners of the times, that it was impossible to return to the discipline of the primitive Church, and treated all these reformers as madmen, as enthusiasts, as tyrants. Dip into the history of Normandy, by Ordericus Vitalius, and you will meet with these complaints at almost every page.

All this seemed greatly in favor of the Church, of its unity, and of its power. While, however, the popes of Rome sought to usurp the government of the world, while the monasteries enforced a better code of morals and a severer form of discipline, a few mighty, though solitary individuals protested in favor of human reason, and asserted its claim to be heard, its right to be consulted, in the formation of man's opinions. The greater part of these philosophers forbore to attack commonly received opinions—I mean religious creeds; all they claimed for reason was the right to be heard—all they declared was, that she had the right to try these truths by her own tests, and that it was not enough that they should be merely affirmed by authority. John Erigena, or John Scotus, as he is more frequently called, Roscelin, Abelard, and others, became the noble interpreters of individual reason, when it now began to claim its lawful inheritance. It was the teaching and writings of these giants of their days that first put in motion that desire for intellectual liberty, which kept pace with the reform of Gregory VII. and St. Bernard. If we examine the general character of this movement of mind, we shall find that it sought not a change of opinion, that it did not array itself against the received system of faith; but that it simply advocated the right of reason to work for itself—in short, the right of free inquiry.

The scholars of Abelard, as he himself tell us, in his *Introduction to Theology*, requested him to give them " some philosophical arguments, such as were fit to satisfy their minds; begged that he would instruct them, not merely to repeat what he taught them, but to understand it; for no one can believe that which he does not comprehend, and it is absurd to set out to preach to others concerning things which neither those who teach nor those who learn can understand. What other end can the study of philosophy have, if not to lead us to a knowledge of God, to which all studies should be subordinate? For what purpose is the reading of profane authors, and of books which treat of worldly affairs, permitted to believers, if not to enable them to understand the truths of the Holy Scriptures, and to give them the abilities necessary to defend them? It is above all things desirable for this purpose, that we should strengthen one another with all the powers of reason; so that in questions so difficult and complicated as those which form the object of Christian faith, you may be able to hinder the subtilties of its enemies from too easily corrupting its purity."

The importance of this first attempt after liberty, or this re-birth of the spirit of free inquiry, was not long in making itself felt. Though busied with its own reform, the Church soon took the alarm, and at once declared war against these new reformers, whose methods gave it more reason to fear than their doctrines. This clamor of human reason was the grand circumstance which burst forth at the close of the eleventh and beginning of the twelfth centuries, just at the time the Church was establishing its theocratic and monastic form. At this epoch, a serious struggle for the first time broke out between the clergy and the advocates of free inquiry. The quarrels of Abelard and St. Bernard, the councils of Soissons and Sens, at which Abelard was condemned, were nothing more than the expresssion of this fact, which holds so important a place in the history of modern civilization. It was the principal occurrence which affected the Church in the twelfth century; the point at which we will, for the present, take leave of it.

But at this same instant another power was put in motion, which, though altogether of a different character, was perhaps one of the most interesting and important in the progress of society during the middle ages—I mean the institution of free cities and boroughs; or what is called the enfranchisement of the commons. How strange is the inconsistency of grossness and ignorance! If it had been told to these early citizens who vindicated their liberties with such enthusiasm, that there were certain men who cried out for the rights of human reason, the right of free inquiry, men whom the Church regarded as heretics, they would have stoned or burned them on the spot. Abelard and his friends more than once ran the risk of suffering this kind of martyrdom. On the other hand, these same philosophers, who were so bold in their demands for the privileges of reason, spoke of the enfranchisement of the commons as an abominable revolution, calculated to destroy civil society. Between the movement of philosophy and the movement of the commons—between political liberty and the liberty of the human mind—a war seemed to be declared; and it has required ages to reconcile these two powers, and to make them understand that their interests are the same. In the twelfth century they had nothing in common, as we shall more fully see in the next lecture, which will be devoted to the formation of free cities and municipal corporations.

LECTURE VII.

RISE OF FREE CITIES.

We have already, in our previous lectures, brought down the history of the two first great elements of modern civilization, the feudal system and the Church, to the twelfth century. The third of these fundamental elements—that of the commons, or free corporate cities—will from the subject of the present, and I propose to limit it to the same period as that occupied by the other two.

It is necessary, however, that I should notice, on entering upon this subject, a difference which exists between corporate cities and the feudal system and the Church. The two latter, although they increased in influence, and were subject to many changes, yet show themselves as completed, as having put on a definite form, between the fifth and the twelfth centuries—we see their rise, growth, and maturity. Not so the free cities. It is not till toward the close of this period—till the eleventh and twelfth centuries—that corporate cities make any figure in history. Not that I mean to assert that their previous history does not merit attention; not that there are not evident traces of their existence before this period; all I would observe is, that they did not, previously to the eleventh century, perform any important part in the great drama of the world, as connected with modern civilization. Again, with regard to the feudal system and the Church; we have seen them, between the fifth century and the twelfth, act with power upon the social system; we have seen the effects they produced; by regarding them as two great principles, we have arrived, by way of induction, by way of conjecture, at certain results which we have verified by referring to facts themselves. This, however, we cannot do with regard to corporations. We only see these in their childhood. I can scarcely go further to-day than inquire into their causes, their origin; and the few observations I shall make respecting their effects—respecting the influence of corporate cities upon modern civilization, will be rather a foretelling of what afterward came to pass, than a recounting of what actually took place. I cannot, at this period, call in the testimony of known and contemporary events, because it was not till between the twelfth and fifteenth centuries that corporations attained any degree of perfection and influence, that these institutions bore any fruit, and that we can verify our assertions by history. I mention this difference of situation, in order to forewarn you of that which you may find incomplete and premature in the sketch I am about to give you.

Let us suppose that in the year 1789, at the commencement of the terrible regeneration of France, a burgess of the twelfth century had risen from his grave, and made his appearance among us and some one had put into his hands (for we will suppose he could read) one of those spirit-stirring pamphlets which caused so much excitement, for instance, that of M. Sieyes, *What is the third estate?* ("*Qu'est-ce que le tiers état?*") If, in looking at this, he had met the following passage, which forms the basis of the pamphlet:—" The third estate is the French nation without the nobility and clergy:" what, let me ask, would be the impression such a sentence would make on this burgess's mind? Is it probable that he would understand it? No: he would not be able to comprehend the meaning of the words, "the French nation," because they remind him of no facts of circumstances with which he would be acquainted, but represent a state of things to the existence of which he is an entire stranger; but if he did understand the phrase, and had a clear apprehension that the absolute sovereignty was lodged in the third estate, it is beyond a question that he would characterize such a proposition as almost absurd and impious, so utterly at variance would it be with his feelings and his ideas of things —so contradictory to the experience and observation of his whole life.

If we now suppose the astonished burgess to be introduced into any one of the free cities of France which had existed in his time—say Rhiems, or Beauvais, or Laon, or Noyon—we shall see him still more astonished and puzzled: he enters the town, he sees no towers, ramparts, militia, or any other kind of defense; everything exposed, everything an easy spoil to the first depredator, the town ready to fall into the hands of the first assailant. The burgess is alarmed at the insecurity of this free city, which he finds in so defenseless and unprotected a condition. He then proceeds into the heart of the town; he inquires how things are going on, what is the nature of its government, and the character of its inhabitants. He learns that there is an authority not resident within its walls, which imposes whatever taxes it pleases to levy upon them without their consent; which requires them to keep up a militia, and to serve in the army without their inclination being consulted. They talk to him about the magistrates, about the mayor and aldermen, and he is obliged to hear that the burgesses have nothing to do with their nomination. He learns that the municipal government is not conducted by the burgesses, but that a servant of the king, a steward living at a distance, has the sole management of their affairs. In addition to this, he is informed that they are prohibited from assembling together to take into consideration matters immediately concerning themselves, that the church bells have ceased to announce public meetings for such purposes. The burgess of the twelfth century is struck dumb with confusion—a moment since he was amazed at the greatness, the importance, the vast superiority which the "*tiers état*" so vauntingly arrogated to itself; but now, upon examination, he finds them deprived of all civic rights, and in a state of thraldom and degradation far more intolerable than he had ever before witnessed. He passes suddenly from one extreme to the other, from the spectacle of a corporation exercising sovereign power to a corporation without any power at all: how is it possible that he should understand this, or be able to reconcile it? his head must be turned, and his faculties lost in wonder and confusion.

Now, let us burgesses of the nineteenth century imagine, in our turn, that we are transported back into the twelfth. A twofold appearance, but exactly reversed, presents itself to us in a precisely similar manner. If we regard the affairs of the public in general—the state, the government, the country, the nation at large—we shall neither see nor hear anything of burgesses; they were mere ciphers—of no importance or consideration whatever. Not only so, but if we would know in what estimation they held themselves as a body, what weight, what influence they attached to themselves with respect to their relations toward the government of France as a nation, we shall receive a reply to our inquiry in language expressive of deep humility and timidity; while we shall find their masters, the lords, from whom they subsequently wrested their franchises, treating them, at least as far as words go, with a pride and scorn truly amazing; yet these indignities do not appear, in the slightest degree, to provoke or astonish their submissive vassals.

But let us enter one of these free cities, and see what is going on within it. Here things take quite another turn: we find ourselves in a fortified town, defended by armed burgesses. These burgesses fix their own taxes, elect their own magistrates, have their own courts of judicature, their own public assemblies for deliberating upon public measures, from which none are excluded. They make war at their own expense, even against their suzerain—maintain their own militia. In short, they govern themselves, they are sovereigns.

Here we have a similar contrast to that which made France, of the eighteenth century, so perplexing to the burgess of the twelfth; the scenes only are changed. In the present day the burgesses, in a national point of view, are everything—municipalities nothing; formerly corporations were everything, while the burgesses, as respects the nation, were nothing. From this it will appear evident that many things, many extraordinary events, and even many revolutions, must have happened between the twelfth and the fifteenth centuries, in order to bring about so great a change as that which has taken place in the social condition of this class of society. But however vast this change, there can be no doubt but that the commons, the third estate of 1789, politically speaking, are the descendants, the heirs of the free towns of the twelfth century. And the present haughty, ambitious French nation, which aspires so high, which proclaims so pompously its sovereignty, and pretends not only to have regenerated and to govern itself, but to regenerate and rule the whole world, is indisputably descended from those very free towns which revolted in the twelfth century —with great spirit and courage it must be allowed, but with no nobler object than that of escaping to some remote corner of the land from the vexatious tyranny of a few nobles.

It would be in vain to expect that the condition of the free towns in the twelfth century will reveal the causes of a metamorphosis such as this, which resulted from a series of events that took place between the twelfth and eighteenth centuries. It is in these events that we shall discover the causes of this change as we go on. Nevertheless, the origin of the "*tiers état*" has played a striking part in its history; and though we may not be able therein to trace out the whole secret of its destiny, we shall, at least, there meet with the seeds of it; that which it was at first, again occurs in that which it is become, and this to a much greater extent than might be presumed from appearances. A sketch, however imperfect, of the state of the free cities in the twelfth century, will, I think, convince you of this fact.

In order to understand the condition of the free cities at that time properly, it is necessary to consider them in two points of view. There are two great questions to be determined: *first*, that of the enfranchisement of the commons, or cities—that is to say, how this revolution was brought about, what were its causes, what alteration it effected in the condition of the burgesses, what in that of society in general, and in that of all the other orders of the state. The second question relates to the government of the free cities, the internal condition of the enfranchised towns, with reference to the burgesses residing within them, the principles, forms, and customs that prevailed among them.

From these two sources—namely, the change introduced into the social position of the burgesses, on the one hand, and from the internal government, by their municipal economy, on the other, has flowed all their influence upon modern civilization. All the circumstances that can be traced to their influence, may be referred to one of those two causes. As soon, then, as we thoroughly understand, and can satisfactorily account for, the enfranchisement of the free cities on the one hand, and the formation of their government on the other, we shall be in possession of the two keys to their history. In conclusion, I shall say a few words on the great diversity of conditions in the free cities of Europe. The facts which I am about to lay before you are not to be applied indiscriminately to all the free cities of the twelfth century—to those of Italy, Spain, England, and France alike; many of them undoubtedly were nearly the same in them all, but the points of difference are great and important. I shall point them out to your notice as I proceed. We shall meet with them again at a more advanced stage of our civilization, and can then examine them more closely.

In acquainting ourselves with the history of the enfranchisement of the free towns, we must remember what was the state of those towns between the fifth and eleventh centuries—from the fall of the Roman empire to the time when municipal revolution commenced. Here, I repeat, the differences are striking: the condition of the towns varied amazingly in the different countries of Europe; still there are some facts which may be regarded as nearly common to them all, and it is to these that I shall confine my observations. When I have gone through these, I shall say a few words more particularly respecting the free towns of France, and especially those of the north, beyond the Rhone and the Loire; these will form prominent figures in the sketch I am about to make.

After the fall of the Roman empire, between the fifth and tenth centuries, the towns were neither in a state of servitude nor freedom. We here again run the same risk of error in the employment of words, that I spoke to you of in a previous lecture in describing the character of men and events. When a society has lasted a considerable time, and its language also, its words acquire a complete, a determinate, a precise, a sort of legal official signification. Time has introduced into the signification of every term a thousand ideas, which are awakened within us every time we hear it pronounced, but which, as they do not all bear the same date, are not all suitable at the same time. The terms "*servitude* and *freedom*," for example, recall to our minds ideas far more precise and definite than the facts of the eighth, ninth, or tenth centuries to which they relate. If we say that the towns in the eighth century were in a state of freedom, we say by far too much: we attach now to the word "*freedom*" a signification which does not represent the fact of the eighth century. We shall fall into the same error, if we say that the towns were in a state of servitude; for this term implies a state of things very different from the circumstances of the municipal towns of those days. I say again, then, that the towns were neither in a state of freedom nor servitude: they suffered all the evils to which weakness is liable: they were a prey to the continual depredations, rapacity, and violence of the strong: yet, notwithstanding these horrid disorders, their impoverished and diminishing population, the towns had, and still maintained, a certain degree of importance: in most of them there was a clergyman, a bishop who exercised great authority, who possessed great influence over the people, served as a tie between them and their conquerors, thus maintaining the city in a sort of independence, by throwing over it the protecting shield of religion. Besides this, there were still left in the towns some valuable fragments of Roman institutions. We are indebted to the careful researches of MM. de Savigny, Hullmann, Mdle. de Lezardiere, etc., for having furnished us with many circumstances of this nature. We hear often, at this period, of the convocation of the senate, of the curiæ, of public assemblies, of municipal magistrates. Matters of police, wills, donations, and a multitude of civil transactions, were concluded in the *curiæ* by the magistrates, in the same way that they had previously been done under the Roman municipal government.

These remains of urban activity and freedom were gradually disappearing, it is true, from day to day. Barbarism and disorder, evils always increasing, accelerated depopulation. The establisment of the lords of the country in the provinces, and the rising preponderance of agricultural life, became another cause of the decline of the cities. The bishops themselves, after they had incorporated themselves into the feudal frame, attached much less importance to their municipal life. Finally, upon the triumph of the feudal system, the towns, without falling into the slavery of the agriculturists, were entirely subjected to the control of a lord, were included in some fief, and lost, by this title, somewhat of the independence which still remained to them, and which, indeed, they had continued to possess, even in the most barbarous times—even in the first centuries of invasion. So that from the fifth century up to the time of the complete organization of the feudal system, the state of the towns was continually getting worse.

When once, however, the feudal system was fairly established, when every man had taken his place, and became fixed as it were to the soil, when the wandering life had entirely ceased, the towns again assumed some importance —a new activity began to display itself within them. This is not surprising. Human activity, as we all know, is like the fertility of the soil—when the disturbing process is over, it reappears and makes all to grow and blossom; wherever there appears the least glimmering of peace and order the hopes of man are excited, and with his hopes his industry. This is what took place in the cities. No sooner was society a little settled under the feudal system, than the proprietors of fiefs began to feel new wants, and to acquire a certain degree of taste for improvement and melioration; this gave rise to some little commerce and industry in the towns of their domains; wealth and population increased within them —slowly for certain, but still they increased. Among other circumstances which aided in bringing this about, there is one which, in my opinion, has not been sufficiently noticed —I mean the asylum, the protection which the churches afforded to fugitives. Before the free towns were constituted, before they were in a condition by their power, their fortifications, to offer an asylum to the desolate population of the country, when there was no place of safety for them but the Church, this circumstance alone was sufficient to draw into the cities many unfortunate persons and fugitives. These sought refuge either in the Church itself or within its precincts; it was not merely the lower orders, such as serfs, villains, and so on, that sought this protection, but frequently men of considerable rank and wealth, who might chance to be proscribed. The chronicles of the times are full of examples of this kind. We find men lately powerful, upon being attacked by some more powerful neighbor, or by the king himself, abandoning their dwellings, and carrying away all the property they could rake together, entering into some city, and placing themselves under the protection of a church: they became citizens. Refugees of this sort had, in my opinion, a considerable influence upon the progress of the cities; they introduced into them, besides their wealth, elements of a population superior to the great mass of their inhabitants. We know, moreover, that when once an assemblage somewhat considerable is formed in any place, that other persons naturally flock to it; perhaps from finding it a place of greater security, or perhaps from that sociable disposition of our nature which never abandons us.

By the concurrence of all these causes, the cities regained a small portion of power as soon as the feudal sytsem became somewhat settled. But the security of the citizens was not restored to an equal extent. The roving, wandering life had, it is true, in a great measure ceased, but to the conquerors, to the new proprietors of the soil, this roving life was one great means of gratifying their passions. When they desired to pillage, they made an excursion, they went afar to seek a better fortune, another domain. When they became more settled, when they considered it necessary to renounce their predatory expeditions, the same passions, the same gross desires, still remained in full force. But the weight of these now fell upon those whom they found ready at hand, upon the powerful of the world, upon the cities. Instead of going afar to pillage, they pillaged what was near. The exactions of the proprietors of fifes upon the burgesses were redoubled at the end of the tenth century. ·Whenever the lord of the domain, by which a city was girt, felt a desire to increase his wealth, he gratified his avarice at the expense of the citizens. It was more particularly at this period that the citizens complained of the total want of commercial security. Merchants, on returning from their trading rounds, could not, with safety, return to their city. Every avenue was taken possession of by the lord of the domain and his vassals. The moment in which industry commenced its career, was precisely that in which security was most wanting. Nothing is more galling to an active spirit, than to be deprived of the long-anticipated pleasure of enjoying the fruits of his industry. When robbed of this, he is far more irritated and vexed than when made to suffer in a state of being fixed and monotonous, than when that which is torn from him is not the fruit of his own activity, has not excited in him all the joys of hope. There is in the progressive movement, which elevates a man of a population toward a new fortune, a spirit of resistance against iniquity and violence much more energetic than in any other situation.

Such, then, was the state of cities during the course of the tenth century. They possessed more strength, more importance, more wealth, more interests to defend. At the same time, it became more necessary than ever to defend them, for these interests, their wealth and their strength, became objects of desire to the nobles. With the means of resistance, the danger and difficulty increased also. Besides, the feudal system gave to all connected with it a perpetual example of resistance; the idea of an organized energetic government, capable of keeping society in order and regularity by its intervention, had never presented itself to the spirits of that period. On the contrary, there was a perpetual recurrence of individual will, refusing to submit to authority. Such was the conduct of the major part of the holders of fiefs toward their suzerains, of the small proprietors of land to the greater; so that at the very time when the cities were oppressed and tormented, at the moment when they had new and greater interests to sustain, they had before their eyes a continual lesson of insurrection. The feudal system rendered this service to mankind—it has constantly exhibited individual will, displaying itself in all its power and energy. The lesson prospered; in spite of their weakness, in spite of the prodigious inequality which existed between them and the great proprietors, their lords, the cities everywhere broke out into rebellion against them.

It is difficult to fix a precise date to this great event—this general insurrection of the cities. The commencement of their enfranchisement is usually placed at the beginning of the eleventh century. But in all great events, how many unknown and disastrous efforts must have been made before the successful one! Providence, upon all occasions, in order to accomplish its designs, is prodigal of courage, virtues, sacrifices—finally, of man; and it is only after a vast number of unknown attempts apparently lost, after a host of noble hearts have fallen into despair—convinced that their cause was lost—that it triumphs. Such, no doubt, was the case in the struggle of the free cities. Doubtless in the eighth, ninth, and tenth centuries there were many attempts at resistance, many efforts made for freedom:—many attempts to escape from bondage, which not only were unsuccessful, but the remembrance of which, from their ill success, has remained without glory. Still we may rest assured that these attempts had a vast influence upon succeeding events: they kept alive and maintained the spirit of liberty—they prepared the great insurrection of the eleventh century.

I say insurrection, and I say it advisedly. The enfranchisement of the towns or communities in the eleventh century was the fruit of a real insurrection, of a real war—a war declared by the population of the cities against their lords. The first fact which we always meet with in annals of this nature, is the rising of the burgesses, who seize whatever arms they can lay their hands on;—it is the expulsion of the people of the lord, who come for the purpose of levying contributions, some extortion; it is an enterprise against the neighboring castle;—such is always the character of the war. If the insurrection fails, what does the conqueror instantly do? He orders the destruction of the fortifications erected by the citizens, not only around their city, but also around each dwelling. We see that at the very moment of confederation, after having promised to act in common, after having taken, in common, the corporation oath, the first act of each citizen was to put this own house in a state of resistance. Some towns, the names of which are now almost forgotten—the little community of Vezelai, in Nevers, for example—sustained against their lord a long and obstinate struggle. At length victory declared for the Abbot of Vezelai; upon the spot he ordered the demolition of the fortifications of the houses of the citizens; and the names of many of the heroes, whose fortified houses were then destroyed, are still preserved.

Let us enter the interior of these habitations of our ancestors; let us examine the form of their construction, and the mode of life which this reveals: all is devoted to war, everything is impressed with its character.

The construction of the house of a citizen of the twelfth century, so far, at least, as we can now obtain an idea of it, was something of this kind: it consisted usually of three stories, one room in each; that on the ground floor served as a general eating room for the family; the first story was much elevated for the sake of security, and this is the most remarkable circumstance in the construction. The room in this story was the habitation of the master of the house and his wife. The house was, in general, flanked with an angular tower, usually square: another symptom of war; another means of defence. The second story consisted again of a single room; its use is not known, but it probably served for the children and domestics. Above this in most houses, was a small platform, evidently intended as an observatory or watch-tower. Every feature of the building bore the appearance of war. This was the decided character, the true name of the movement, which wrought out the freedom of the cities.

After a war has continued a certain time, whatever may be the belligerent parties, it naturally leads to a peace. The treaties of peace between the cities and their adversaries were so many charters. These charters of the cities were so many positive treaties of peace between the burgesses and their lords.

The insurrection was general. When I say *general*, I do not mean that there was any concerted plan, that there was any coalition between all the burgesses of a country; nothing like it took place. But the situation of all the towns being nearly the same, they all were liable to the same danger; a prey to the same disasters. Having acquired similar means of resistance and defence, they made use of those means at nearly the same time. It may be possible, also, that the force of example did something; that the success of one or two communities was contagious. Sometimes the charters appear to have been drawn up from the same model; for instance, that of Noyon served as a pattern for those of Beauvais, St. Quentin, and others; I doubt, however, whether example had so great an influence as is generally conjectured. Communication between different provinces was difficult and of rare occurrence; the intelligence conveyed and received by hearsay and general report was vague and uncertain; and there is much reason for believing that the insurrection was rather the result of a similarity of situation and of a general spontaneous movement. When I say *general*, I wish to be understood simply as saying that insurrections took place everywhere; they did not, I repeat, spring from any unanimous concerted movement: all was particular, local; each community rebelled on its own account, against its own lord, unconnected with any other place.

The vicissitudes of the struggle were great. Not only did success change from one side to the other, but even after peace was in appearance concluded, after the charter had been solemnly sworn to by both parties, they violated and eluded its articles in all sorts of ways. Kings acted a prominent part in the alternations of these struggles. I shall speak of these more in detail when I come to royalty itself. Too much has probably been said of the effects of royal influence upon the struggles of the people for freedom. These effects have been often contested, sometimes exaggerated, and in my opinion, sometimes greatly underrated. I shall here confine myself to the assertion that royalty was often called upon to interfere in these contests, sometimes by the cities, sometimes by their lords; and that it played very different parts; acting now upon one principle, and soon after upon another; that it was ever changing its intentions, its designs, and its conduct; but that, taking it altogether, it did much, and produced a greater portion of good than of evil.

In spite of all these vicissitudes, notwithstanding the perpetual violation of charters in the twelfth century—the freedom of the cities was consummated. Europe, and particularly France, which, during a whole century, had abounded in insurrections, now abounded in charters; cities rejoiced in them with more or less security, but still they rejoiced; the event succeeded, and the right was acknowledged.

Let us now endeavor to ascertain the more immediate results of this great fact, and what changes it produced in the situation of the burgesses as regarded society.

And, at first, as regards the relations of the burgesses with the general government of the country, or with what we now call the state, it effected nothing; they took no part in this more than before; all remained local, enclosed within the limits of the fief.

One circumstance, however, renders this assertion not strictly true: a connexion now began to be formed between the cities and the king. At one time the people called upon the king for support and protection, or solicited him to guaranty the charter which had been promised or sworn to. At another the barons invoked the judicial interference of the king between them and the burgesses. At the request of one or other of the two parties, from a multitude of various causes, royalty was called upon to interfere in the quarrel, whence resulted a frequent and close connexion between the citizens and the king. In consequence of this connexion the cities became a part of the state, they began to have relations with the general governmnt.

Although all still remained local, yet a new general class of society became formed by the enfranchisement of the commons. No coalition of the burgesses of different cities had taken place; as yet they had as a class no public or general existence. But the country was covered with men engaged in similar pursuits, possessing the same views and interests, the same manners and customs; between whom there could not fail to be gradually formed a certain tie, from which originated the general class of burgesses. This formation of a great social class was the necessary result of the local enfranchisement of the burgesses. It must not, however, be supposed that the class of which we are speaking was then what it has since become. Not only is its situation greatly changed, but its elements are totally different. In the twelfth century, this class was almost entirely composed of merchants or small traders, and little landed or house proprietors who had taken up their residence in the city. Three centuries afterward there were added to this class lawyers, physicians, men of letters, and the local magistrates. The class of burgesses was formed gradually and of very different elements: history gives us no accurate account of its progress, nor of its diversity. When the body of citizens is spoken of, it is erroneously conjectured to have been, at all times, composed of the same elements. Absurd supposition! It is, perhaps, in the diversity of its composition at different periods of history that we should seek to discover the secret of its destiny; so long as it was destitute of magistrates and of men of letters, so long it remained totally unlike what it became in the sixteenth century; as regards the state, it neither possessed the same character nor the same importance. In order to form a just idea of the changes in the rank and influence of this portion of society, we must take a view of the new professions, the new moral situations, of the new intellectual state which gradually arose within it. In the twelfth century, I must repeat, the body of citizens consisted only of small merchants or traders, who, after having finished their purchases and sales, retired to their houses in the city or town; and of little proprietors of houses or lands who had there taken up their residence. Such was the European class of citizens, in its primary elements.

The third great result of the enfranchisement of the cities was the struggle of classes; a struggle which constitutes the very fact of modern history, and of which it is full.

Modern Europe, indeed, is born of this struggle between the different classes of society. I have already shown that in other places this struggle has been productive of very different consequences; in Asia, for example, one particular class has completely triumphed, and the system of castes has succeeded to that of classes, and society has there fallen into a state of immobility. Nothing of this kind, thank God! has taken place in Europe. One of the classes has not conquered, has not brought the others into subjection; no class has been able to overcome, to subjugate the others; the struggle, instead of rendering society stationary, has been a principal cause of its progress; the relations of the different classes with one another; the necessity of combating and of yielding by turns; the variety of interests, passions, and excitements; the desire to conquer without the power to do so: from all this has probably sprung the most energetic, the most productvie principle of development in European civilization. This struggle of the classes has been constant; enmity has grown up between them; the infinite diversity of situation, of interests, and of manners, has produced a strong moral hostility; yet they have progressively approached, assimilated, and understood each other; every country of Europe has seen arise and develop itself within a certain public mind, a certain community of interests, of ideas, of sentiments, which have triumphed over this diversity and war. In France, for example, in the seventeenth and eighteenth centuries, the moral and social separation of classes was still very profound, yet there can be no doubt but that their fusion, even then, was far advanced; that even then there was a real French nation, not consisting of any class exclusively, but of a commixture of the whole; all animated with the same feeling, actuated by one common social principle, firmly knit together by the bond of nationality.

Thus, from the bosom of variety, enmity, and discord, has issued that national unity, now become so conspicuous in modern Europe; that nationality whose tendency is to develop and purify itself more and more, and every day to increase its splendor.

Such are the great, the important, the conspicuous social effects of the revolution which now occupies our attention. Let us now endeavor to show what were its moral effects, what changes it produced in the minds of the citizens themselves, what they became in consequence, and what they should morally become, in their new situation.

When we take into our consideration the connexion of the citizens with the state in general, with the government of the state, and with the interests of the country, as that connexion existed not only in the twelfth century, but also in after ages, there is one circumstance which must strike us most forcibly: I mean the extraordinary mental timidity of the citizens: their humility; the excessive modesty of their pretensions to a right of interference in the government of their country; and the little matter that, in this respect, contented them. Nothing was to be seen in them which discovered that genuine political feeling which aspires to the possession of influence, and to the power of reforming and governing; nothing attests in them either energy of mind, or loftiness of ambition; one feels ready to exclaim, Poor, prudent, simple-hearted citizens!

There are not, properly, more than two sources whence, in the political world, can flow loftiness of ambition and energy of mind. There must be either the feeling of possessing a great importance, a great power over the destiny of others, and this over a large sphere; or there must be in one's self a powerful feeling of personal independence, the assurance of one's own liberty, the consciousness of having a destiny with which no will can intermeddle beyond that in one's own bosom. To one or other of these two conditions seem to be attached energy of mind, the loftiness of ambition, the desire to act in a large sphere, and to obtain corresponding results.

Neither of these conditions is to be found in the situation of the burgesses of the middle ages. These were, as we have just seen, only important to themselves; except within the walls of their own city, their influence amounted to but little; as regarded the state, to almost nothing. Nor could they be possessed of any great feeling of personal independence: their having conquered—their having obtained a character did but little in the way of promoting this noble sentiment. The burgess of a city, comparing himself with the little baron who dwelt near him, and who had just been vanquished by him, would still be sensible of his own extreme inferiority; he was ignorant of that proud sentiment of independence which animated the proprietor of a fief; the share of freedom which he possessed was not derived from himself alone, but from his association with others—from the difficult and precarious succor which they afforded. Hence that retiring disposition, that timidity of mind, that trembling shyness, that humility of speech (though perhaps coupled with firmness of purpose) which is so deeply stamped on the character of the burgesses, not only of the twelfth century, but even of their most remote descendants. They had no taste for great enterprises; if chance pushed them into such, they became vexed and embarrassed; any responsibility was a burden to them; they felt themselves out of their sphere, and endeavored to return into it; they treated upon easy terms. Thus, in running over the history of Europe, and especially of France, we may occasionally find municipal communities esteemed, consulted, perhaps respected, but rarely feared; they seldom impressed their adversaries with the notion that they were a great and formidable power, a power truly political. There is nothing to be astonished at in the weakness of the modern burgess; the great cause of it may be traced to his origin, in those circumstances of his enfranchisement which I have just placed before you. The loftiness of ambition, independent of social conditions, breadth and boldness of political views, the desire to be employed in public affairs, the full consciousness of the greatness of man, considered as such, and of the power that belongs to him, if he be capable of exercising it; it is these sentiments, these dispositions, which, of entirely modern growth in Europe, are the offspring of modern civilization, and of that glorious and powerful generality which characterizes it, and which will never fail to secure to the public an influence, a weight in the government of the country, that were constantly wanting, and deservedly wanting, to the burgesses our ancestors.

As a set-off to this, in the contests which they had to sustain respecting their local interests—in this narrow field, they acquired and displayed a degree of energy, devotedness, perseverance, and patience, which has never been surpassed. The difficulty of the enterprise was so great, they had to struggle against such perils, that a display of courage almost beyond example became necessary. Our notions of the burgess of the twelfth and thirteenth centuries, and of his life, are very erroneous. The picture which Sir Walter Scott has drawn in *Quentin Durward* of the burgomaster of Liege, fat, inactive, without experience, without daring, and caring for nothing but passing his life in ease and enjoyment, is only fitted for the stage; the real burgess of that day had a coat of mail continually on his back, a pike constantly in his hand; his life was nearly as stormy, as warlike, as rigid as that of the nobles with whom he contended. It was in these every-day perils, in combating the varied dangers of practical life, that he acquired that bold and masculine character, that determined exertion, which have become more rare in the softer activity of modern times.

None, however, of these social and moral effects of the enfranchisement of corporations became fully developed in the twelfth century; it is only in the course of the two following centuries that they showed themselves so as to be clearly discerned. It is nevertheless certain that the seeds of these effects existed in the primary situation of the commons, in the mode of their enfranchisement, and in the position which the burgesses from that time took in society; I think, therefore, that I have done right in bringing these circumstances before you to-day.

Let us now penetrate into the interior of one of those corporate cities of the twelfth century, that we may see how it was governed, that we may now see what principles and what facts prevailed in the relations of the burgesses with one another. It must be remembered, that in speaking of the municipal system bequeathed by the Roman empire to the modern world, I took occasion to say, that the Roman world was a great coalition of municipalities, which had previously been as sovereign and independent as Rome itself. Each of these cities had formerly been in the same condition as Rome, a little free republic, making peace and war, and governing itself by its own will. As fast as these became incorporated into the Roman world, those rights which constitute sovereignty—the right of war and peace, of legislation, taxation, etc.—were transferred from each city to the central government at Rome. There remained then but one municipal sovereignty. Rome reigned over a vast number of municipalities, which had nothing left beyond a civic existence. The municipal system became essentially changed: it was no longer a political government, but simply a mode of administration. This was the grand revolution which was consummated under the Roman empire. The municipal system became a mode of administration; it was reduced to the government of local affairs, to the civic interests of the city. This is the state in which the Roman empire, at its fall, left the cities and their institutions. During the chaos of barbarism, notions and facts of all sorts became embroiled and confused; the various attributes of sovereignty and administration were confounded. Distinctions of this nature were no longer regarded. Affairs were suffered to run on in the course dictated by necessity. The municipalities became sovereigns or administrators in the various places, as need might require. Where cities rebelled, they re-assumed the sovereignty, for the sake of security, not out of respect for any political theory, nor from any feeling of their dignity, but that they might have the means of contending with the nobles, whose yoke they had thrown off; that they might take upon themselves the right to call out the militia, to tax themselves to support the war, to name their own chiefs and magistrates; in a word, to govern themselves. The internal government of the city was their means of defence, of security. Thus, sovereignty again returned to the municipal system, which had been deprived of it by the conquests of Rome. City corporations again became sovereigns. This is the political characteristic of their enfranchisement.

I do not, however, mean to assert, that this sovereignty was complete. Some trace of an exterior sovereignty always may be found; sometimes it was the baron who retained the right to send a magistrate into the city, with whom the municipal magistrates acted as assessors; perhaps he had the right to collect certain revenues; in some cases a fixed tribute was assured to him Sometimes the exterior sovereignty of the community was in the hands of the king.

The cities themselves, in their turn, entered, into the feudal system; they had vassals, and became suzerains; and by this title possessed that portion of sovereignty which was inherent in the suzerainty. A great confusion arose between the rights which they held from their feudal position, and those which they had acquired by their insurrection; and by this double title they held the sovereignty. . .

Let us see, as far as the very scanty sources left us will
allow, how the internal government of the cities, at least in
the more early times, was managed. The entire body of the
inhabitants formed the communal assembly: all those who
had taken the communal oath—and all who dwelt within the
walls were obliged to do so—were summoned, by the tolling
of the bell, to the general assembly. In this were named
the magistrates. The number chosen, and the power and
proceedings of the magistrates, differed very considerably.
After choosing the magistrates, the assemblies dissolved;
and the magistrates governed almost alone, sufficiently
arbitrarily, being under no further responsibility than the
new elections, or, perhaps, popular outbreaks, which were,
at this time, the great guarantee for good government.

You will observe that the internal organization of the
municipal towns is reduced to two very simple elements, the
general assembly of the inhabitants, and a government invested with almost arbitrary power, under the responsibility
of insurrections—general outbreaks. It was impossible,
especially while such manners prevailed, to establish anything like a regular government, with proper guarantees of
order and duration. The greater part of the population of
these cities were ignorant, brutal, and savage to a degree
which rendered them exceedingly difficult to govern. At
the end of a very short period, there was but little more
security within these communities than there had been, previously, in the relations of the burgesses within the baron.
There soon, however, became formed a burgess aristocracy.
The causes of this are easily understood. The notions of
that day, coupled with certain social relations, led to the
establishment of trading companies legally constituted. A
system of privileges became introduced into the interior of
the cities, and, in the end, a great inequality. There soon
grew up in all of them a certain number of considerable,
opulent burgesses, and a population, more or less numerous,
of workmen, who, notwithstanding their inferiority, had no
small influence in the affairs of the community. The free
cities thus became divided into an upper class of burgesses,
and a population subject to all the errors, all the vices of a
mob. The superior citizens thus found themselves pressed
between two great difficulties: first, the arduous one of
governing this inferior turbulent population; and, secondly,
that of withstanding the continual attempts of the ancient
master of the borough, who sought to regain his former

power. Such was the situation of their affairs, not only in France, but in Europe, down to the sixteenth century. This, perhaps, is the cause which prevented these communities from taking, in several countries of Europe, and especially in France, that high political station which seemed properly to belong to them. Two spirits were unceasingly at work within them: among the inferior population, a blind, licentious, furious spirit of democracy; among the superior burgesses, a spirit of timidity, of caution, and an excessive desire to accommodate all differences, whether with the king, or with its ancient proprietors, so as to preserve peace and order in the bosom of the community. Neither of these spirits could raise the cities to a high rank in the state.

All these effects did not become apparent in the twelfth century; still we may foresee them, even in the character of the insurrection, in the manner in which it broke out, in the state of the different elements of the city population.

Such, if I mistake not, are the principal characteristics, the general results, both of the enfranchisement of the cities and of their internal government. I have already premised, that these facts were not so uniform, not so universal, as I have represented them. There are great diversities in the history of the European free cities. In the south of France and in Italy, for example, the Roman municipal system prevailed; the population was not nearly so divided, so unequal, as in the north. Here, also, the municipal organization was much better; perhaps the effect of Roman traditions, perhaps of the better state of the population. In the north, it was the feudal system that prevailed in the city arrangements. Here all seemed subordinate to the struggle against the barons. The cities of the south paid much more regard to their internal constitution, to the work of melioration and progress. We see, from the beginning, that they will become free republics. The career of those of the north, above all those of France, showed itself, from the first, more rude, more incomplete, destined to less perfect, less beautiful developments. If we run over those of Germany, Spain, and England, we shall find among them many other differences. I cannot particularize them, but shall notice some of them, as we advance in the history of civilization. All things at their origin are nearly confounded in one and the same physiognomy; it is only in their after-growth that their variety shows itself. Then begins a new development which urges forward societies toward that free and lofty unity, the glorious object of the efforts and wishes of mankind.

LECTURE VIII.

SKETCH OF EUROPEAN CIVILIZATION—STATE OF EUROPE FROM THE TWELFTH TO THE FOURTEENTH CENTURIES—THE CRUSADES.

I HAVE not yet laid before you the whole plan of my course. I began by pointing out its object, and I then went straight forward, without taking any comprehensive view of European civilization, and without indicating at once its starting-point, its path, and its goal—its beginning, middle, and end. We are now, however, arrived at a period when this comprehensive view, this general outline, of the world through which we travel, becomes necessary. The times which have hitherto been the subject of our study, are explained in some measure by themselves, or by clear and immediate results. The times into which we are about to enter can neither be understood nor excite any strong interest, unless we connect them with their most indirect and remote consequences. In an inquiry of such vast extent, a time arrives when we can no longer submit to go forward with a dark and unknown path before us; when we desire to know not only whence we have come and where we are, but whither we are going. This is now the case with us. The period which we approach cannot be understood, or its importance appreciated, unless by means of the relations which connect it with modern times. Its true spirit has been revealed only by the lapse of many subsequent ages.

We are in possession of almost all the essential elements of European civilization. I say almost all, because I have not yet said anything on the subject of monarchy. The crisis which decidedly developed the monarchical principle, hardly took place before the twelfth or even the thirteenth century. It was then only that the institution of monarchy was really established, and began to occupy a definite place in modern society. It is on this account that I have not sooner entered on the subject. With this exception we possess, I repeat it, all the great elements of European society. You have seen the origin of the feudal aristocracy, the Church and the municipalities; you have observed the institutions which would naturally correspond with these facts; and not only the institutions, but the principles and ideas which these facts naturally give rise to. Thus, with reference to feudalism, you have watched the origin of modern domestic life; you have comprehended, in all its energy, the feeling of personal independence, and the place which it must have occupied in our civilization. With reference to the Church, you have observed the appearance of the purely religious form of society, its relations with civil society, the principle of theocracy, the separation between the spiritual and temporal powers, the first blows of persecution, the first cries of liberty of conscience. The infant municipalities have given you a view of a social union founded on principles quite different from those of feudalism; the diversity of the classes of society, their contests with each other, the first and strongly marked features of the manners of the modern inhabitants of towns; timidity of judgment combined with energy of soul, proneness to be excited by demagogues joined to a spirit of obedience to legal authority; all the elements, in short, which have concurred in the formation of European society have already come under your observation.

Let us now transport ourselves into the heart of modern Europe; I do not mean Europe in the present day, after the prodigious metamorphosis we have witnessed, but in the seventeenth and eighteenth centuries. What an immense difference! I have already insisted on this difference with reference to communities; I have endeavored to show you how little resemblance there is between the burgesses of the eighteenth century and those of the twelfth. Make the same experiment on feudalism and the Church, and you will be struck with a similar metamorphosis. There was no more resemblance between the nobility of the court of Louis XV. and the feudal aristocracy, or between the Church in the days of Cardinal de Bernis and those of the Abbe Suger, than there is between the burgesses of the eighteenth century and the same class in the twelfth. Between these two periods, though society had already acquired all its elements, it underwent a total transformation.

I am now desirous to trace clearly the general and essential character of this transformation.

From the fifth century, society contained all that I have already found and described as belonging to it—kings, a lay aristocracy, a clergy, citizens, husbandmen, civil and religious authorities; the germs, in short, of everything necessary to form a nation and a government; and yet there was no government, no nation. In all the period that has occupied our attention, there was no such thing as a people, properly so called, or a government, in the modern acceptation of the word. We have fallen in with a number of particular forces, special facts, and local institutions; but nothing general, nothing public, nothing political, nothing, in short, like real nationality.

Let us, on the other hand, survey Europe in the seventeenth and eighteenth centuries: we everywhere see two great objects make their appearance on the stage of the world—the government and the people. The influence of a general power over an entire country, and the influence of the country in the power which governs it, are the materials of history; the relations between these great forces, their alliances or their contests, are the subjects of its narration. The nobility, the clergy, the citizens, all these different classes and particular powers are thrown into the background, and effaced, as it were, by these two great objects, the people and its government.

This, if I am not deceived, is the essential feature which distinguishes modern Europe from the Europe of the early ages; and this was the change which was accomplished between the thirteenth and the sixteenth century.

It is, then, in the period from the thirteenth to the sixteenth century, into which we are about to enter, that we must endeavor to find the cause of this change. It is the distinctive character of this period, that it was employed in changing Europe from its primitive to its modern state; and hence arise its importance and historical interest. If we did not consider it under this point of view, if we did not endeavor to discover the events which arose out of this period, not only we should never be able to comprehend it, but we should soon become weary of the inquiry.

Viewed in itself and apart from its results, it is a period without character, a period in which confusion went on increasing without apparent causes, a period of movement without direction, of agitation without result; a period when monarchy, nobility, clergy, citizens, all the elements of social order, seemed to turn round in the same circle, incapable alike of progression and of rest. Experiments of all kinds were made and failed; endeavors were made to establish goverments and lay the foundations of public liberty; reforms in religion were even attempted; but nothing was accomplished or came to any result. If ever the human race seemed destined to be always agitated, and yet always stationary, condemned to unceasing and yet barren labors, it was from the thirteenth to the fifteenth century that this was the complexion of its condition and history.

I am acquainted only with one work in which this appearance of the period in question is faithfully described; I allude to M. de Barante's *History of the Dukes of Burgandy*. I do not speak of the fidelity of his pictures of manners and narratives of adventures, but of that general fidelity which renders the work an exact image, a true mirror of the whole period, of which it at the same time displays both the agitation and the monotony.

Considered, on the contrary, in relation to what has succeeded it, as the transition from Europe in its primitive, to Europe in its modern state, this period assumes a more distinct and animated aspect; we discover in it a unity of design, a movement in one direction, a progression; and its unity and interest are found to reside in the slow and hidden labor accomplished in the course of its duration.

The history of European civilization, then, may be thrown into three great periods: first, a period which I shall call that of origin, or formation; during which the different elements of society disengage themselves from chaos, assume an existence, and show themselves in their native forms, with the principles by which they are animated; this period lasted almost to the twelfth century. The second period is a period of experiments, attempts, groping; the different elements of society approach and enter into combination, feeling each other, as it were, but producing anything general, regular, or durable; this state of things, to say the truth, did not terminate till the sixteenth century. Then comes the third period, or the period of development, in which human society in Europe takes a definite form, follows a determinate direction, proceeds rapidly and with a general movement, toward a clear and precise object; this is the period which began in the sixteenth century, and is now pursuing its course.

Such appears, on a general view, to be the aspect of European civilization. We are now about to enter into the second of the above periods; and we have to inquire what were the great and critical events which occurred during its course, and which were the determining causes of the social transformation which was its result.

The first great event which presents itself to our view, and which opened, so to speak, the period we are speaking of, was the crusades. They began at the end of the eleventh century, and lasted during the twelfth and thirteenth. It was, indeed, a great event; for, since its occurrence, it has never ceased to occupy the attention of philosophical historians, who have shown themselves aware of its influence in changing the conditions of nations, and of the necessity of study in order to comprehend the general course of its facts.

The first character of the crusades is their universality; all Europe concurred in them; they were the first European event. Before the crusades, Europe had never been moved by the same sentiment, or acted in a common cause; till then, in fact, Europe did not exist. The crusades made manifest the existence of Christian Europe. The French formed the main body of the first army of crusaders; but there were also Germans, Italians, Spaniards, and English. But look at the second and third crusades, and we find all the nations of Christendom engaged in them. The world had never before witnessed a similar combination.

But this is not all. In the same manner as the crusades were a European event, so, in each separate nation, they were a national event. In every nation, all classes of society were animated with the same impression, yielded to the same idea, and abandoned themselves to the same impulse. Kings, nobles, priests, citizens, country people, all took the same interest and the same share in the crusades. The moral unity of nation was thus made manifest; a fact as new as the unity of Europe.

When such events take place in what may be called the youth of nations; in periods when they act spontaneously, freely, without premeditation or political design, we recognize what history calls heroic events, the heroic ages of nations. The crusades were the heroic event of modern Europe; a movement at the same time individual and general; national, and yet not under political direction.

That this was really their primitive character is proved by every fact, and every document. Who were the first crusaders? Bands of people who set out under the conduct of Peter the Hermit, without preparations, guides, or leaders, followed rather than led by a few obscure knights, traversed Germany and the Greek empire, and were dispersed, or perished, in Asia Minor.

The higher class, the feudal nobility, next put themselves in motion for the crusade. Under the command of Godfrey of Bouillon, the nobles and their men departed full of ardor. When they had traversed Asia Minor, the leaders of the crusaders were seized with a fit of lukewarmness and fatigue. They became indifferent about continuing their course; they were inclined rather to look to their own interest, to make conquests and possess them. The mass of the army, however, rose up, and insisted on marching to Jerusalem, the deliverance of the holy city being the object of the crusade. It was not to gain principalities for Raymond of Toulouse, or for Bohemond, or any other leader, that the crusaders had taken arms. The popular, national, European impulse overcame all the intentions of individuals; and the leaders had not sufficient ascendancy over the masses to make them yield to their personal interests.

The sovereigns, who had been strangers to the first crusade, were now drawn into the general movement as the people had been. The great crusades of the twelfth century were commanded by kings.

I now go at once to the end of the thirteenth century. A great deal was still said in Europe about crusades, and they were even preached with ardor. The popes excited the sovereigns and the people; councils were held to recommend the conquest of the holy land; but no expeditions of any importance were now undertaken for this purpose, and it was regarded with general indifference. Something had entered into the spirit of European society which put an end to the crusades. Some private expeditions still took place; some nobles and some bands of troops still continued to depart for Jerusalem; but the general movement was evidently arrested. Neither the necessity, however, nor its facility of continuing it, seemed to have ceased. The Moslems triumphed more and more in Asia. The Christian kingdom founded at Jerusalem had fallen into their hands. It still appeared necessary to regain it; and the means of success were greater than at the commencement of the crusades. A great number of Christians were established and still powerful in Asia Minor, Syria, and Palestine. The proper means of transport, and of carrying on the war, were better known. Still, nothing could revive the spirit of the crusades. It is evident that the two great forces of society —the sovereigns on the one hand, and the people on the other—no longer desired their continuance.

It has been often said that Europe was weary of these constant inroads upon Asia. We must come to an understanding as to the meaning of the word *weariness*, frequently used on such occasions. It is exceedingly incorrect. It is not true that generations of mankind can be weary of what has not been done by themselves; that they can be wearied by the fatigues of their fathers. Weariness is personal; it cannot be transmitted like an inheritance. The people of the thirteenth century were not weary of the crusades of the twelfth; they were influenced by a different cause. A great change had taken place in opinions, sentiments, and social relations. There were no longer the same wants, or the same desires: the people no longer believed, or wished to believe, in the same things. It is by these moral or political changes, and not by weariness, that the differences in the conduct of successive generations can be explained. The pretended weariness ascribed to them is a metaphor wholly destitute of truth.

Two great causes, the one moral, the other social, impelled Europe into the crusades.

The *moral* cause, as you are aware, was the impulse of religious feeling and belief. From the end of the seventh century, Christianity maintained a constant struggle against Mohammedanism. It had overcome Mohammedanism in Europe, after having been threatened with great danger from it; and had succeeded in confining it to Spain. Even from thence the expulsion of Mohammedanism was constantly attempted. The crusades have been represented as a sort of accident, an unforeseen event, sprung from the recitals of pilgrims returned from Jerusalem, and the preaching of Peter the Hermit. They were nothing of the kind. The crusades were the continuation, the height of the great struggle which had subsisted for four centuries between Christianity and Mohammedanism. The theatre of this contest had hitherto been in Europe; it was now transported into Asia. If I had attached any value to those comparisons, those parallels, into which historical facts are sometimes made willing or unwillingly to enter, I might show you Christianity running exactly the same course, and undergoing the same destiny in Asia, as Mohammedanism in Europe. Mohammedanism established itself in Spain, where it conquered, founded a kingdom and various principalities. The Christians did the same thing in Asia. They were there in regard to the Mohammedans, in the same situation as the Mohammedans in Spain with regard to the Christians. The kingdom of Jerusalem corresponds with the kingdom of Granada: but these similitudes, after all, are of little importance. The great fact was the struggle between the two religious and social systems: the crusades were its principal crisis. This is their historical character; the chain which connects them with the general course of events.

Another cause, the social state of Europe in the eleventh century, equally contributed to the breaking out of the crusades. I have been careful to explain why, from the fifth to the eleventh century, there was no such thing as generality in Europe; I have endeavored to show how everything had assumed a local character; how states, existing institutions, and opinions, were confined within very narrow bounds: it was then that the feudal system prevailed. After the lapse of some time, such a narrow horizon was no longer sufficient; human thought and activity aspired to pass beyond the narrow sphere in which they were confined. The people no longer led their former wandering life, but had not lost the taste for its adventures; they threw themselves into the crusades as into a new state of existence, in which they were more at large, and enjoyed more variety; which reminded them of the freedom of former barbarism, while it opened boundless prospects of futurity.

These were, in my opinion, the two determining causes of the crusades in the twelfth century. At the end of the thirteenth, neither of these causes continued to exist. Mankind and society were so greatly changed, that neither the moral nor the social incitements which had impelled Europe upon Asia were felt any longer. I do not know whether many of you have read the original historians of the crusades, or have ever thought of comparing the contemporary chroniclers of the first crusades with those of the end of the twelfth and thirteenth centuries; for example, Albert de Aix, Robert the Monk, andd Raynard d'Argile, who were engaged in the first crusade with William of Tyre and Jacques de Vitry. When we compare these two classes of writers, it is impossible not not be struck with the distance between them. The first are animated chroniclers, whose imagination is excited, and who relate the events of the crusade with passion: but they are narrow-minded in the extreme, without an idea beyond the little sphere in which they lived; ignorant of every science, full of prejudices, incapable of forming an opinion on what was passing around them, or the events which were the subject of their narratives. But open, on the other hand, the history of the crusades by William of Tyre, and you will be surprised to find almost a modern historian; a cultivated, enlarged, and liberal mind, great political intelligence, general views and opinions upon causes and effects. Jacques de Vitry is an example of another species of cultivation; he is a man of learning, who does not confine himself to what immediately concerns the crusades, but describes the state of manners, the geography, the religion, and natural history of the country to which his history relates. There is, in short, an immense distance between the historians of the first and of the last crusades; a distance which manifests an actual revolution in the state of the human mind.

This revolution is most conspicuous in the manner in which these two classes of writers speak of the Mohammedans. For the first chroniclers—and consequently for the first crusaders, of whose sentiments the first chroniclers are merely the organs—the Mohammedans are only an object of hatred; it is clear that those who speak of them do not know them, form no judgment respecting them, nor consider them under any point of view but that of the religious hostility which exists between them. No vestige of social relation is discoverable between them and the Mohammedans: they detest them, and fight with them; and nothing more. William of Tyre, Jacques de Vitry, Bernard le Tresorier, speak of the Mussulmans quite differently. We see that, even while fighting with them, they no longer regard them as monsters; that they have entered to a certain extent into their ideas, that they have lived with them, and that certain social relations, and even a sort of sympathy, have arisen between them. William of Tyre pronounces a glowing eulogium on Noureddin and Bernard le Tresorier on Saladin. They sometimes even go the length of placing the manners and conduct of the Mussulmans in opposition to those of the Christians; they adopt the manners and sentiments of the Mussulmans in order to satirise the Christians, in the same manner as Tacitus delineated the manners of the Germans in contrast with those of Rome. You see, then, what an immense change must have taken place between these two periods, since you find in the latter, in regard to the very enemies of the Christians, the very peeple against whom the crusades were directed, an impartiality of judgment which would have filled the first crusaders with surprise and horror.

The principal effect, then, of the crusades was a great step toward the emancipation of the mind, a great progress toward enlarged and liberal ideas. Though begun under the name and influence of religous belief, the crusades deprived religious ideas, I shall not say of their legitimate share of influence, but of their exclusive and despotic possession of the human mind. This result, though undoubtedly unforeseen, arose from various causes. The first was evidently the novelty, extent, and variety of the scene which displayed itself to the crusaders; what generally happens to travelers happened to them. It is mere common-place to say that travelling gives freedom to the mind; that the habit of observing different nations, different manners, and different opinions, enlarges the ideas, and disengages the judgment from old prejudices. The same thing happened to those nations of travelers who have been called the crusaders; their minds were opened and raised by having seen a multitude of different things, by having become acquainted with other manners than their own. They found themselves also placed in connexion with two states of civilization, not only different from their own, but more advanced—the Greek state of society on the one hand, and the Mussulman on the other. There is no doubt that the society of the Greeks, though enervated, perverted, and decaying, gave the crusaders the impression of something more advanced, polished, and enlightened than their own. The society of the Mussulmans presented them a scene of the same kind. It is curious to observe in the chronicles the impression made by the crusaders on the Mussulmans, who regarded them at first as the most brutal, ferocious, and stupid barbarians they had ever seen. The crusaders, on their part, were struck with the riches and elegance of manners which they observed among the Mussulmans. These first impressions were succeeded by frequent relations between the Mussulmans and Christians. These became more extensive and important than is commonly believed. Not only had the Christians of the east habitual relations with the Mussulmans, but the people of the east and the west became acquainted with, visited, and mingled with each other. It is but lately that one of those learned men who do honor to France in the eyes of Europe, M. Abel Remusat, has discovered the relations which subsisted between the Mongol emperors and the Christian kings. Mongol ambassadors were sent to the kings of the Franks, and to St. Louis among others, in order to persuade them to enter into alliance, and to resume the crusades for the common interest of the Mongols and the Christians against the Turks. And not only were diplomatic and official relations thus established between the sovereigns, but there was much and various intercourse between the nations of the east and west. I shall quote the word of M. Abel Remusat:—

"Many men of religious orders—Italians, French, and Flemings—were charged with diplomatic missions to the court of the Great Khan. Mongols of distinction came to Rome, Barcelona, Valentia, Lyons, Paris, London, and Northampton; and a Franciscan of the kingdom of Naples was Archbishop of Pekin. His successor was a professor of theology in the University of Paris. But how many other people followed in the train of those personages, either as slaves, or attracted by the desire of profit, or led by curiosity into regions hitherto unknown! Chance has preserved the names of some of these; the first envoy who visited the King of Hungary on the part of the Tartars was an Englishman, who had been banished from his country for certain crimes, and who, after having wandered over Asia, at last entered into the service of the Mongols. A Flemish Cordelier, in the heart of Tartary, fell in with a woman of Metz called "Paquette," who had been carried off into Hungary, a Parisian goldsmith, and a young man from the neighborhood of Rouen, who had been at the taking of Belgrade. In the same country he fell in also with Russians, Hungarians, and Flemings. A singer, called "Robert," after having travelled through Eastern Asia, returned to end his days in the cathedral of Chartres. A Tartar was a furnisher of helmets in the armies of Philip the Fair. Jean de Plancarpin fell in, near Gayouk, with a Russian gentleman whom he calls "Temer," and who acted as an interpreter; and many merchants of Breslaw, Poland, and Austria, accompanied him in his journey into Tartary. Others returned with him through Russia; they were Genoese, Pisans, and Venetians. Two Venetians, merchants, whom chance had brought to Bokhara, followed a Mongol ambassador, sent by Houlagou to Khoubilai. They remained many years in China and Tartary, returned with letters from the Great Khan to the Pope, and afterward went back to the Khan, taking with them the son of one of their number, the celebrated Marco Polo, and once more left the court of Khoubilai to return to Venice. Travels of this nature were not less frequent in the following century. Of this number are those of John Mandeville, an English physician; Oderic de Frioul, Pegoletti, Guilleaume de Bouldeselle, and several others. It may well be supposed, that those travels of which the memory is preserved form but a small part of those which were undertaken, and there were in those days many more people who were able to perform those long journeys than to write accounts of them. Many of those adventurers must have remained and died in the countries they went to visit. Others returned home as obscure as before, but having their imagination full of the things they had seen, relating them to their families, with much exaggeration no doubt, but leaving behind them, among many ridiculous fables, useful recollections and traditions capable of bearing fruit. Thus, in Germany, Italy, and France, in the monasteries, among the nobility, and even down to the lowest classes of society, there were deposited many precious seeds destined to bud at a somewhat later period. All these unknown travelers, carrying the arts of their own country into distant regions, brought back other pieces of knowledge not less precious, and, without being aware of it, made exchanges more advantageous than those of commerce. By these means, not only the traffic in the silks, porcelain, and other commodities of Hindostan, became more extensive and practicable, and new paths were opened to commercial industry and enterprise; but, what was more valuable still, foreign manners, unknown nations, extraordinary productions, presented themselves in abundance to the minds of the Europeans, which, since the fall of the Roman empire, had been confined within too narrow a circle. Men began to attach some importance to the most beautiful, the most populous, and the most anciently civilized of the four quarters of the world. They began to study the arts, the religions, the languages, of the nations by whom it was inhabited; and there was even an intention of establishing a professorship of the Tartar language in the University of Paris. The accounts of travelers, strange and exaggerated indeed, but soon discussed and cleared up, diffused more correct and varied notions of those distant regions. The world seemed to open, as it were, toward the east; geography made an immense stride; and ardor for discovery became the new form assumed by European spirit of adventure. The idea of another hemisphere, when our own came to be better known, no longer seemed an improbable paradox; and it was when in search of the Zipangri of Marco Polo that Christopher Columbus discovered the New World."

You see, then, what a vast and unexplored world was laid open to the view of European intelligence by the consequences of the crusade. It cannot be doubted that the impulse which led to them was one of the most powerful causes of the development and freedom of mind which arose out of that great event.

There is another circumstance which is worthy of notice. Down to the time of the crusades, the court of Rome, the centre of the Church, had been very little in communication with the laity, unless through the medium of ecclesiastics; either legates sent by the court of Rome, or the whole body of the bishops and clergy. There were always some laymen in direct relation with Rome; but upon the whole, it was by means of churchmen that Rome had any communication with the people of different countries. During the crusades, on the contrary, Rome became a halting-place for a great portion of the crusaders, either in going or returning. A multitude of laymen were spectators of its policy and its manner, and were able to discover the share which personal interest had in religious disputes. There is no doubt that this newly-acquired knowledge inspired many minds with a boldness hitherto unknown

When we consider the state of the general mind at the termination of the crusades, especially in regard to ecclesiastical matters, we cannot fail to be struck with a singular fact: religious notions underwent no change, and were not replaced by contrary or even different opinions. Thought, notwithstanding, had become more free; religious creeds were not the only subjects on which the human mind exercised its faculties; without abandoning them, it began occasionally to wander from them, and to take other directions. Thus, at the end of the thirteenth century, the moral causes which had led to the crusades, or which, at least, had been their most energetic principle, had disappeared; the moral state of Europe had undergone an essential modification.

The social state of society had undergone an analogous change. Many inquiries have been made as to the influence of the crusades in this respect; it has been shown in what manner they had reduced a great number of feudal proprietors to the necessity of selling their fiefs to the kings, or to sell their privileges to the communities, in order to raise money for the crusades.

It has been shown that, in consequence of their absence, many of the nobles lost a great portion of their power. Without entering into the details of this question, we may collect into a few general facts the influence of the crusades on the social state of Europe.

They greatly diminished the number of petty fiefs, petty domains, and petty proprietors; they concentrated property and power in a smaller number of hands. It is from the time of the crusades that we may observe the formation and growth of great fiefs—the existence of feudal power on a large scale.

I have often regretted that there was not a map of France divided into fiefs, as we have a map of France divided into departments, *arrondissments*, cantons and *communes*, in which all the fiefs were marked, with their boundaries, relations with each other, and successive changes. If we could have compared, by the help of such maps, the state of France before and after the crusades, we should have seen how many small fiefs had disappeared, and to what extent the greater ones had increased. This was one of the most important results of the crusades.

Even in those cases where small proprietors preserved their fiefs, they did not live upon them in such an insulated state as formerly. The possessors of great fiefs became so many centres around which the smaller ones were gathered, and near which they came to live. During the crusades, small proprietors found it necessary to place themselves in the train of some rich and powerful chief, from whom they received assistance and support. They lived with him, shared his fortune, and passed through the same adventures that he did. When the crusaders returned home, this social spirit, this habit of living in intercourse with superiors continued to subsist, and had its influence on the manners of the age. As we see that the great fiefs were increased after the crusades, so we see, also, that the proprietors of these fiefs held, within their castles, a much more considerable court than before, and were surrounded by a greater number of gentlemen, who preserved their little domains, but no longer kept within them.

The extension of the great fiefs, and the creation of a number of central points in society, in place of the general dispersion which previously existed, were the two principal effects of the crusades, considered with respect to their influence upon feudalism.

As to the inhabitants of the towns, a result of the same nature may easily be perceived. The crusades created great civic communities. Petty commerce and petty industry were not sufficient to give rise to communities such as the great cities of Italy and Flanders. It was commerce on a great scale—maritime commerce, and, especially, the commerce of the east and west, which gave them birth; now it was the crusades which gave to maritime commerce the greatest impulse it had yet received.

On the whole, when we survey the state of society at the end of the crusades, we find that the movement tending to dissolution and dispersion, the movement of universal localization (if I may be allowed such an expression) had ceased, and had been succeeded by a movement in the contrary direction, a movement of centralization. All things tended to mutual approximation; small things were absorbed in great ones, or gathered round them. Such was the direction then taken by the progress of society.

You now understand why, at the end of the thirteenth and in the fourteenth century, neither nations nor sovereigns wished to have any more crusades. They neither needed nor desired them; they had been thrown into them by the impulses of religious spirit, and the exclusive dominion of religious ideas; but this dominion had now lost its energy. They had also sought in the crusades a new way of life, of a less confined and more varied description; but they began to find this in Europe itself, in the progress of the social relations. It was at this time that kings began to see the road to political aggrandizement. Why go to Asia in search of kingdoms, when there were kingdoms to conquer at their very doors? Philip Augustus embarked in the crusade very unwillingly; and what could be more natural? His desire was to make himself king of France. It was the same thing with the people. The road to wealth was open to them; and they gave up adventures for industry. Adventures were replaced, for sovereigns, by political projects; for the people, by industry on a large scale. One class only of society still had a taste for adventure; that portion of the feudal nobility, who, not being in a condition to think of political aggrandizement, and not being disposed to industry, retained their former situation and manners. This class, accordingly, continued to embark in crusades, and endeavored to renew them.

Such, in my opinion, are the real effects of the crusades; on the one hand the extension of ideas and the emancipation of thought; on the other, a general enlargement of the social sphere, and the opening of a wider field for every sort of activity: they produced, at the same time, more individual freedom and more political unity. They tended to the independence of man and the centralization of society. Many inquiries have been made respecting the means of civilization which were directly imported from the east. It has been said that the largest part of the great discoveries which, in the course of the fourteenth and fifteenth centuries, contributed to the progress of European civilization—such as the compass, printing, and gunpowder—were known in the east, and that the crusades brought them into Europe. This is true to a certain extent; though some of these assertions may be disputed. But what cannot be disputed is this influence, this general effect of the crusades upon the human mind on the one hand, and the state of society on the other. They drew society out of a very narrow road, to throw it into new and infinitely broader paths; they began that transformation of the various elements of European society into governments and nations, which is the characteristic of modern civilization. The same period witnessed the development of one of those institutions which has most powerfully contributed to this great result—monarchy; the history of which, from the birth of the modern states of Europe to the thirteenth century, will form the subject of our next lecture.

The following chronological table may serve to put before the student's eye a connected outline of the principal facts Eight crusades are enumerated.

First Crusade.—A.D. 1096-1100.   Urban II. Pope.

A.D.
1094. Peter the Hermit returned from a pilgrimage—by direction of the Pope, preaches throughout Europe.
1095. Council of Clermont in France. (A previous council had been held at Placenza.) Attended by the Pope and an immense concourse of clergy and nobles. The crusade proclaimed—great privileges, civil and ecclesiastical, to all who should "assume the cross" —a year allowed to prepare. Peter the Hermit, not waiting, sets out at the head of a vast rabble of undisciplined fanatics and marauders, who perish by disease, famine, and the sword, in Asia Minor.
1096. An army of 100,000 mounted and mailed warriors, 600,000 men capable of bearing arms, and a multitude of monks, women, and children, depart from Europe and assemble on the plains of Bythinia, east of Constantinople. Principal leaders of the expedition: Godfrey of Boulongne, with his brothers, Baldwin and Eustace; Robert II., Duke of Normany; Robert II., Count of Flanders; Raymond of Toulouse; Hugh of Vermandois; Stephen de Blois; Bohemond, Prince of Tarento, with his nephew Tancred.
1097. Nice taken by the crusaders.
1098. Antioch and Edessa taken.
1099. Jerusalem taken—a Christian kingdom, on feudal principles, established—the crown conferred on Godfrey of Boulougne.

Interval between the First and Second Crusades.—1100-1147.

Baldwin I. succeeds his brother Godfrey as King of Jerusalem. A new army of crusaders destroyed by the Saracens in Asia Minor, and the remnant of the first army cut to pieces at Rama. St. Jean d'Acre (Ptolemais), Berytus, and Sidon, taken by Baldwin II., successor of Baldwin I. The Christian army unsuccessful—Edessa taken by the Turks in 1144—continued ill success of the Christians leads to a new crusade.

Second Crusade.—1147-1149. Eugene III. Pope.

Leaders of this expedition: Conrad III., Emperor of Germany, and Louis VII., King of France, who set out separately on their march. Both armies destroyed in Asia Minor by famine and the sword. The fugitives assemble at Jerusalem. Conrad, Louis, and Baldwin III., King of Jerusalem, lay siege to Damascus—the enterprise fails through the quarrels of the princes—Conrad and Louis return to Europe.

Interval between the Second and Third Crusades.—1149-1189.

Saladin takes possession of Egypt and founds a dynasty in 1175. Makes war upon the Christian kingdom of Jerusalem ; defeats Guy of Lusignan at the battle of Tiberias; Guy taken prisoner; St. Jean d'Acre and Jerusalem taken. Conrad of Montferrat lays claim to the crown of Jerusalem, and rallies the remains of the Christian forces at Tyre.

Third Crusade.—1189-1193. Clement III. Pope.

Leaders: Frederick I. (Barbarossa), Emperor of Germany; Philip Augustus, King of France ; and Richard I. of England.

Frederick departs first with an army of 100,000 men, which is entirely destroyed in Asia Minor. The emperor himself dies in Cilicia, 1190. His son, Frederick of Suabia, afterward killed at St. Jean d'Acre.

1190. The kings of France and England embark by sea, and pass the winter in Sicily; the armies embroiled by the artifices of Tancred, usurping king of Jerusalem, and by dissension between the kings

1191. The armies of France and England, with the Christian princes of Syria, take St. Jean d'Acre. Philip Augustus returns to France, leaving a part of his army with Richard—who displays his bravery in some useless battles, but is unable to regain Jerusalem.

1192. Richard concludes a truce with Saladin and returns to Europe.

Third Interval.—1193-1202.

Saladin dies—his dominions divided among the princes of his family.

Fourth Crusade.—1202-1204. Innocent III. Pope.

Leaders: Baldwin IX., Count of Flanders; Boniface II., Marquis of Montferrat; Henry Dandolo, Doge of Venice, etc. The *kings* of Europe could not be aroused to engage in this crusade, notwithstanding all the urgency of the Holy See. The chief command was conferred by the crusaders on Boniface of Montferrat. This expedition, however, never reached the Holy Land—but engaged in putting down a usurpation at Constantinople, which finally led to the taking and plundering of that city by the crusaders, and the division of the empire among the conquerors, of whom Baldwin was raised to the imperial dignity. The French empire of Constantinople was destroyed in 1261, by Michael Paleologus.

Fourth Interval.—1204-1217.

Meantime the Christians in the east, though despoiled of most of their possessions, and weakened by divisions, bravely defended themselves against the sultans of Egypt. They continually invoked aid from Europe ; but more powerful interests at home made the European princes regardless of their calls. Only those of more exalted imaginations could be influenced. There was a crusade of children in 1212.

Fifth Crusade.—1217-1221. Honorius III. Pope.

Three kings—John de Brienne, titular king of Jerusalem; Andrew II., King of Hungary; and Hugh of Lusignan, King of Cyprus—united their forces at St. Jean d'Acre. The King of Hungary was soon recalled by troubles at home; Hugh of Lusignan died; and John de Brienne went to attack Egypt alone. He conquered Damietta, and would have obtained the restitution of Jerusalem but for the obstinacy of the Papal legate, who forbade any truce with the infidels. In 1221 the crusaders, after many reverses, submitted to an humiliating peace; and John of Brienne, returning to Europe, gave his daughter in marriage to Frederick II., Emperor of Germany, who thereby became titular king of Jerusalem.

Fifth Interval.—1221-1228.

Nothing remarkable took place in Syria.

Sixth Crusade.—1228-1229. Gregory IX. Pope.

Leader, Frederick II. This emperor had taken the vows of the cross five years before, and though anathematized by the Pope, had failed to fulfil his engagement. At length he set out by invitation of the Sultan Maledin, who yielded Jerusalem to him by treaty without battle. Frederick was desirous to be crowned king of Jerusalem, but no bishop dared anoint an excommunicated prince. Threatened with the loss of his Italian dominions, he returned to Europe.

Sixth Interval.—1229-1248.

Anarchy throughout the East, both among the Christians and Mohammedans. Jerusalem, after being taken successively by several Saracen chiefs, fell into the hands of the Sultan of Egypt.

Seventh Crusade.—1248-1254. Innocent IV. Pope.

Leaders: St. Louis (IX.) and the French princes. The King of France engaged in this crusade in consequence of a vow made during a dangerous illness. Most of the princes of the blood and great vassals accompanied him. He turned his arms first against Egypt and took Damietta in 1250; but his army, surprised by a sudden rising of the Nile, and carried off in great numbers by pestilence, was surrounded by the Mussulmen, and Louis himself, with 20,000 of his army, was made prisoner. He obtained his liberty, however, by payment of a heavy ransom and the surrender of Damietta. He remained four years in Palestine, repairing the fortifications of the towns which yet remained in the hands of the Christians (Ptolemais, Jaffa, Sidon, etc.), and mediating between the Christian and Mohammedan princes.

Seventh Interval.—1254-1272.

The Mongols, who, under Gengis Khan, had before overrun the greatest part of Asia, now entered Syria under his son, having already destroyed the Califate of Bagdad in 1258. They were driven from Syria by the Sultan of Egypt, Bibars, by whom also Damascus, Tyre, Jaffa, and Antioch were seized.

Eighth Crusade.—1270. Clement IV. Pope.

Leaders: Louis IX., Charles of Anjou, Edward, Prince of England, afterward Edward I. This expedition was first directed to the coast of Africa; Louis debarked before Tunis and laid siege to that city; but

the army was cut down by the plague, to which Louis himself and one
of his sons fell victims. Charles of Anjou, his brother, made peace
with the Mohammedans and renounced the expedition to the Holy
Land. This was the last crusade.

End of the Christian power in Syria.—1270-1291.

There remained now but four places in the possession of the Christians on the eastern shore of the Mediterranean—Tripoli, Tyre, Berytus, and St. Jean d'Acre. These successively yielded to the Saracens, the last in 1291. The vaiious orders of religious knights, sworn to the defence of the Holy Land, withdrew at first to the Island of Cyprus. In 1310, the Hospitallers established themselves at Rhodes; in 1312, the order of the Templars was abolished; in 1300, the Teutonic knights transferred the seat of their order to Courland, where they laid the foundation of a dominion which continued powerful for a long period.
—See *Des Michels' Hist. du Moyen Age.*

LECTURE IX.

OF MONARCHY.

I ENDEAVORED, at our last meeting, to determine the essential and distinctive character of modern society as compared with the primitive state of society in Europe; and I believed I had found it in this fact, that all the elements of the social state, at first numerous and various, were reduced to two—the government on one hand, and the people on the other. Instead of finding, in the capacity of ruling forces and chief agents in history, the clergy, kings, citizens, husbandmen, and serfs, we now find in modern Europe, only two great objects which occupy the historical stage—the government and the nation.

If such is the fact to which European civilization has led, such, also, is the result to which our researches should conduct us. We must see the birth, the growth, the progressive establishment of this great result. We have entered upon the period to which we can trace its origin: it was, as you have seen, between the twelfth and the sixteenth centuries that those slow and hidden operations took place which brought society into this new form, this definite state. We have also considered the first great event which, in my opinion, evidently had a powerful effect in impelling Europe into this road; I mean the crusades.

About the same period, and almost at the very time when the crusades broke out, that institution began to increase, which has perhaps chiefly contributed to the formation of modern society, and to the fusion of all the social elements into two forces, the government and the people. This institution is monarchy.

It is evident that monarchy has played a vast part in the history of European civilization. Of this we may convince ourselves by a single glance. We see the development of monarchy proceed, for a considerable time, at the same rate as that of society itself: they had a common progression. And not only had they a common progression, but with every step that society made toward its definite and modern character, monarchy seemed to increase and prosper; so that when the work was consummated—when there remained, in the great states of Europe, little or no important and decisive influence but that of the government and the public—it was monarchy that became the government.

It was not only in France, where the fact is evident, that this happened, but in most of the countries of Europe. A little sooner or later, and under forms somewhat different, the history of society in England, Spain, and Germany, offer us the same result. In England, for example, it was under the Tudors that the old particular and local elements of English society were dissolved and mingled, and gave way to the system of public authorities; this, also, was the period when monarchy had the greatest influence. It was the same thing in Germany, Spain, and all the great European states.

If we leave Europe, and cast our eyes over the rest of the world, we shall be struck with an analogous fact. Everywhere we shall find monarchy holding a great place, and appearing as the most general and permanent, perhaps, of all institutions; as that which is the most difficult to preclude where it does not exist, and, where it does exist, the most difficult to extirpate. From time immemorial it has had possession of Asia. On the discovery of America, all the great states of that continent were found, with different combinations, under monarchical governments. When we penetrate into the interior of Africa, wherever we meet with nations of any extent, this is the government which prevails. And not only has monarchy penetrated everywhere, but it has accommodated itself to the most various situations, to civilization and barbarism: to the most peaceful manners, as in China, and to those in which a warlike spirit predominates. It has established itself not only in the midst of the system of *castes*, in countries whose social economy exhibits the most rigorous distinction of ranks, but also in the midst of a system of equality, in countries where society is most remote from every kind of legal and permanent classification. In some places despotic and oppressive; in others favorable to the progress of civilization and even of liberty; it is like a head that may be placed on many different bodies, a fruit that may grow from many different buds.

In this fact we might discover many important and curious consequences. I shall take only two; the first is, that such a result cannot possibly be the offspring of mere chance, of force or usurpation only; that there must necessarily be, between the nature of monarchy considered as an institution, and the nature either of man as an individual or of human society, a strong and intimate analogy. Force, no doubt, has had its share, both in the origin and progress of the institution; but as often as you met with a result like this, as often as you see a great event develop itself or recur during a long series of ages, and in the midst of so many different situations, never ascribe it to force. Force performs a great and daily part in human affairs; but it is not the principle which governs their movements: there is always, superior to force, and the part which it performs, a moral cause which governs the general course of events. Force, in the history of society, resembles the body in the history of man. The body assuredly holds a great place in the life of man, but is not the principle of life. Life circulates in it, but does not emanate from it. Such is also the case in human society; whatever part force may play in them, it does not govern them, or exercise a supreme control over their destinies; this is the province of reason, of the moral influences which are hidden under the accidents of force, and regulate the course of society. We may unhesitatingly declare that it was to a cause of this nature, and not to mere force, that monarchy was indebted for its success.

A second fact of almost equal importance is the flexibility of monarchy, and its faculty of modifying itself and adapting itself to a variety of different circumstances. Observe the contrast which it presents; its form reveals unity, permanence, simplicity. It does not exhibit that variety of combinations which are found in other institutions; yet it accommodates itself to the most dissimilar states of society. It becomes evident then that it is susceptible of great diversity, and capable of being attached to many different elements and principles both in man as an individual and in society.

It is because we have not considered monarchy in all its extent; because we have not, on the one hand, discovered the principle which forms its essence and subsists under every circumstance to which it may be applied; and because, on the other hand, we have not taken into account all the variations to which it accommodates itself, and all the principles with which it can enter into alliance;—it is, I say, because we have not considered monarchy in this twofold, this enlarged point of view, that we have not thoroughly understood the part it has performed in the history of the world, and have often been mistaken as to its nature and effects.

This is the task which I should wish to undertake with you, so as to obtain a complete and precise view of the effects of this institution in modern Europe; whether they have flowed from its intrinsic principle, or from the modifications which it has undergone.

There is no doubt that the strength of monarchy, that moral power which is its true principle, does not reside in the personal will of the man who for the time happens to be king; there is no doubt that the people in accepting it as an institution, that philosophers in maintaining it as a system, have not meant to accept the empire of the will of an individual—a will essentially arbitrary, capricious, and ignorant.

Monarchy is something quite different from the will of an individual, though it presents itself under that form. It is the personification of legitimate sovereignty—of the collective will and aggregate wisdom of a people—of that will which is essentially reasonable, enlightened, just, impartial—which knows naught of individual wills, though by the title of legitimate monarchy, earned by these conditions, it has the right to govern them. Such is the meaning of monarchy as understood by the people, and such is the motive of their adhesion to it.

Is it true that there is a legitimate sovereignty, a will which has a right to govern mankind? They certainly believe that there is; for they endeavor, have always endeavored, and cannot avoid endeavoring, to place themselves under its empire. Conceive, I shall not say a people, but the smallest community of men; conceive it in subjection to a sovereign who is such only *de facto*, to a power which has no other right but that of force, which does not govern by the title of reason and justice; human nature instantly revolts against a sovereignty such as this. Human nature, therefore, must believe in legitimate sovereignty. It is this sovereignty alone, the sovereignty *de jure*, which man seeks for, and which alone he consents to obey. What is history but a demonstration of this universal fact? What are most of the struggles which harass the lives of nations but so many determined impulses toward this legitimate sovereignty, in order to place themselves under its empire? And it is not only the people, but philosophers, who firmly believe in its existence and incessantly seek it. What are all the systems of political philosophy but attempts to discern the legitimate sovereignty? What is the object of their investigations but to discover who has the right to govern society? Take theocracy, monarchy, aristocracy, democracy; they all boast of having discovered the seat of legitimate sovereignty; they all promise to place society under the authority of its rightful master. This, I repeat, is the object of all the labor of philosophers, as well as of all the efforts of nations.

How can philosophers and nations do otherwise than believe in this legitimate sovereignty? How can they do otherwise than strive incessantly to discover it? Let us suppose the simplest case; for instance, some act to be performed, either affecting society in general, or some portion of its members, or even a single individual; it is evident that in such a case there must be some rule of action, some legitimate will to be followed and applied. Whether we enter into the most minute details of social life, or participate in its most momentous concerns, we shall always meet with a truth to be discovered, a law of reason to be applied to the realities of human affairs. It is this law which constitutes that legitimate sovereignty toward which other philosophers and nations have never ceased, and can never cease, to aspire.

But how far can legitimate sovereignty be represented, generally and permanently, by an earthly power, by a human will? Is there anything necessarily false and dangerous in such an assumption? What are we to think in particular of the personification of legitimate sovereignty under the image of royalty? On what conditions, and within what limits, is this personification admissible? These are great questions, which it is not my business now to discuss, but which I cannot avoid noticing, and on which I shall say a few words in passing.

I affirm, and the plainest common sense must admit, that legitimate sovereignty, in its complete and permanent form, cannot belong to any one; and that every attribution of legitimate sovereignty to any human power whatever is radically false and dangerous. Thence arises the necessity of the limitation of every power, whatever may be its name or form; thence arises the radical illegitimacy of every sort of absolute power, whatever may be its origin, whether conquest, inheritance, or election We may differ as to the best means of finding the legitimate sovereignty; they vary according to the diversities of place and time; but there is no place or time at which any power can legitimately be the independent possessor of this sovereignty.

This principle being laid down, it is equally certain that monarchy, under whatever system we consider it, presents itself as the personification of the legitimate sovereignty. Listen to the supporters of theocracy; they will tell you that kings are the image of God upon earth, which means nothing more than that they are the personification of supreme justice, truth and goodness. Turn to the jurists; they will tell you that the king is the living law; which means, again, that the king is the personification of the legitimate sovereignty, of that law of justice which is entitled to govern society. Interrogate monarchy itself in its pure and unmixed form; it will tell you that it is the personification of the state, of the commonwealth. In whatever combination, in whatever situation, monarchy is considered, you will find that it is always held out as representing this legitimate sovereignty, this power, which alone is capable of lawfully governing society.

We need not be surprised at this. What are the characteristic of this legitimate sovereignty, and which are derived from its very nature? In the first place, it is single; since there is but one truth, one justice, so there can be but one legitimate sovereignty. It is, moreover, permanent, and always the same, for truth is unchangeable. It stands on a high vantage-ground, beyond the reach of the vicissitudes and chances of this world, with which it is only connected in the character, as it were, of a spectator and a judge. Well, then, these being the rational and natural characteristics of the legitimate sovereignty, it is monarchy which exhibits them under the most palpable forms, and seems to be their most faithful image. Consult the work in which M. Benjamin Constant has so ingeniously represented monarchy, as a neutral and moderating power, raised far above the struggles and casualties of society, and never interfering but in great and critical conjunctures. Is not this, so to speak, the attitude of the legitimate sovereignty, in the government of human affairs? There must be something in this idea peculiarly calculated to strike the mind, for it has passed, with singular rapidity, from books into the actual conduct of affairs. A sovereign has made it, in the constitution of Brazil, the very basis of his throne. In that constitution, monarchy is represented as a moderating power, elevated above the active powers of the state, like their spectator and their judge.

Under whatever point of view you consider monarchy, when you compare it with the legitimate sovereignty, you will find a great outward resemblance between them—a resemblance with which the human mind must necessarily have been struck. Whenever the reflection or the imagination of men has especially turned toward the contemplation or study of legitimate sovereignty, and of its essential qualities, it has inclined toward monarchy. Thus in the times when religious ideas preponderated, the habitual contemplation of the nature of God impelled mankind toward the monarchical system. In the same manner, when the influence of jurists prevailed in society, the habit of studying, under the name of law, the nature of the legitimate sovereignty, was favorable to the dogma of its personification in the institution of monarchy. The attentive application of the human mind to the contemplation of the nature and qualities of the legitimate sovereignty, when there were no other causes to destroy its effect, has always given strength and consideration to monarchy, as being its image.

There are, too, certain junctures, which are particularly favorable to this personification; such, for example, as when individual forces display themselves in the world with all their uncertainties; all their waywardness; when selfishness predominates in individuals, either through ignorance and brutality, or through corruption. At such times, society, distracted by the conflict of individual wills, and unable to attain, by their free concurrence, to a general will, which might hold them in subjection, feels an ardent desire for a sovereign power, to which all individuals must submit; and, as soon as any institution presents itself which bears any of the characteristics of legitimate sovereignty, society rallies round it with eagerness; as people, under proscription, take refuge in the sanctuary of a church. This is what has taken place in the wild and disorderly youth of nations, such as those we have passed through. Monarchy is wonderfully suited to those times of strong and fruitful anarchy, if I may so speak, in which society is striving to form and regulate itself, but is unable to do so by the free concurrence of individual wills. There are other times when monarchy, though from a contrary cause, has the same merit. Why did the Roman world, so near dissolution at the end of the republic, still subsist for more than fifteen centuries, under the name of an empire, which, after all, was nothing but a lingering decay, a protracted death-struggle? Monarchy, alone, could produce such an effect; monarchy, alone, could maintain a state of society which the spirit of selfishness incessantly tended to destroy. The imperial power contended for fifteen centuries against the ruin of the Roman world.

It thus appears that there are times when monarchy, alone, can retard the dissolution, and times when it, alone, can accelerate the formation of society. And it is, in both cases, because it represents, more clearly than any other form of government can do, the legitimate sovereignty, that it exercises this power over the course of events.

Under whatever point of view you consider this institution, and at whatever period you take it, you will find, therefore, that its essential character, its moral principle, its true meaning, the cause of its strength, is, its being the image, the personification, the presumed interpreter, of that single, superior, and essentially legitimate will, which alone has a right to govern society.

Let us now consider monarchy under the second point of view, that is to say, in its flexibliity, the variety of parts it has performed and of effects it has produced. Let us endeavor to account for this character, and ascertain its causes.

Here we have an advantage; we can at once return to history, and to the history of our own country. By a concurrence of singular circumstances, monarchy in modern Europe has but one very character which it has ever exhibited in the history of the world. European monarchy has been, in some sort, the result of all the possible kinds of monarchy. In running over its history, from the fifth to the twelfth century, you will see the variety of aspects under which it appears, and the extent to which we everywhere find that variety, complication, and contention, which characterize the whole course of European civilization.

In the fifth century, at the time of the great invasion of the Germans, two monarchies were in existence—the barbarian monarchy of Clovis, and the imperial monarchy of Constantine. They were very different from each other in principles and effects.

The barbarian monarchy was essentially elective. The German kings were elected, though their election did not take place in the form to which we are accustomed to attach that idea. They were military chiefs, whose power was freely accepted by a great number of their companions, by whom they were obeyed as being the bravest and most competent to rule. Election was the true source of this barbarian monarchy, its primitive and essential character.

It is true that this character, in the fifth century, was already somewhat modified, and that different elements were introduced into monarchy. Different tribes had possessed their chiefs for a certain space of time; families had arisen, more considerable and wealthier than the rest. This produced the beginning of hereditary succession; the chief being almost always chosen from these families. This was the first principle of a different nature which became associated with the leading principle of election.

Another element had already entered into the institution of barbarian monarchy—I mean the element of religion. We find among some of the barbarian tribes—the Goths, for example—the conviction that the families of their kings were descended from the families of their gods or of their deified heroes, such as Odin. This, too, was the case with Homer's monarchs, who were the issue of gods or demi-gods, and, by this title, objects of religious veneration, notwithstanding the limited extent of their power.

Such was the barbarian monarchy of the fifth century, whose primitive principle still predominated, though it had itself grown diversified and wavering.

I now take the monarchy of the Roman empire, the principle of which was totally different. It was the personification of the state, the heir of the sovereignty and majesty of the Roman people. Consider the monarchy of Augustus of Tiberius: the emperor was the representative of the senate; the assemblies of the people, the whole republic.

Was not this evident from the modest language of the first emperors—of such of them, at least, as were men of sense and understood their situation? They felt that they stood in the presence of the people, who themselves had lately possessed the sovereign power, which they had abdicated in their favor; and addressed the people as their representatives and ministers. But in reality they exercised all the power of the people, and that, too, in its most exaggerated and fearful form. Such a transformation it is easy for us to comprehend; we have witnessed it ourselves; we have seen the sovereignty transferred from the people to the person of a single individual; this was the history of Napoleon. He also was a personification of the sovereignty of the people; and constantly expressed himself to that effect. "Who has been elected," he said, "like me, by eighteen millions of men? who is, like me, the representative of the people?" and when, upon his coins, we read on one side *Republique Francaise*, and on the other *Napoleon Empereur*, what is this but an example of the fact which I am describing, of the people having become the monarch?

Such was the fundamental character of the imperial monarchy; it preserved this character during the three first centuries of the empire; and it was, indeed, only under Diocletian that it assumed its complete and definitive form. It was then, however, on the eve of undergoing a great change; a new kind of monarchy was about to appear. During three centuries Christianity had been endeavoring to introduce into the empire the element of religion. It was under Constantine that Christianity succeeded, not in making religion the prevailing element, but in giving it a prominent part to perform. Monarchy here presents itself under a different aspect; it is not of earthly origin: the prince is not the representative of the sovereignty of the public; he is the image, the representative, the delegate of God. Power descends to him from on high, while, in the imperial monarchy, power had ascended from below. These were totally different situations., with totally different results. The rights of freedom and political securities are difficult to combine with the principle of religious monarchy; but the principle itself is high, moral, and salutary. I shall show you the idea which was formed of the prince, in the seventh century, under the system of religious monarchy. I take it from the canons of the Council of Toledo.

"The king is called *rex* because he governs with justice. If he acts justly (*recté*) he has a legitimate title to the name of king; if he acts unjustly, he loses all claim to it. Our fathers, therefore, said with reason, *rex ejus eris si recta facis; si autem non facis, non eris.* The two principal virtues of a king are justice and truth (the science of truth, reason).

"The depository of the royal power, no less than the whole body of the people, is bound to respect the laws. While we obey the will of Heaven, we make for ourselves, as well as our subjects, wise laws, obedience to which is obligatory on ourselves and our successors, as well as upon all the population of our kingdom. . . . . .

"God, the creator of all things, in constructing the human body, has raised the head aloft, and has willed that from it should proceed the nerves of all the members, and he has placed in the head the torches of the eyes, in order to throw light upon every dangerous object. In like manner he has established the power of intelligence, giving it the charge of governing all the members, and of prudently regulating their action. . . . . . .

"It is necessary then to regulate, first of all, those things which relate to princes, to provide for their safety, and protect their life, and then those things which concern the people, in such a manner, that in properly securing the safety of kings, that of the people may be, at the same time, and so much the more effectually, secured."

But, in the system of religious monarchy, there is almost always another element introduced besides monarchy itself. A new power takes its place by its side; a power nearer to God, the source whence monarchy emanates, than monarchy itself. This is the clergy, the ecclesiastical power which interposes between God and kings, and between kings and people, in such sort, that monarchy, though the image of the Divinity, runs the hazard of falling to the rank of an instrument in the hands of the human interpreters of the Divine will. This is a new cause of diversity in the destinies and effects of the institution.

The different kinds of monarchy, then, which, in the fifth century, made their appearance on the ruins of the Roman empire, were, the barbarian monarchy, the imperial monarchy, and religious monarchy in its infancy. Their fortunes were as different as their principles.

In France, under the first race, barbarian monarchy prevailed. There were, indeed, some attempts on the part of the clergy to impress upon it the imperial or religious character; but the system of election, in the royal family, with some mixture of inheritance and of religious notions, remained predominant.

In Italy, among the Ostrogoths, the imperial monarchy overcame the barbarous customs. Theodoric considered himself as successor of the emperors. It is sufficient to read Cassiodorus to perceive that this was the character of his government.

In Spain, monarchy appeared more religious than elsewhere. As the councils of Toledo, though I shall not call them absolute, were the influencing power, the religious character predominated, if not in the government, properly so called, of the Visigothic kings, at least in the laws which the clergy suggested to them, and the language they made them speak.

In England, among the Saxons, manners remained almost wholly barbarous. The kingdoms of the heptarchy were little else than the territories of different bands, every one having its chief. Military election appears more evidently among them than anywhere else. The Anglo-Saxon monarchy is the most faithful type of the barbarian monarchy.

Thus, from the fifth to the seventh century, at the same time that all these three sorts of monarchy manifested themselves in general facts, one or other of them prevailed, according to circumstances, in the different states of Europe.

Such was the prevailing confusion at this period, that nothing of a general or permanent nature could be established; and, from vicissitude to vicissitude, we arrive at the eighth century without finding that monarchy has anywhere assumed a definitive character.

Toward the middle of the eighth century, and with the triumph of the second race of the Frank kings, events assume a more general character, and become clearer; as they were transacted on a larger scale, they can be better understood and have more evident results. The different kinds of monarchy were shortly destined to succeed and combine with one another in a very striking manner.

At the time when the Carlovingians replaced the Merovingians, we perceive a return of the barbarian monarchy. Election reappeared; Pepin got himself elected at Soissons. When the first Carlovingians gave kingdoms to their sons, they took care that they should be acknowledged by the chief men of the states assigned to them. When they divided a kingdom, they desired that the partition should be sanctioned in the national assemblies. In short, the elective principle, under the form of popular acceptance, again assumed a certain reality. You remember that this change of dynasty was like a new inroad of the Germans into the west of Europe, and brought back some shadow of their ancient institutions and manners.

At the same time, we see the religious principle more clearly introducing itself into monarchy, and performing a part of greater importance. Pepin was acknowledged and consecrated by the pope. He felt that he stood in need of the sanction of religion; it was already become a great power, and he sought its assistance. Charlemagne adopted the same policy; and religious monarchy thus developed itself. Still, however, under Charlemagne, religion was not the prevailing character of his government; the imperial system of monarchy was that which he wished to revive. Although he allied himself closely with the clergy, he made use of them, and was not their instrument. The idea of a great state, of a great political combination—the resurrection, in short, of the Roman empire, was the favorite day-dream of Charlemagne.

He died, and was succeeded by Louis le Debonnaire. Everybody knows the character to which the royal power was then, for a short time, reduced. The king fell into the hands of the clergy, who censured, deposed, re-instated, and governed him; a monarchy subordinate to religious authority seemed on the point of being established.

Thus, from the middle of the eighth to the middle of the ninth century, the diversity of the three kinds of monarchy became manifested by events important, closely connected and clear.

After the death of Louis le Debonnaire, during the state of disorder into which Europe fell, the three kinds of monarchy almost equally disappeared: everything became confounded. At the end of a certain time, when the feudal system had prevailed, a fourth kind of monarchy presented itself, differing from all those which had been hitherto observed: this was feudal monarchy. It is confused in its nature, and cannot easily be defined. It has been said that the king, in the feudal system of government, was the *suzerain* over *suzerains*, the lord over lords; that he was connected by firm links, from degree to degree, with the whole frame of society; and that, in calling around him his own vassals, then the vassals of his vassals, and so on in gradation, he exercised his authority over the whole mass of the people, and showed himself to be really a king. I do not deny that this is the theory of feudal monarchy: but it is a mere theory, which has never governed facts. This pretended influence of the king by means of a hierarchical organization, these links which are supposed to have united monarchy to the whole body of feudal society, are the dreams of speculative politicians. In fact, the greatest part of the feudal chieftains at that period were completely independent of the monarchy; many of them hardly knew it even by name, and had few or no relations with it: every kind of sovereignty was local and independent. The name of king, borne by one of these feudal chiefs, does not so much express a fact as a remembrance.

Such is the state in which monarchy presents itself in the course of the tenth and eleventh centuries.

In the twelfth, at the accession of Louis le Gros, things began to change their aspect. The king was more frequently spoken of; his influence penetrated into places which it had not previously reached; he assumed a more active part in society. If we inquire into this title, we recognize none of those titles of which monarchy had previously been accustomed to avail itself. It was not by inheritance from the emperors, or by the title of imperial monarchy, that this institution aggrandized itself, and assumed more consistency. Neither was it in virtue of election, or as being an emanation from divine power: every appearance of election had vanished; the principle of inheritance definitively prevailed; and notwithstanding the sanction given by religion to the accession of kings, the minds of men did not appear to be at all occupied with the religious character of the monarchy of Louis le Gros. A new element, a character hitherto unknown, was introduced into monarchy; a new species of monarchy began to exist.

Society, I need hardly repeat, was at this period in very great disorder, and subject to constant scenes of violence. Society, in itself, was destitute of means to struggle against this situation, and to recover some degree of order and unity. The feudal institutions—those parliaments of barons, those seignorial courts—all those forms under which, in modern times, feudalism has been represented as a systematic and orderly state of government—all these things were unreal and powerless; there was nothing in them which could afford the means of estabishing any degree of order or justice; so that, in the midst of social anarchy, no one knew to whom recourse could be had, in order to redress a great injustice, remedy a great evil, to constitute something like a state. The name of king remained, and was borne by some chief whose authority was acknowledged by a few others. The different titles, however, under which the royal power had been formerly exercised, though they had no great influence, yet were far from being forgotten, and were recalled on various occasions. It happened that, in order to re-establish some degree of order in a place near the king's residence, or to terminate some difference which had lasted a long time, recourse was had to him; he was called upon to intervene in affairs which were not directly his own; and he intervened as a protector of public order, as arbitrator, as redresser of wrongs. The moral authority which continued to be attached to his name gained for him, by little and little, this great accession of power.

'Such was the character which monarchy began to assume under Louis le Gros, and under the administration of Suger. Now, for the first time, seems to have entered the minds of men the idea, though very incomplete, confused, and feeble, of a public power, unconnected with the local powers which had possession of society, called upon to render justice to those who could not obtain it by ordinary means, and capable of producing, or at least commanding, order;—the idea of a great magistracy, whose essential character was to maintain or re-establish the peace of society, to protect the weak, and to decide differences which could not be otherwise settled.. Such was the entirely new character, in which, reckoning from the twelfth century, monarchy appeared in Europe, and especially in France. It was neither as barbarian monarchy, as religious monarchy, nor as imperial monarchy, that the royal power was exercised; this kind of monarchy possessed only a limited, incomplete, and fortuitous power;—a power which I cannot more precisely describe than by saying that it was, in some sort, that of the chief conservator of the public peace.

This is the true origin of modern monarchy; this is its vital principle, if I may so speak; it is this which has been developed in the course of its career, and, I have no hesitation in saying, has ensured its success. At different periods of history we observe the re-appearance of the various characters of monarchy; we see the different kinds of monarchy which I have described, endeavoring, by turns, to recover the preponderance. Thus, the clergy have always preached religious monarchy; the civilians have labored to revive the principle of imperial monarchy; the nobility would sometimes have wished to renew elective monarchy, or maintain feudal monarchy. And not only have the clergy, the civilians, and the nobility, attempted to give such or such a character a predominance in the monarchy, but monarchy itself has made them all contribute toward the aggrandizement of its own power. Kings have represented themselves sometimes as the delegates of God, sometimes as the heirs of the emperors, or as the first noblemen of the land, according to the occasion or public wish of the moment; they have illegitimately availed themselves of these various titles, but none of them has been the real title of modern monarchy, or the source of its preponderating influence. It is, I repeat, as depository and protector of public order, of general justice, and of the common interest—it is under the aspect of a chief magistracy, the centre and bond of society, that modern monarchy has presented itself to the people, and, in obtaining their adhesion, has made their strength its own.

You will see, as we proceed, this characteristic of the monarchy of modern Europe, which began, I repeat, in the twelfth century, and in the reign of Louis le Gros, confirm and develop itself, and become at length, if I may so speak, the political physiognomy of the institution. It is by this that monarchy has contributed to the great result which now characterizes European society, the reduction of all the social elements to two—the government and the nation.

Thus it appears, that, at the breaking out of the crusades, Europe entered upon the path which was to conduct her to her present state: you have just seen monarchy assume the important part which it was destined to perform in this great transformation. We shall consider, at our next meeting, the different attempts at political organization, made from the twelfth to the sixteenth century, in order to maintain, by regulating it, the order of things that was about to perish. We shall consider the efforts of feudalism, of the Church, and even of the free cities, to constitute society according to its ancient principles, and under its primitive forms, and thus to defend themselves against the general change which was preparing.

LECTURE X.

VARIOUS ATTEMPTS TO FORM THE SEVERAL SOCIAL ELEMENTS INTO ONE SOCIETY.

At the commencement of this lecture I wish, at once, to determnine its object with precision. It will be recollected, that one of the first facts that struck us, was the diversity, the separation, the independence, of the elements of ancient European society. The feudal nobility, the clergy, and the commons, had each a position, laws, and manners, entirely different; they formed so many distinct societies whose mode of government was independent of each other. they were in some measure connected, and in contact, but no real union existed between them; to speak correctly, they did not form a nation—a state.

The fusion of these distinct portions of society into one is, at length, accomplished; this is precisely the distinctive organization, the essential characteristic of modern society. The ancient social elements are now reduced to two—the government and the people; that is to say, diversity ceased and similitude introduced union. Before, however, this result took place, and even with a view to its prevention, many attempts were made to bring all these separate portions of society together, without destroying their diversity and independence. No positive attack was made on the peculiar position and privileges of each portion, on their distinctive nature, and yet there was an attempt made to form them into one state, one national body, to bring them all under one and the same government.

All these attempts failed. The result which I have noticed above, the union of modern society, attests their want of success. Even in those parts of Europe where some traces of the ancient diversity of the social elements are still to be met with, in Germany, for instance, where a real feudal nobility and a distinct body of burghers still exist; in England, where we see an established Church enjoying its own revenues and its own peculiar jurisdiction; it is clear that this pretended distinct existence is a shadow, a falsehood: that these special societies are confounded in general society, absorbed in the state, governed by the public authorities, controlled by the same system of polity, carried away by the same current of ideas, the same manners. Again I assert, that even where the form still exists, the separation and independence of the ancient social elements have no longer any reality.

At the same time, these attempts at rendering the ancient and social elements co-ordinate, without changing their nature, at forming them into national unity without annihilating their variety, are entitled to an important place in the history of Europe. The period which now engages our attention—that period which separates ancient from modern Europe, and in which was accomplished the metamorphosis of European society—is almost entirely filled with them. Not only do they form a principal part of the history of this period, but they had a considerable influence on after events, on the manner in which was effected the reduction of the various social elements to two—the government and the people. It is clearly, then, of great importance, that we should become well acquainted with all those endeavors at political organization which were made from the twelfth to the sixteenth century, for the purpose of creating nations and governments, without destroying the diversity of secondary societies placed by the side of each other. These attempts form the subject of the present lecture—a laborious and even painful task.

All these attempts at political organization did not, certainly, originate from a good motive; too many of them arose from selfishness and tyranny. Yet some of them were pure and disinterested; some of them had, truly, for their object the moral and social welfare of mankind. Society, at this time, was in such a state of incoherence, of violence and iniquity, as could not but be extremely offensive to men of enlarged views—to men who possessed elevated sentiments, and who labored incessantly to discover the means of improving it. Yet even the best of these noble attempts miscarried; and is not the loss of so much courage—of so many sacrifices and endeavors—of so much virtue, a melancholy spectacle? And what is still more painful, a still more poignant sorrow, not only did these attempts at social melioration fail, but an enormous mass of error and of evil was mingled with them. Notwithstanding good intention, the majority of them were absurd, and show a profound ignorance of reason, of justice, of the rights of humanity, and of the conditions of the social state; so that not only were they unsuccessful, but it was right that they should be so. We have here a specacle, not only of the hard lot of humanity, but also of its weakness. We may here see how the smallest portion of truth suffices so to engage the whole attention of men of superior intellect, that they forget everything else, and become blind to all that is not comprised within the narrow horizon of their ideas. We may here see how the existence of ever so small a particle of justice in a cause is sufficient to make them lose sight of all the injustice which it contains and permits. This display of the vices and follies of man is, in my opinion, still more melancholy to contemplate than the misery of this condition; his faults affect me more than his sufferings. The attempts already alluded to will bring man before us in both these situations; still we must not shun the painful retrospect; it behooves us not to flinch from doing justice to those men, to those ages that have so often erred, so miserably failed, and yet have displayed such noble virtues, made such powerful efforts, merited so much glory.

The attempts at political organization which were formed from the twelfth to the sixteenth centuries were of two kinds; one having for its object the predominance of one of the social elements; sometimes the clergy, sometimes the feudal nobility, sometimes the free cities, and making all the others subordinate to it, and by such a sacrifice to introduce unity; the other proposed to cause all the different societies to agree and to act together, leaving to each portion its liberty, and ensuring to each its due share of influence.

The attempts of the former kind are much more open to supicion of self-interest and tyranny than the latter; in fact, they were not spotless; from their very nature they were essentially tyrannical in their mode of execution; yet some of them might have been, and indeed were, conceived in a spirit of pure intention, and with a view to the welfare and advancement of mankind.

The first attempt which presents itself, is the attempt at theocratical organization; that is to say, the design of bringing all the other societies into a state of submission to the principles and sway of ecclesiastical society.

I must here refer to what I have already said relative to the history of the Church. I have endeavored to show what were the principles it developed—what was the legitimate part of each—how these principlse arose from the natural course of events—the good and the evil produced by them. I have characterized the different stages through which the Church passed from the eighth to the twelfth century. I have pointed out the state of the Imperial Church, of the Barbarian Church, of the Feudal Church, and lastly, of the Theocratic Church. I take it for granted that all this is present in your recollection, and I shall now endeavor to show you what the clergy did in order to obtain the government of Europe, and why they failed in obtaining it.

The attempt at theocratic organization appeared at an early period, both in the acts of the court of Rome, and in those of the clergy in general; it naturally proceeded from the political and moral superiority of the Church; but, from the commencement, such obstacles were thrown in its way, that, even in its greatest vigor, it never had the power to overcome them.

The first obstacle was the nature itself of Christianity. Very different, in this respect, from the greater part of religious creeds, Christianity established itself by persuasion alone, by simple moral efforts; even at its birth it was not armed with power; in its earliest years it conquered by words alone, and its only conquest was the souls of men. Even after its triumph, even when the Church was in possession of great wealth and consideration, the direct government of society was not placed in its hands. Its origin, purely moral, springing from mental influence alone, was implanted in its constitution. It possessed a vast influence, but it had no power. It gradually insinuated itself into the municipal magistracies; it acted powerfully upon the emperors and upon all their agents; but the positive administration of public affairs—the government, properly so called—was not possessed by the Church. Now, a system of government, a theocracy, as well as any other, cannot be established in an indirect manner, by mere influence alone; it must possess the judicial and ministerial offices, the command of the forces, be in receipt of the imposts, have the disposal of the revenues, in a word, it must govern—take possession of society. Force of persuasion may do much, it may obtain great influence over a people, and even over governments its sway may be very powerful; but it cannot govern, it cannot found a system, it cannot take possession of the future. Such has been, even from its origin, the situation of the Christian Church; it has always sided with government, but hever superseded it, and taken its place; a great obstacle, which the attempt at theocratic organization was never able to surmount.

The attempt to establish a theocracy very soon met with a second obstacle. When the Roman empire was destroyed, and the barbarian states were established on its ruins, the Christian Church was found among the conquered. It was necessary for it to escape from this situation; to begin by converting the conquerors, and thus to raise itself to their rank. This accomplished, when the Church aspired to dominion, it had to encounter the pride and the resistance of the feudal nobility. Europe is greatly indebted to the laic members of the feudal system in the eleventh century: the people were almost completely subjugated by the Church; sovereigns could scarcely protect themselves from its domination; the feudal nobility alone would never submit to its yoke, would never give way to the power of the clergy. We have only to recall to our recollection the general appearance of the middle ages, in order to be struck with the singular mixture of loftiness and submission, of blind faith and liberty of mind, in the connexion of the lay nobility with the priests. We there find some of the remnants of their primitive situation. It may be remembered how I endeavored to describe the origin of the feudal system, its first elements, and the manner in which feudal society first formed itself around the habitation of the possessor of the fief. I remarked how much the priest was there below the lord of the fief. Yes, and there always remained, in the hearts of the feudal nobility, a feeling of this situation; they always considered themselves as not only independent of the Church, but as its superior—as alone called upon to possess, and in reality to govern, the country; they were willing always to live on good terms with the clergy, but at the same time insisting that each should perform his own part, the one not infringing upon the duties of the other. During many centuries it was the lay aristocracy who maintained the independence of society with regard to the Church; they boldly defended it when the sovereigns and the people were subdued. They were the first to oppose, and probably contributed more than any other power to the failure of the attempt at theocratic organization of society

A third obstacle stood much in the way of this attempt, an obstacle which has been but little noticed, and the effect of which has often been misunderstood.

In all parts of the world where a clergy made itself master of society, and forced it to submit to a theocratic organization, the government always fell into the hands of a married clergy, of a body of priests who were enabled to recruit their ranks from their own society. Examine history; look to Asia and Egypt; every powerful theocracy you will find to have been the work of a priesthood, of a society complete within itself, and which had no occasion to borrow of any other.

But the celibacy of the clergy placed the Christian priesthood in a very different situation; it was obliged to have recourse incessantly to lay society in order to continue its existence; it was compelled to seek at a distance, among all stations, all social professions, for the means of its duration. In vain, attachment to their order induced them to labor assiduously for the purpose of assimilating these discordant elements; some of the original qualities of these new-comers ever remain; citizens or gentlemen, they always retained some vestige of their former disposition, of their early habits. Doubtless the Catholic clergy, by being placed in a lonely situation by celibacy, by being cut off, as it were, from the common life of men, became more isolated, and separate from society; but then it was forced continually to have recourse to this same lay society, to recruit, to renew itself from it, and consequently to participate in the moral revolutions which it underwent; and I have no hesitation in stating it as my opinion, that this necessity, which was always arising, did much more to prevent the success of the attempt at theocratic organization, than the *esprit de corps*, strongly supported as it was by celibacy, did to forward it.

The clergy, indeed, found within its own body the most powerful opponents of this attempt. Much has been said of the unity of the Church, and it is true that it has constantly endeavored to obtain this unity, and in some particulars has had the good fortune to succeed. But we must not suffer ourselves to be imposed upon by high-sounding words, nor by partial facts. What society has offered to our view a greater number of civil dissensions, has been subject to more dismemberments than the clergy. What society has suffered more from divisions, from agitations, from disputes than the ecclesiastical nation? The national churches of the majority of European states have been incessantly at variance with the Roman court; the councils have been at war with the popes: heresies have been innumerable and ever springing up anew; schism always breaking out; nowhere was ever witnessed such a diversity of opinions, so much rancor in dispute, such minute parcelling out of power. The internal state of the Church, the disputations which have taken place, the revolutions by which it has been agitated, have been perhaps the greatest of all obstacles to the triumph of that theocratical organization which the Church endeavored to impose upon society.

All these obstacles were visibly in action even so early as the fifth century, even at the commencement of the great attempt of which we are now speaking. They did not, however, prevent the continuance of its exertions, nor retard its progress during several centuries. The period of its greatest glory, its crisis, as it may be termed, was the reign of Gregory the Seventh, at the end of the eleventh century. We have already seen that the predominant wish of Gregory was to render the world subservient to the clergy, the clergy to the pope, and to form Europe into one immense and regular theocracy. In the scheme by which this was to be effected, this great man appears, so far as one can judge of events which took place so long ago, to have committed two great faults—one as a theorist, the other as a revolutionist. The first consisted in the pompous proclamation of his plan; in his giving a systematical detail of his principles relative to the nature and the rights of spiritual power, of drawing from them beforehand, like a severe logician, their remotest, their ultimate consequences. He thus threatened and even attacked all the lay sovereigns of Europe, without having secured the means of success: not considering that success in human affairs is not to be obtained by such absolute proceedings, or by a mere appeal to a philosophic argument. Gregory the Seventh also fell into the common error of all revolutionists—that of attempting more than they can perform, and of not fixing the measure and limits of their enterprises within the bounds of possibility. In order to hasten the predominance of his opinions, he entered into a contest against the empire, against all sovereigns, even against the great body of the clergy itself. He never temporized—he consulted no particular interests, but openly proclaimed his determinaion to reign over all kingdoms as well as over all intellects; and thus raised up against him, not only all temporal powers, who discovered the pressing danger of their situation, but also all those who advocated the right of free inquiry, a party which now began to show itself, and dreaded and exclaimed against all tyranny over the human mind. It seemed indeed probable, on the whole, that Gregory the Seventh injured rather than advanced the cause which he wished to serve.

This cause, however, still continued to prosper throughout the whole of the twelfth and down to the middle of the thirteenth century. This was the epoch of the greatest power and splendor of the Church. I do not think it can be said that during this period she made much progress; to the end of the reign of Innocent III. she rather displayed her glory and power than increased them. But at this very moment of her apparently greatest success, a popular reaction seemed to declare war against her in almost every part of Europe. In the south of France broke out the heresy of the Albigenses, which carried away a numerous and powerful society. Almost at the same time similar notions and desires appeared in the north, in Flanders. Wickliffe, only a little later, attacked in England, with great talent, the power of the Church, and founded a sect which was not destined to perish. Sovereigns soon began to follow the bent of their nations. It was only at the beginning of the thirteenth century, that the emperors of the house of Hohenstaufen, who deservedly rank among the most able and powerful sovereigns of Europe, were overcome in their struggle with the Holy See; yet before the end of the same century, Saint Louis, the most pious of monarchs, proclaimed the independence of temporal power, and published the first pragmatic sanction, which has served as the basis of all the following. At the opening of the fourteenth century began the quarrel between Philip the Bel with Boniface VIII. Edward I. of England was not more obedient to the court of Rome. At this epoch it is evident that the attempt at theocratic oganization had failed; the Church henceforward acted only upon the defensive; she no longer attempted to force her system upon Europe; but only considered how she might keep what she possessed. It is at the end of the thirteenth century that truly dates the emancipation of the laic society of Europe; it was then that the Church gave up her pretensions to its possession.

For a long time before this she had renewed this pretension in the very sphere in which it appeared most likely for her to be successful. For a long time in Italy itself, even around the very throne of the Church, theocracy had completely failed, and given way to a system its very opposite in character: to that attempt at democratic organization, of which the Italian republics are the type, and which displayed so brilliant a career in Europe from the eleventh to the sixteenth century.

It will be remembered, that, when speaking of the free cities, of their history, and of the manner of their formation, I observed that their growth had been more precocious and vigorous in Italy than in any other country; they were here more numerous, as well as more wealthy, than in Gaul, England, or Spain; the Roman municipal system had been preserved with more life and regularity. Besides this, the provinces of Italy were less fitted to become the habitation of its new masters than the rest of Europe. The lands had been cleared, drained, and cultivated; it was not covered with forests, and the barbarians could not here devote their lives to the chase, or find occupations similar to what had amused them in Germany. A part of this country, moreover, did not belong to them. The south of Italy, the Campania, Romana, Ravenna, were still dependant on the Greek emperors. Favored by distance from the seat of government, and by the vicissitudes of war, the republican system soon took root, and grew very fast in this portion of the country. Italy, too, besides having never been entirely subdued by the barbarians, was favored by the circumstance, that the conquerors who overran it did not remain its tranquil and lasting possessors. The Ostrogoths were destroyed and driven off by Belisarius and Narses: the kingdom of the Lombards was not permanent. The Franks overthrew it under Pepin and Charlemagne, who, without exterminating the Lombard population, found it their interest to ally themselves with the ancient Italian inhabitants, in order to contend against the Lombards with more success. The barbarians, then, never became in Italy, as in the other parts of Europe, the exclusive and quiet masters of the territory and people. And thus it happened that the feudal system never made much progress beyond the Alps, where it was but weakly established, and its members few and scattered. Neither did the great territorial proprietors ever gain that preponderance here, which they did in Gaul and other countries, but it continued to rest with the towns. When this result clearly showed itself, a great number of the possessors of fiefs, moved by choice or necessity, left their country dwellings and took up their abode within the walls of some city. The barbarian nobles made themselves burgesses. It is easy to imagine what strength and superiority the towns of Italy acquired, compared with the other communities of Europe, by this single circumstance. What we have chiefly dwelt upon, as most observable in the character of town populations, is their timidity and weakness. The burgesses appear like so many courageous freedmen, struggling with toil and care against a master, always at their gates. The fate of the Italian towns was widely different; the conquering and conquered populations here mixed together within the same walls; the towns had not the trouble to defend themselves against a neighboring master; their inhabitants were citizens, who, at least for the most part, had always been free; who defended their independence and their rights against distant foreign sovereigns; at one time against the kings of the Franks, and, at a later period, against the emperors of Germany. This will in some measure account for the immense and precocious superiority of the Italian cities: while in other countries we see poor insignificant communities arise after great trouble and exertion; we here see shoot up, almost at once, republics—states.

Thus becomes explained, why the attempt at republican organization was so successful in this part of Europe. It repressed, almost in its childhood, the feudal system, and became the prevailing form in society. Still it was but little adapted to spread or endure; it contained but few germs of melioration, a necessary condition for the extension and duration of any form of government.

In looking at the history of the Italian republics, from the eleventh to the fifteenth century, we are struck with two facts, seemingly contradictory, yet still indisputable. We see passing before us a wonderful display of courage, of activity, and of genius; an amazing prosperity is the result: we see a movement and a liberty unknown to the rest of Europe. But if we ask what was the real state of the inhabitants, how they passed their lives, what was their real share of happiness, the scene changes; there is, perhaps, no history so sad, so gloomy: no period, perhaps, during which the lot of man appears to have been so agitated, subject to so many deplorable chances, and which so abounds in dissensions, crimes, and misfortunes. Another fact strikes us at the same moment; in the political life of the greater part of these republics, liberty was always growing less and less. The want of security was so great, that the people were unavoidably driven to take shelter in a system less stormy, less popular, than that in which the state existed Look at the history of Florence, Venice, Genoa, Milan, or Pisa; in all of them we find the course of events, instead of aiding the progress of liberty, instead of enlarging the circle of institutions, tending to repress it; tending to concentrate power in the hands of a smaller number of individuals. In a word, we find in these republics, otherwise so energetic, so brilliant, and so rich, two things wanting—security of life, the first requisite in the social state, and the progress of institutions.

From these causes sprung a new evil, which prevented the attempt at republican organization from extending itself. It was from without—it was from foreign sovereigns, that the greatest danger was threatened to Italy. Still this danger never succeeded in reconciling these republics, in making them all act in concert; they were never ready to resist in common the common enemy. This has led many Italians, the most enlightened, the best of patriots, to deplore, in the present day, the republican system of Italy in the middle ages, as the true cause which hindered it from becoming a nation; it was parcelled out, they say, into a multitude of little states, not sufficiently master of their passions to confederate, to constitute themselves into one united body They regret that their country has not, like the rest of Europe, been subject to a despotic centralization which would have formed it into a nation, and rendered it independent of the foreigner.

It appears, then, that republican organization, even under the most favorable circumstances. did not contain, at this period, any more than it has done since, the principle of progress. duration, and extension. We may compare, up to a certain point, the organization of Italy, in the middle ages, to that of ancient Greece. Greece, like Italy, was a country covered with little republics, always rivals, sometimes enemies, and sometimes rallying together for a common object. In this comparison the advantage is altogether on the side of Greece. There is no doubt, notwithstanding the frequent iniquities that history makes known, but that there was much more order, security, and justice in the interior of Athens, Lacedemon, and Thebes, than in the Italian republics. See, however, notwithstanding this, how short was the political career of Greece, and what a principle of weakness is contained in this parcelling out of territory and power. No sooner did Greece come in contact with the great neighboring states, with Macedon and Rome, than she fell. These little republics, so glorious and still so flourishing, could not coalesce to resist. How much more likely was this to be the case in Italy, where society and human reason had made no such strides as in Greece, and consequently possessed much less power.

If the attempt at republican organization had so little chance of stability in Italy, where it had triumphed, where the feudal system had been overcome, it may easily be supposed that it was much less likely to succeed in the other parts of Europe.

I shall take a rapid survey of its fortunes.

There was one portion of Europe which bore a great resemblance to Italy; the south of France, and the adjoining provinces of Spain, Catalonia, Navarre, and Biscay. In these districts the cities had made nearly the same progress, and had risen to considerable importance and wealth. Many little feudal nobles had here allied themselves with the citizens; a part of the clergy had likewise embraced their cause; in a word, the country in these respects was another Italy. So also, in the course of the eleventh and beginning of the twelfth century, the towns of Provence, of Languedoc, and Acquitaine, made a political effort and formed themselves into free republics, as had been done by the towns on the other side of the Alps. But the south of France was connected with a very powerful branch of the feudal system, that of the north. The heresy of the Albigenses appeared. A war broke out between feudal France and municipal France. The history of the crusade against the Albigenses, commanded by Simon de Montfort, is well known: it was the struggle of the feudalism of the north against the attempt at democratic organization of the south. Notwithstanding the efforts of southern patriotism, the north gained the day; political unity was wanting in the south, but civilization was not yet sufficiently advanced there to enable men to bring it about. This attempt at republican organization was put down, and the crusade re-established the feudal system in the south of France.

A republican attempt succeeded better a little later, among the Swiss mountains. Here, the theatre was very narrow, the struggle was only against a foreign monarch, who, although much more powerful than the Swiss, was not one of the most formidable sovereigns of Europe. The contest was carried on with a great display of courage. The Swiss feudal nobility allied themselves, for the most part, with the cities: a powerful help, which also raised the character of the revolution it sustained, and stamped it with more aristocratical and stationary character than it seemingly ought to have borne.

I cross to the north of France, to the free towns of Flanders, to those on the banks of the Rhine, and belonging to the Hanseatic league. Here the democratic organization completely triumphed in the internal government of the cities; but from its origin, it is evident, that it was not destined to take entire possession of society. The free towns of the north were surrounded, pressed on every side by feudalism, by barons, and sovereigns, to such an extent that they were constantly obliged to stand upon the defensive. It is scarcely necessary to say, that they did not trouble themselves to make conquests; they defended themselves sometimes well and sometimes badly. They preserved their privileges, but they remained confined to the inside of their walls. Within these, democratic organization was shut up and arrested; if we walk abroad over the face of the country, we find no semblance of it.

Such, then, was the state of the republican attempt: triumphant in Italy, but with little hope of duration and progress; vanquished in the south of Gaul; victorious upon a small scale in the mountains of Switzerland; while in the north, in the free communities of Flanders, the Rhine, and Hanseatic league, it was condemned not to appear outside their walls. Still, even in this state, evidently inferior to the other elements of society, it inspired the feudal nobility with prodigious terror. The barons became jealous of the wealth of the cities, they feared their power; the spirit of democracy stole into the country; insurrections of the peasantry became more frequent and obstinate. In nearly every part of Europe a coalition was formed among the nobles against the free cities. The parties were not equal; the cities were isolated; there was no correspondence or intelligence between them; all was local. It may be true that there existed, between the burgesses of different countries, a certain degree of sympathy; the success or reverses of the towns of Flanders, in their struggles with the dukes of Burgandy, excited a lively sensation in the French cities: but this was very fleeting, and led to no result; no tie, no true union became established between them; the free communities lent no assistance to one another. The position of feudalism was much superior; yet divided, and without any plan of its own, it was never able to destroy them. After the struggle had lasted a considerable time, when the conviction became settled that a complete victory was impossible, concession became necessary; these petty burgher republics were acknowledged, negotiated with, and admitted as members of the state. A new plan was now begun, a new attempt was made at political organization. The object of this was to conciliate, to reconcile, to make to live and act together, in spite of their rooted hostility, the various elements of society; that is to say, the feudal nobility, the free cities, the clergy, and monarchs. It is to this attempt at mixed organization that I have still to claim your attention.

I presume there is no one who is not acquainted with the nature of the States-general of France, the Cortes of Spain and Portugal, the Parliament of England, and the States of Germany. The elements of these various assemblies were much the same; that is to say, the feudal nobility, the clergy, and the cities or commons, there met together and labored to unite themselves into one sole society, into one same state, under one same law, one same authority. Whatever their various names, this was the tendency, the design of all.

Let us take, as the type of this attempt, the fact which most interests us, as well as being best known to us—the States-general of France. I say this fact is best known, while I am still sure that the term States-general awakens in none of you more than a vague and incomplete idea. Who can say what there was in it of stability, of regularity; the number of its members, the subjects of their deliberations, the times at which they were convoked, or the length of their sessions? Of all this we know nothing, and it is impossible to obtain from history any clear, general, satisfactory information respecting it. The best accounts we can gather from the history of France, as regards the character of these assemblies, would almost lead us to consider them as pure accidents, as the last political resort both of people and kings; the last resort of the kings, when they had no money and knew not how to free themselves from embarrassment; the last resort of the people, when some evil became so great that they knew not what remedy to apply to it. The nobles formed part of the States-general; so did the clergy; but they came to them with little interest, for they knew well that it was not in these assemblies that they possessed the greatest influence, that it was not there that they took a true part in the government. The burgesses themselves were not eager to attend them; it was not a right which they were anxious to exercise, but rather a necessity to which they submitted. Again, what was the character of the political proceedings of these assemblies? At one time we find them perfectly insignificant, at others terrible. If the king was the stronger, their humility and docility were extreme; if the situation of the monarch was unfortunate, if he really needed the assistance of the States, they then became factious, either the instrument of some aristocratic intrigue, or of some ambitious demagogues. Their works died almost always with them; they promised much, they attempted much—and did nothing. No great measure which has truly had any influence upon society in France, no important reform either in the general legislation or administration, ever emanated from the States-general. It must not, however, be supposed that they have been altogether useless, or without effect; they had a moral effect, of which in general we take too little account; they served from time to time as a protestation against political servitude, a forcible proclamation of certain guardian principles—such, for example, as that a nation has the right to vote its own taxes, to take part in its own affairs, to impose a responsibility upon the agents of power. That these maxims have never perished in France, is mainly owing to tne States-general; and it is no slight service rendered to a country, to maintain among its virtues, to keep alive in its thoughts, the remembrance and claims of liberty. The States-general has done us this service, but it never became a means of government; it never entered upon political organization; it never attained the object for which it was formed, that is to say, the fusion into one only body of the various societies which divided the country.

The Cortes of Portugal and Spain offered the same general result, though in a thousand circumstances they differ. The importance of the Cortes varied according to the kingdoms, and times at which they were held; they were most powerful and most frequently convoked in Aragon and Biscay, during the disputes for the successions to the crown, and the struggles against the Moors. To some of the Cortes —for example, that of Castile, 1370 and 1373—neither the nobles nor the clergy were called. There were a thousand accidents which it would be necessary to notice, if we had time to look closely into events; but in the general sketch to which I am obliged to confine myself it will be enough to state that the Cortes, like the States-general of France, have been an accident in history, and never a system—never a political organization, or regular means of government.

The lot of England has been different. I shall not, however, enter into any detail upon this subject at present, as it is my intention to devote a future lecture to the special consideration of the political life of England. All I shall now do is to say a few words upon the causes which gave it a direction totally different from that of the continental states.

And, first, there were no great vassals, no subjects sufficiently powerful to enter single-handed into a contest with the crown. The great barons were obliged, at a very early period, to coalesce, in order to make a common resistance. Thus the principle of association, and proceedings truly political, were forced upon the high aristocracy. Besides this, English feudalism—the little holders of fiefs—were brought by a train of circumstances, which I cannot here recount, to unite themselves with the burgher class, to sit with them in the House of Commons; and by this, the Commons obtained in England a power much superior to those on the Continent, a power really capable of influencing the government of the country. In the fourteenth century the character of the English Parliament was already formed: the House of Lords was the great council of the king, a council effectively associated in the exercise of authority. The House of Commons, composed of deputies from the little possessors of fiefs, and from the cities, took, as yet, scarcely any part in the government, properly so called; but it asserted and established rights, it defended with great spirit private and local interests. Parliament, considered as a whole, did not yet govern; but already it was a regular institution, a means of government adopted in principle, and often indispensable in fact. Thus the attempt to bring together the various elements of society, and to form them into one body politic, one true state or commonwealth, did succeed in England while it failed in every part of the Continent.

I shall not offer more than one remark upon Germany, and that only to indicate the prevailing character of its history. The attempts made here at political organization, to melt into one body the various elements of society, were spiritless and coldly followed up. These social elements had remained here more distinct, more independent than in the rest of Europe. Were any proof of this wanting, it might be found in its later usages. Germany is the only country of Europe (I say nothing of Poland and the Sclavonian nations, which entered so very late into the European system of civilization) in which feudal election has for a long time taken part in the election of royalty; it is likewise the only country of Europe in which ecclesiastical sovereigns were continued; the only one in which were preserved free cities with a true political existence and sovereignty. It is clear, therefore, that the attempt to fuse the elements of primitive European society into one social body, must have been much less active and effective in Germany than in any other nation.

I have now run over all the great attempts at political organization which were made in Europe, down to the end of the fourteenth or beginning of the fifteenth century. All these failed. I have endeavored to point out, in going along, the causes of these failures; to speak truly, they must all be summed up in one: society was not yet sufficiently advanced to adapt itself to unity; all was yet too local, too special, too narrow; too many differences prevailed both in things and in minds. There were no general interests, no general opinions capable of guiding, of bearing sway over particular interests and particular opinions. The most enlightened minds, the boldest thinkers, had as yet no just idea of administration or justice truly public. It was evidently necessary that a very active, powerful civilization should first mix, assimilate, grind together, as it were, all these incoherent elements; it was necessary that there should first be a strong centralization of interests, laws, manners, ideas; it was necessary, in a word, that there should be created a public authority and a public opinion. We are now drawing near to the period in which this great work was at last consummated. Its first symptoms—the state of manners, mind, and opinions, during the fifteenth century, their tendency toward the formation of a central government and a public opinion—will be the subject of the following lecture.

LECTURE XI.

CENTRALIZATION OF NATIONS AND GOVERNMENTS.

WE have now reached the threshold of modern history, in the proper sense of the term. We now approach that state of society which may be considered as our own, and the institutions, the opinions, and the manners which were those of France forty years ago, are those of Europe still, and, notwithstanding the changes produced by our revolution, continue to exercise a powerful influence upon us. It is in the sixteenth century, as I have already told you, that modern society really commences.

Before entering into a consideration of this period, let us review the ground over which we have already passed. We have discovered among the ruins of the Roman empire, all the essential elements of modern Europe; we have seen them separate themselves and expand, each on its own account, and independently of the others. We have observed, during the first historical period, the constant tendency of these elements to separation, and to a local and special existence. But scarcely has this object appeared to be attained; scarcely have feudalism, municipal communities, and the clergy, each taken their distinct place and form, when we have seen them tend to approximate, unite, and form themselves into a general social system, into a national body, a national government. To arrive at this result, the various countries of Europe had recourse to all the different systems which existed among them: they endeavored to lay the foundations of social union, and of political and moral obligations, on the principles of theocracy, of aristocracy, of democracy, and of monarchy. Hitherto all these attempts have failed. No particular system has been able to take possession of society, and to secure it, by its sway, a destiny truly public. We have traced the cause of this failure to the absence of general interests and general ideas: we have found that everything, as yet, was too special, too individual, too local; that a long and powerful process of centralization was necessary, in order that society might become at once extensive, solid, and regular, the object which it necessarily seeks to attain. Such was the state in which we left Europe at the close of the fourteenth century.

Europe, however, was then very far from understanding her own state, such as I have now endeavored to explain it to you. She did not know distinctly what she required, or what she was in search of. Yet she set about endeavoring to supply her wants as if she knew perfectly what they were. When the fourteenth century had expired, after the failure of every attempt at political organization, Europe entered naturally, and as if by instinct, into the path of centralization. It is the characteristic of the fifth century that it constantly tended to this result, that it endeavored to create general interests and general ideas, to raise the minds of men to more enlarged views, and to create, in short, what had not, till then, existed on a great scale—nations and governments.

The actual accomplishment of this change belongs to the sixteenth and seventeenth centuries, though it was in the fifteenth that it was prepared. It is this preparation, this silent and hidden process of centralization, both in the social relations and in the opinions of men—a process accomplished, without premeditation or design, by the natural course of events—that we have now to make the subject of our inquiry.

It is thus that man advances in the execution of a plan which he has not conceived, and of which he is not even aware. He is the free and intelligent artificer of a work which is not his own. He does not perceive or comprehend it, till it manifests itself by external appearances and real results; and even then he comprehends it very incompletely. It is through his means, however, and by the development of his intelligence and freedom, that it is accomplished. Conceive a great machine, the design of which is centred in a single mind, though its various parts are instructed to different workmen, separated from, and strangers to each other. No one of them understands the work as a whole, nor the general result which he concurs in producing; but every one executes, with intelligence and freedom, by rational and voluntary acts, the particular task assigned to him. It is thus, that by the hand of man, the designs of Providence are wrought out in the government of the world. It is thus that the two great facts which are apparent in the history of civilization come to co-exist; on the one hand, those portions of it which may be considered as fated, or which happen without the control of human knowledge or will; on the other hand, the part played in it by the freedom and intelligence of man, and what he contributes to it by means of his own judgment and will.

In order that we may clearly understand the fifteenth century; in order that we may give a distinct account of this prelude, if we may use the expression, to the *state* of society in modern times, we will separate the facts which bear upon the subject into different classes. We will first examine the *political* facts—the changes which have tended to the formation either of nations or of governments. From thence we will proceed to the *moral* facts: we will consider the changes which took place in ideas and in manners; and we shall then see what *general opinions* began, from that period, to be in a state of preparation.

In regard to *political* facts, in order to proceed with quickness and simplicity, I shall survey all the great countries of Europe, and place before you the influence which the fifteenth century had upon them—how it found them, how it left them.

I shall begin with France. The last half of the fourteenth, and the first half of the fifteenth century, were, as you all know, a time of great national wars against the English. This was the period of the struggle for the independence of the French territory and the French name against foreign domination. It is sufficient to open the book of history, to see with what ardor, notwithstanding a multitude of treasons and dissensions, all classes of society in France joined in this struggle, and what patriotism animated the feudal nobility, the burghers, and even the peasantry. If we had nothing but the story of Joan of Arc to show the popular spirit of the time, it alone would suffice for that purpose. Joan of Arc sprang from among the people; it was by the sentiments, the religious belief, the passions of the people, that she was inspired and supported. She was looked upon with mistrust, with ridicule, with enmity even, by the nobles of the court and the leaders of the army; but she had always the soldiers and the people on her side. It was the peasants of Lorraine who sent her to succor the citizens of Orleans. No event could show in a stronger light the popular character of that war, and the feeling with which the whole country engaged in it.

Thus the nationality of France began to be formed. Down to the reign of the house of Valois, the feudal character prevailed in France; a French nation, a French spirit, French patriotism, as yet had no existence. With the princes of the house of Valois begins the history of France, properly so called. It was in the course of their wars, amid the various turns of their fortune, that, for the first time, the nobility, the citizens, the peasants, were united by a moral tie, by the tie of a common name, a common honor, and by one burning desire to overcome the foreign invader. We must not, however, at this time, expect to find among them any real political spirit, any great design of unity in government and institutions, according to the conceptions of the present day. The unity of France, at that period, dwelt in her name, in her national honor, in the existence of a national monarchy, no matter of what character, provided that no foreigner had anything to do with it. It was in this way that the struggle against the English contributed strongly to form the French nation, and to impel it toward unity.

At the same time that France was thus forming herself in a moral point of view, she was also extending herself physically, as it may be called, by enlarging, fixing, and consolidating her territory. This was the period of the incorporation of most of the provinces which now constitute France. Under Charles VII. [1422-1461] after the expulsion of the English, almost all the provinces which they had occupied—Normandy, Angoumois, Touraine, Poitou, Saintonge, etc., became definitely French. Under Louis XI. [1461-1483] ten provinces, three of which have been since lost and regained, were also united to France—Roussillon and Cerdagne, Burgundy, Franche-Conte, Picardy, Artois, Provence, Maine, Anjou, and Perche. Under Charles VIII. and Louis XII. [1483-1515] the successive marriages of Anne with these two kings gave her Britany. Thus, at the same period, and during the course of the same events, France, morally as well as physically, acquired at once strength and unity.

Let us turn from the nation to the government, and we shall see the accomplishment of events of the same nature; we shall advance toward the same result. The French government had never been more destitute of unity, of cohesion, and of strength, than under the reign of Charles VI. [1380-1422], and during the first part of the reign of Charles VII. At the end of this reign [1461], the appearance of everything was changed. There were evident marks of a power which was confirming, extending, organizing itself. All the great resources of government, taxation, military force, and administration of justice, were created on a great scale, and almost simultaneously. This was the period of the formation of a standing army, of permanent militia, and of *compagnies-d'ordonnance*, consisting of cavalry, free archers, and infantry. By these companies, Charles VII. re-established a degree of order in the provinces, which had been desolated by the license and exactions of the soldiery, even after the war had ceased. All contemporary historians expatiate on the wonderful effects of the *compagnies-d'ordonnance*. It was at this period that the *taille*, one of the principal revenues of the crown, was made perpetual; a serious inroad on the liberty of the people, but which contributed powerfully to the regularity and strength of the government. At the same time the great instrument of power, the administration of justice, was extended and organized; parliaments were multiplied, five new parliaments having been instituted in a short space of time:—under Louis XI., the parliaments of Grenoble (in 1451), of Bordeaux (in 1462), and of Dijon (in 1477); under Louis XII., the parliaments of Roun (in 1499), and of Aix (in 1501). The parliament of Paris also acquired, about the same time, much additional importance and stability, both in regard to the administration of justice, and the superintendence of the police within its jurisdiction.

Thus, in relation to the military force, the power of taxation, and the administration of justice, that is to say, in regard to those things which form its essence, government acquired in France, in the fifteenth century, a character of unity, regularity, and permanence, previously unknown; and the feudal powers were finally superseded by the power of the state.

At the same time, too, was accomplished a change of very different character; a change not so visible, and which has not so much attracted the notice of historians, but still more important, perhaps, than those which have been mentioned: the change effected by Louis XI. in the mode of governing.

A great deal has been said about the struggle of Louis XI. [1461-1483] against the grandees of the kingdom, of their depression, and of his partiality for the citizens and the inferior classes. There is truth in all this, though it has been much exaggerated, and though the conduct of Louis XI. toward the different classes of society more frequently disturbed than benefited the state. But he did something of deeper import. Before his time the government had been carried on almost entirely by force, and by mere physical means. Persuasion, address, care in working upon men's minds, and in bringing them over to the views of the government—in a word, what is properly called policy—a policy, indeed, of falsehood and deceit, but also of management and prudence—had hitherto been little attended to. Louis XI. substituted intellectual for material means, cunning for force, Italian for feudal policy. Take the two men whose rivalry engrosses this period of our history, Charles the Bold and Louis XI.: Charles is the representative of the old mode of governing; he has recourse to no other means than violence; he constantly appeals to arms; he is unable to act with patience, or to address himself to the dispositions and tempers of men in order to make them the instruments of his designs. Louis XI., on the contrary, takes pleasure in avoiding the use of force, and in gaining an ascendency over men, by conversation with individuals, and by skilfully bringing into play their interests and peculiarities of character. It was not the public institutions or the external system of government that he changed; it was the secret proceedings, the tactics, of power. It was reserved for modern times to attempt a still greater revolution; to endeavor to introduce into the means, as well as the objects, of public policy, justice in place of self-interest, publicity instead of cunning. Still, however, a great step was gained by renouncing the continued use of force, by calling in the aid of intellectual superiority, by governing through the understandings of men, and not by overturning everything that stood in the way of the exercise of power. This is the great change which, among all his errors and crimes, in spite of the perversity of his nature, and solely by the strength of his powerful intellect, Louis XI. has the merit of having begun.

From France I turn to Spain; and there I find movements of the same nature. It was also in the fifteenth century that Spain was consolidated into one kingdom. At this time an end was put to the long struggle between the Christians, and Moors, by the conquest of Grenada. Then, too, the Spanish territory became centralized: by the marriage of Ferdinand the Catholic, and Isabella, the two principal kingdoms, Castile and Arragon, were united under the same dominion. In the same manner as in France, the monarchy was extended and confirmed. It was supported by severer institutions, which bore more gloomy names. Instead of parliaments, it was the inquisition that had its origin in Spain. It contained the germ of what it afterward became; but at first it was of a political rather than a religious nature and was destined to maintain civil order rather than defend religious faith. The analogy between the countries extends beyond their institutions; it is observable even in the persons of the sovereigns. With less subtlety of intellect, and a less active and intriguing spirit, Ferdinand the Catholic, in his character and government, strongly resembles Louis XI. I pay no regard to arbitrary comparisons or fanciful parallels, but here the analogy is strong, and observable in general facts as well as in minute details.

A similar analogy may be discovered in Germany. It was in the middle of the fifteenth century, in 1438, that the house of Austria came to the empire; and that the imperial power acquired a permanence which it had never before possessed. From that time election was merely a sanction given to hereditary right. At the end of the fifteenth century, Maximilian I. definitively established the preponderance of his house and the regular exercise of the central authority; Charles VII. was the first in France who, for the preservation of order, created a permanent militia; Maximilian, too, was the first in his hereditary dominions, who accomplished the same end by the same means. Louis XI. had established in France, the post-office for the conveyance of letters; Maximilian I. introduced it into Germany. In the progress of civilization the same steps were everywhere taken, in a similar way, for the advantage of central government.

The history of England in the fifteenth century consists of two great events—the war with France abroad, and the contest of the two Roses at home. These two wars, though different in their nature, were attended with similar results. The contest with France was maintained by the English people with a degree of ardor which went entirely to the profit of royalty. The people, already remarkable for the prudence and determination with which they defended their resources and treasures, surrendered them at that period to their monarchs, without foresight or measure. It was in the reign of Henry V. that a considerable tax, consisting of custom-house duties, was granted to the king for his lifetime, almost at the beginning of his reign. The foreign war was scarcely ended, when the civil war, which had already broken out, was carried on; the houses of York and Lancaster disputed the throne. When at length these sanguinary struggles were brought to an end, the English nobility were ruined, diminished in number, and no longer able to preserve the power which they had previously exercised. The coalition of the great barons was no longer able to govern the throne. The Tudors ascended it; and with Henry VII., in 1485, begins the era of political centralization, the triumph of royalty.

Monarchy did not establish itself in Italy, at least under that name; but this made little difference as to the result. It was in the fifteenth century that the fall of the Italian republics took place. Even where the name was retained, the power became concentrated in the hands of one, or of a few families. The spirit of republicanism was extinguished. In the north of Italy, almost all the Lombard republics merged in the Dutchy of Milan. In 1434, Florence fell under the dominion of the Medicis. In 1464, Genoa became subject to Milan. The greater part of the republics, great and small, yielded to the power of sovereign houses; and soon afterward began the pretensions of foreign sovereigns to the dominion of the north and south of Italy; to the Milanese and kingdom of Naples.

Indeed, to whatever country of Europe we cast our eyes, whatever portion of its history we consider, whether it relates to the nations themselves or their governments, to their territories or their institutions, we everywhere see the old elements, the old forms of society, disappearing. Those liberties which were founded on tradition were lost; new powers arose, more regular and concentrated than those which previously existed. There is something deeply melancholy in this view of the fall of the ancient liberties of Europe. Even in its own time it inspired feelings of the utmost bitterness. In France, in Germany, and above all, in Italy, the patriots of the fifteenth century resisted with ardor, and lamented with despair, that revolution which everywhere produced the rise of what they were entitled to call despotism. We must admire their courage and feel for their sorrow; but at the same time we must be aware that this revolution was not only inevitable, but useful. The primitive system of Europe—the old feudal and municipal liberties—had failed in the organization of a general society. Security and progress are essential to social existence. Every system which does not provide for present order, and progressive advancement for the future, is vicious, and speedily abandoned. And this was the fate of the old political forms of society, of the ancient liberties of Europe in the fifteenth century. They could not give to society either security or progress. These objects naturally became sought for elsewhere; to obtain them, recourse was had to other principles and other means: and this is the import of all the facts to which I have just called your attention.

To this same period may be assigned another circumstance which has had a great influence on the political history of Europe. It was in the fifteenth century that the relations of governments with each other began to be frequent, regular, and permanent. Now, for the first time, became formed those great combinations by means of alliance, for peaceful as well as warlike objects, which, at a later period, gave rise to the system of the balance of power. European diplomacy originated in the fifteenth century. In fact you may see, toward its close, the principal powers of the continent of Europe, the popes, the dukes of Milan, the Venetians, the German emperors, and the kings of France and Spain, entering into a closer correspondence with each other than had hitherto existed; negotiating, combining, and balancing their various interests. Thus at the very time when Charles VIII. set on foot his expedition to conquer the kingdom of Naples, a great league was formed against him, between Spain, the Pope, and the Venetians. The league of Cambray was formed some years later (in 1508), against the Venetians. The holy league directed against Louis XII. succeeded, in 1511, to the league of Cambray. All these combinations had their rise in Italian policy; in the desire of different sovereigns to possess its territory; and in the fear lest any of them, by obtaining an exclusive possession, should acquire an excessive preponderance. This new order of things was very favorable to the career of monarchy. On the one hand, it belongs to the very nature of the external relations of states that they can be conducted only by a single person, or by a very small number, and that they require a certain degree of secrecy: on the other hand, the people were so little enlightened that the consequences of a combination of this kind quite escaped them. As it had no direct bearing on their individual or domestic life, they troubled themselves little about it; and, as usual, left such transactions to the discretion of the central government. Thus diplomacy, in its very birth, fell into the hands of kings; and the opinion, that it belongs to them exclusively; that the nation, even when free, and possessed of the right of voting its own taxes, and interfering in the management of its domestic affairs, has no right to intermeddle in foreign matters; —this opinion, I say, became established in all parts of Europe, as a settled principle, a maxim of common law. Look into the history of England in the sixteenth and seventeenth centuries; and you will observe the great influence of that opinion, and the obstacles it presented to the liberties of England in the reigns of Elizabeth, James I., and Charles I. It is always under the sanction of the principle, that peace and war, commercial relations, and all foreign affairs, belong to the royal prerogative, that absolute power defends itself against the rights of the country. The people are remarkably timid in disputing this portion of the prerogative; and their timidity has cost them the dearer, for this reason, that, from the commencement of the period into which we are now entering (that is to say, the sixteenth century), the history of Europe is essentially diplomatic. For nearly three centuries, foreign relations form the most important part of history. The domestic affairs of countries began to be regularly conducted; the internal government, on the Continent at least, no longer produced any violent convulsions, and no longer kept the public mind in a state of agitation and excitement. Foreign relations, wars, treaties, alliances, alone occupy the attention and fill the page of history; so that we find the destinies of nations abandoned in a great measure to the royal prerogative, to the central power of the state.

It could scarcely have happened otherwise. Civilization must have made great progress, intelligence, and political habits must be widely diffused, before the public can interfere with advantage in matters of this kind. From the sixteenth to the eighteenth century, the people were far from being sufficiently advanced to do so. Observe what occurred in England, under James I., at the beginning of the seventeenth century. His son-in-law, the Elector Palatine, who had been elected king of Bohemia, had lost his crown, and had even been stripped of his hereditary dominions, the Palatinate. Protestanism everywhere espoused his cause; and, on this ground, England took a warm interest in it. There was a great manifestation of public opinion in order to force James to take the part of his son-in-law, and obtain for him the restoration of the Palatinate. Parliament insisted violently for war, promising ample means to carry it on. James was indifferent on the subject; he made several attempts to negotiate, and sent some troops to Germany; he then told parliament that he required £900,000 sterling, to carry on the war with any chance of success. It is not said, and indeed it does not appear, that his estimate was exaggerated. But parliament shrunk back with astonishment and terror at the sound of such a sum, and could hardly be prevailed upon to vote £70,000 sterling, to reinstate a prince, and reconquer a country three hundred leagues distant from England. Such were the ignorance and political incapacity of the public in affairs of this nature; they acted without any knowledge of facts, or any consideration of consequences. How then could they be capable of interfering in a regular and effectual manner? This is the cause which principally contributed to make foriegn relations fall into the hands of the central power; no other was in a condition to conduct them, I shall not say for the public benefit, which was very far from being always consulted, but with anything like consistency and good sense.

It may be seen, then, that in whatever point of view we regard the political history of Europe at this period—whether we look upon the internal condition of different nations, or upon their relation with each other—whether we consider the means of warfare, the administration of justice, or the levying of taxes, we find them pervaded by the same character; we see everywhere the same tendency to centralization, to unity, to the formation and preponderance of general interests and public powers. This was the hidden working of the fifteenth century, which, at the period we are speaking of, had not yet produced any very apparent result, or any actual revolution in society, but was preparing all those consequences which afterward took place.

I shall now bring before you a class of facts of a different nature; *moral* facts, such as stand in relation to the development of the human mind and the ormation of general ideas. In these again we shall discover the same phenomena, and arrive at the same result.

I shall begin with an order of facts which has often engaged our attention, and under the most various forms, has always held an important place in the history of Europe—the facts relative to the Church. Down to the fifteenth century, the only general ideas which had a powerful influence on the masses were those connected with religion. The

Church alone was invested with the power of regulating, promulgating, and prescribing them. Attempts, it is true, at independence, and even at. separation, were frequently made; and the Chucrh had much to do to overcome them. Down to this period, however, she had been successful. Creeds rejected by the Church had never taken any general or permanent hold on the minds of the people: even Albigenses had been repressed. Dissension and strife were incessant in the Church, but without any decisive and striking result. The fifteenth century opened with the appearance of a different state of things. New ideas, and a public and avowed desire of change and reformation, began to agitate the Church herself. The end of the fourteenth and beginning of the fifteenth century were marked by the great schism of the west, resulting from the removal of the papal chair to Avignon, and the creation of two popes, one at Avignon, and the other at Rome. The contest between these two papacies is what is called the great schism of the west. It began in 1378. In 1409, the Council of Pisa endeavored to put an end to it by deposing the two rival popes and electing another. But instead of ending the schism, this step only rendered it more violent.

There were now three popes instead of two, and disorders and abuses went on increasing. In 1414, the Council of Constance assembled, convoked by desire of the Emperor Sigismund. This council set about a matter of far more importance than the nomination of a new pope; it undertook the reformation of the Church. It began by proclaiming the indissolubility of the universal council, and its superiority over the papal power. It endeavored to establish these principles in the Church, and to reform the abuses which had crept into it, particularly the exactions by which the Court of Rome obtained money. To accomplish this object the council appointed what we should call a commission of inquiry, in other words, a *Reform College*, composed of deputies to the council, chosen in the different Christian nations. This college was directed to inquire into the abuses which polluted the Church, and into the means of remedying them, and to make a report to the council, in order that it might deliberate on the proceedings to be adopted. But while the council was thus engaged, the question was started, whether it could proceed to the reform of abuses without the visible concurrence of the head of the Church, without the sanction of the pope. It was carried in the negative through the influence of the Roman party, supported by some well-meaning but timid individuals. The council elected a new pope, Martin V., in 1417. The pope was instructed to present, on his part, a plan for the reform of the Church. This plan was rejected, and the council separated. In 1431, a new council assembled at Bale with the same design. It resumed and continued the reforming labors of the Council of Constance, but with no better success. Schism broke out in this assembly as it ha1 done in Christendom. The pope removed the council to Ferrara, and afterward to Florence. A portion of the prelates refused to obey the pope, and remained at Bale; and, as there had been formerly two popes, so now there were two councils. That of Bale continued its projects of reform; named as its pope, Felix V.; some time afterward removed to Lausanne; and dissolved itself in 1449, without having effected anything.

In this manner papacy gained the day, remained in possession of the field of battle, and of the government of the Church. The council could not accomplish that which it had set about; but it did something else which it had not thought of, and which survived its dissolution. Just at the time the Council of Bale failed in its attempts at reform, sovereigns were adopting the ideas which it had proclaimed, and some of the institutions which it had suggested. In France, and with the decrees of the Council of Bale, Charles VII. formed the pragmatic sanction, which he proclaimed at Bourges in 1438; it authorized the election of bishops, the suppression of annates (or first-fruits), and the reform of the principal abuses introduced into the Church. The pragmatic sanction was declared in France to be a law of the state. In Germany, the Diet of Mayence adopted it in 1439, and also made it a law of the German empire. What spiritual power had tried without success, temporal power seemed determined to accomplish.

But the projects of the reformers met with a new reverse of fortune. As the council had failed, so did the pragmatic sanction. It perished very soon in Germany. It was abandoned by the Diet in 1448, in virtue of a negotiation with Nicholas V. In 1516, Francis I. abandoned it also, substituting for it his *concordat* with Leo X. The reform attempted by princes did not succeed better than that set on foot by the clergy. But we must not conclude that it was entirely thrown away. In like manner as the council had done things which survived it, so the pragmatic sanction had effects which survived it also, and will be found to make an important figure in modern history. The principles of the Council of Bale were strong and fruitful. Men of superior minds, and of energetic characters, had adopted and maintained them. John of Paris, D'Ailly, Gerson, and many distinguished men of the fifteenth century, had devoted themselves to their defence. It was in vain that the council was dissolved; it was in vain that the pragmatic sanction was abandoned; their general doctrines respecting the government of the Church, and the reforms which were necessary, took root in France. They were spread abroad, found their way into parliaments, took a strong hold of the public mind, and gave birth first to the Jansenists, and then to the Gallicans. This entire series of maxims and efforts tending to the reform of the Church, which began with the Council of Constance, and terminated in the four propositions of Bossuet, emanated from the same source, and was directed to the same object. It is the same fact which has undergone successive transformations. Notwithstanding the failure of the legal attempts at reform made in the fifteenth century, they indirectly had an immense influence upon the progress of civilization; and must not be left out of its history.

The councils were right in trying for a legal reform, for it was the only way to prevent a revolution. Nearly at the same time when the Council of Pisa was endeavoring to put an end to the great western schism, and the Council of Constance to reform the Church, the first attempts at popular religious reform broke out in Bohemia. The preaching of John Huss, and his progress as a reformer, commenced in 1404, when he began to teach at Prague. Here, then, we have two reforms going on side by side; the one in the very bosom of the Church—attempted by the ecclesiastical aristocracy itself—cautious, embarrassed, and timid; the other originating without the Church, and directed against it—violent, passionate, and impetuous. A contest began between these two powers, these two parties. The council enticed John Huss and Jerome of Prague to Constance, and condemned them to the flames as heretics and revolutionists. These events are perfectly intelligible to us now. We can very well understand this simultaneous existence of separate reforms, one undertaken by governments, the other by the people, hostile to each other, yet springing from the same cause, and tending to the same object, and, though opposed to each other, finally concurring in the same result. This is what happened in the fifteenth century. The popular reform of John Huss was stifled for the moment; the war of the Hussites broke out three or four years after the death of their master; it was long and violent, but at last the empire was successful in subduing it. The failure of the councils in the work of reform, their not being able to attain the object they were aiming at, only kept the public mind in a state of fermentation. The spirit of reform still existed; it waited but for an opportunity again to break out, and this it found at the beginning of the sixteenth century. Had the reform undertaken by the councils been brought to any good issue, perhaps the popular reform would have been prevented. But it was impossible that one or the other of them should not succeed, for their coincidence shows their necessity.

Such, then, is the state, in respect to religious creeds, in which Europe was left by the fifteenth century: an aristocratic reform attempted without success, with a popular suppressed reform begun, but still ready to break out anew.

It was not solely to religious creeds that the human mind was directed, and busied itself about at this period. It was in the course of the fourteenth century, as you all know, that Greek and Roman antiquity was (if I may use the expression) restored to Europe. You know with what ardor Dante, Petrarch, Bocaccio, and all their contemporaries, sought for Greek and Latin manuscripts, published them, and spread them abroad; and what general joy was produced by the smallest discovery in this branch of learning. It was in the midst of this excitement that the classical school took its rise; a school which has performed a much more important part in the development of the human mind than has generally been ascribed to it. But we must be cautious of attaching to this term, classical school, the meaning given to it at present. It had to do, in those days, with matters very different from literary systems and disputes. The classical school of that period inspired its disciples with admiration, not only for the writings of Virgil and Homer, but for the entire frame of ancient society, for its institutions, its opinions, its philosophy, as well as its literature. Antiquity, it must be allowed, whether as regards politics, philosophy, or literature, was greatly superior to the Europe of the fourteenth and fifteenth centuries. It is not surprising, therefore, that it should have exercised so great an influence; that lofty, vigorous, elegant, and fastidious minds should have been disgusted with the coarse manners, the confused ideas, the barbarous modes of their own time, and should have devoted themselves with enthusiasm, and almost with veneration, to the study of a state of society, at once more regular and more perfect than their own. Thus was formed that school of bold thinkers which appeared at the commencement of the fifteenth century, and in which prelates, jurists, and men of learning were united by common sentiments and common pursuits.

In the midst of this movement happened the taking of Constantinople by the Turks, 1453, the fall of the Eastern empire, and the influx of the fugitive Greek into Italy. These brought with them a greater knowledge of antiquity, numerous manuscripts, and a thousand new means of studying the civilization of the ancients. You may easily imagine how this must have redoubled the admiration and ardor of the classic school. This was the most brilliant period of the Church, especially in Italy, not in respect of political power, but of wealth and luxury. The Church gave herself up to all the pleasures of an indolent, elegant, licentious civilization; to a taste for letters, the arts, and social and physical enjoyments. Look at the way in which the men who played the greatest political and literary parts at that period passed their lives; Cardinal Bembo, for example; and you will be surprised by the mixture which it exhibits of luxurious effeminacy and intellectual culture, of enervated manners and mental vigor. In surveying this period, indeed, when we look at the state of opinions and of social relations, we might imagine ourselves living among the French of the eighteenth century. There was the same desire for the progress of intelligence, and for the acquirement of new ideas; the same taste for an agreeable and easy life, the same luxury, the same licentiousness; there was the same want of political energy and of moral principles, combined with singular sincerity and activity of mind. The literati of the fifteenth century stood in the same relation to the prelates of the Church as the men of letters and philosophers of the eighteenth did to the nobility. They had the same opinions and manners, lived agreeably together, and gave themselves no uneasiness about the storms that were brewing round them. The prelates of the fifteenth century, and Cardinal Bembo among the rest, no more foresaw Luther and Calvin, than the courtiers of Louis XIV. foresaw the French revolution. The analogy between the two cases is striking and instructive.

We observe, then, three great facts in the moral order of society at this period: on one hand, an ecclesiastical reform attempted by the Church itself; on another a popular, religious reform; and lastly, an intellectual revolution, which formed a school of free-thinkers; and all these transformations were prepared in the midst of the greatest political change that has ever taken place in Europe, in the midst of the process of the centralization of nations and governments.

But this is not all. The period in question was also one of the most remarkable for the display of physical activity among men. It was a period of voyages, travels, enterprises, discoveries, and inventions of every kind. It was the time of the great Portuguese expedition along the coast of Africa; of the discovery of the new passage to India by the Cape of Good Hope, by Vasco de Gama; of the discovery of America, by Christopher Columbus; of the wonderful extension of European commerce. A thousand new inventions started up; others already known, but confined within a narrow sphere, became popular and in general use. Gunpowder changed the system of war; the compass changed the system of navigation. Painting in oil was invented, and filled Europe with masterpieces of art. Engraving on copper, invented in 1406, multiplied and diffused them. Paper made of linen became common. Finally, between 1436 and 1452, was invented printing;—printing, the theme of so many declamations and common-places, but to whose merits and effect no common-places or declamations will ever be able to do justice.

From all this, some idea may be formed of the greatness and activity of the fifteenth century; a greatness which, at the time, was not very apparent; an activity of which the results did not immediately take place. Violent reforms seemed to fail; governments acquired stability. It might have been supposed that society was now about to enjoy the benefits of better order, and more rapid progress. The mighty revolutions of the sixteenth century were at hand; the fifteenth century prepared them. They shall be the subject of the following lecture.

LECTURE XII.

THE REFORMATION.

I HAVE often referred to and lamented the disorder, the chaotic situation of European society; I have complained of the difficulty of comprehending and describing a state of society so loose, so scattered, and incoherent; and I have kept you waiting with impatience for the period of general interests, order, and social union. This period we have now reached; but, in treating of it, we encounter a difficulty of another kind. Hitherto, we have found it difficult to connect historical facts one with another, to class them together, to seize their common features, to discover their points of resemblance. The case is different in modern Europe; all the elements, all the incidents of social life modify, act and re-act upon each other; the mutual relations of men are much more numerous and complicated; so also are their relations with the government and the state, the relations of states with each other, and all the ideas and operations of the human mind. In the periods through which we have already travelled, we have found a great number of facts which were insulated, foreign to each other, and without any reciprocal influence. From this time, however, we find nothing insulated; all things press upon one another, and become modified and changed by their mutual contact and friction. What, let me ask, can be more difficult than to seize the real point of unity in the midst of such diversity, to determine the direction of such a widely spread and complicated movement, to sum up this prodigious number of various and closely connected elements, to point out at last the general and leading fact which is the sum of a long series of facts; which characterizes an era, and is the true expression of its influence, and of the part it has performed in the history of civilization? You will be able to measure at a glance the extent of this difficulty, in the great event which is now to engage our attention.

In the twelfth century we met with an event which was religious in its origin if not in its nature; I mean the crusades. Notwithstanding the greatness of this event, its long duration, and the variety of incidents which it brought about it was easy enough for us to discover its general character, and to determine its influence with some degree of precision

We have now to consider the religious revolution of the sixteenth century, which is commonly called THE REFORMATION. Let me be permitted to say in passing, that I shall use this word *reformation* as a simple ordinary term, synonymous with *religious revolution*, and without attaching it to any opinion. You must, I am sure, foresee at once, how difficult it is to discover the real character of this great crisis, and to explain in a general manner what has been its nature and its effects.

The period of our inquiry must extend from the beginning of the sixteenth to the middle of the seventeenth century; for this period embraces, so to speak, the life of this event from its birth to its termination. All historical events have in some sort a determinate career. Their consequences are prolonged to infinity; they are connected with all the past and all the future; but it is not the less true, on this account, that they have a definite and limited existence; that they have their origin and their increase, occupy with their development a certain portion of time, and then diminish and disappear from the scene, to make way for some new event which runs a similar course.

The precise date which may be assigned to the Reformation is not of much importance. We may take the year 1520, when Luther publicly burnt at Wittenberg the bull of Leo X., containing his condemnation, and thus formally separated himself from the Romish Church. The interval between this period and the middle of the seventeenth century, the year 1648, when the treaty of Westphalia was concluded, comprehends the life of the Reformation. That this is the case, may be thus proved. The first and greatest effect of the religious revolution was to create in Europe two classes of states, the Catholic and the Protestant, to set them against each other and force them into hostilities. With many vicissitudes, the struggle between these two parties lasted from the beginning of the sixteenth century to the middle of the seventeenth. It was by the treaty of Westphalia, in 1648, that the Catholic and Protestant states reciprocally acknowledged each other, and engaged to live in amity and peace, without regard to difference of religion. After this, from 1648, difference of religion ceased to be the leading principle of the classification of states, of their external policy, their relations and alliances. Down to that time, notwithstanding great variations, Europe was essentially divided into a Catholic league and a Protestant league. After the treaty of Westphalia this distinction disappeared; and alliances or divisions among states took place from considerations altogether foreign to religious belief. At this point, therefore, the preponderance, or, in other words, the career of the Reformation came to an end, although its consequences, instead of decreasing, continued to develop themselves.

Let us now take a rapid survey of this career, and merely mentioning names and events, point out its course. You will see from this simple indication, from this dry and incomplete outline, what must be the difficulty of summing up a series of such various and complicated facts into one general fact; of determining what is the true character of the religious revolution of the sixteenth century, and of assigning to it its true part in the history of civilization.

The moment in which the Reformation broke out is remarkable for its political importance. It was in the midst of the great struggle between Francis and Charles V.—between France and Spain; a struggle at first for the possession of Italy, but afterward for the German empire, and finally for preponderance in Europe. It was the moment in which the house of Austria elevated itself and became predominant in Europe. It was also the moment in which England, through Henry VIII., interfered in continental politics, more regularly, permanently, and extensively than she had ever done before.

If we follow the course of the sixteenth century in France, we shall find it entirely occupied by the great religious wars between Protestants and Catholics; wars which became the means and the occasion of a new attempt of the great nobles to repossess themselves of the power which they had lost, and to obtain an ascendency over the sovereign. This was the political meaning of the religious wars of France, of the League, of the struggle between the houses of Guise and Valois—a struggle which was put an end to by the accession of Henry IV.

In Spain, the revolution of the United Provinces broke out about the middle of the reign of Philip II. The inquisition on one hand and civil and religious liberty on the other made these provinces the theatre of war under the names of the Duke of Alva and the Prince of Orange. Perseverance and prudence secured the triumph of liberty in Holland, but it perished in Spain, where absolute power, ecclesiastical and civil, reigned without control.

In England the circumstances to be noted are, the reigns of Mary and Elizabeth; the struggle of Elizabeth, as head of the Protestant interests against Philip II.; the accession of James Stuart to the throne of England; and the rise of the great dispute between the monarchy and the people.

About the same time we note the creation of new powers in the north. Sweden was raised into existence by Gustavus Vasa, in 1523. Prussia was created by the secularization of the Teutonic order. The northern powers assumed a place in the politics of Europe which they had not occupied before, and the importance of which soon afterward showed itself in the thirty years' war.

I now come back to France, to note the reign of Louis XIII.; the change in the internal administration of this country effected by Cardinal Richelieu; the relations of France with Germany, and the support which she afforded to the Protestant party. In Germany, during the latter part of the sixteenth century, there was the war with the Turks; in the beginning of the seventeeth, the thirty years' war, the greatest of modern events in eastern Europe; Gustavus Adolphus, Wallenstein, Tilly, the Duke of Brunswick, the Duke of Weimar, are the greatest names which Germany at this time could boast of.

At the same period, in France, took place the accession of Louis XIV. and the commencement of the Fronde; in England broke out the great revolution, or, as it is sometimes improperly called, the grand rebellion, which dethroned Charles I.

In this survey, I have only glanced at the most prominent events of history, events which everybody has heard of; you see their number, their variety, their importance. If we seek for events of another kind, events less conspicuous and less distinguished by great names, we shall find them not less abundant during this period; a period remarkable for the great changes which took place in the political institutions of almost every country; the period in which pure monarchy prevailed in most of the great states, while in Holland there arose the most powerful republic in Europe; and in England constitutional monarchy achieved, or nearly achieved, a final triumph. Then, in the Church, it was during this period that the old monastic orders lost almost all their political power, and were replaced by a new order of a different character, and whose importance, erroneously perhaps, is considered much superior to that of its precursors—I mean the Jesuits. At the same period the Council of Trent obliterated all that remained of the influence of the Councils of Constance and Bale, and secured the definitive ascendency of the Court of Rome in ecclesiastical affairs. Leaving the Church, and taking a passing glance at the philosophy of the age, at the unfettered career of the human mind, we observe two men, Bacon and Descartes, the authors of the greatest philosophical revolution which the modern world has undergone, the chiefs of the two schools which contended for supremacy. It was in this period too that Italian literature shone forth in its fullest splendor, while that of France and England was still in its infancy. Lastly, it was in this period that the colonial system of Europe had its origin; that great colonies were founded; and that commercial activity and enterprise were carried to an extent never before known.

Thus, under whatever point of view we consider this era, we find its political, ecclesiastical, philosophical, and literary events, more numerous, varied, and important, than in any of the preceding ages. The activity of the human mind displayed itself in every way; in the relations of men with each other—in their relations with the governing powers—in the relations of states, and in the intellectual labors of individuals. In short, it was the age of great men and of great things. Yet, among the great events of this period, the religious revolution which now engages our attention was the greatest. It was the leading fact of the period; the fact which gives it its name, and determines its character. Among the many powerful causes which have produced so many powerful effects, the Reformation was the most powerful; it was that to which all the others contributed; that which has modified, or been modified by, all the rest. The task which we have now to perform, then, is to review, with precision this event; to examine this cause, which, in a period of the greatest causes, produced the greatest effects—this event, which, in this period of great events, prevailed over all the rest.

You must, at once, perceive how difficult it is to link together facts so diversified, so immense, and so closely connected, into one great historical unity. It must, however, be done; when events are once consummated, when they have become matter of history, the most important business is then to be attempted; that which man most seeks for are general facts—the linking together of causes and effects. This is what I may call the immortal portion of history, which all generations must study, in order to understand the past as well as the present time. This desire after generalization, of obtaining rational results, is the most powerul and noblest of all our intellectual desires; but we must beware of being satisfied with hasty and incomplete generalizations. No pleasure is more seducing than that of indulging ourselves in determining on the spot, and at first sight, the general character and permanent results of an era or an event. The human intellect, like the human will, is eager to be in action, impatient of obstacles, and desirous of coming to conclusions. It willingly forgets such facts as impede and constrain its operations; but while it forgets, it cannot destroy them; they still live to convict it of error at some after period. There is only one way of escaping this danger; it is by a resolute and dogged study of facts, till their meaning is exhausted, before attempting to generalize, or coming to conclusions respecting their effects. Facts are, for the intellect, what the rules of morals are for the will. The mind must be thoroughly acquainted with facts, and must know their weight; and it is only when she has fulfilled this duty—when she has completely traversed, in every direction, the ground of investigation and inquiry—that she is permitted to spread her wings and take her flight toward that higher region, whence she may survey all things in their general bearings and results. If she endeavor to ascend prematurely, without having first acquired a thorough knowledge of the territory which she desires to contemplate from above, she incurs the most imminent risk of error and downfall. As, in a calculation of figures, an error at the outset leads to others, *ad infinitum*, so, in history, if we do not, in the first instance, take every fact into account—if we allow ourselves to indulge in a spirit of precipitate generalization—it is impossible to tell how far we may be led astray from the truth.

In these observations, I am, in some measure, putting you on your guard against myself. In this course I have been able to do little more than make some attempts at generalization, and take some general views of facts which we had not studied closely and together. Being now arrived at a period where this task is much more difficult, and the chances of error greater than before, I think it necessary to make you aware of the danger, and warn you against my own speculations. Having done so, I shall now continue them, and treat the Reformation in the same way as I have done other events. I shall endeavor to discover its leading fact, to describe its leading fact, to describe its general character, and to show the part which this great event has performed in the process of European civilization.

You remember the situation in which we left Europe, at the end of the fifteenth century. We saw, in the course of it, two great attempts at religious revolution or reform; an attempt at legal reform by the councils, and an attempt at revolutionary reform, in Bohemia, by the Hussites; we saw both these stifled and rendered abortive; and yet we concluded that the event was one which could not be staved off, but that it must necessarily reappear in one shape or another; and that what the fifteenth century attempted would be inevitably accomplished by the sixteenth. I shall not enter into any details respecting the religious revolution of the sixteenth century, which I consider as being generally known. I shall confine myself solely to the consideration of its general influence on the destinies of mankind.

In the inquiries which have been made into the causes which produced this great event, the enemies of the Reformation have imputed it to accidents and mischances, in the course of civilization; for instance, to the sale of indulgences having been intrusted to the Dominicans, and excited the jealousy of the Augustines. Luther was an Augustine; and this, therefore, was the moving power which put the Reformation in action. Others have ascribed it to the ambition of sovereigns—to their rivalry with the ecclesiastical power, and to the avidity of the lay nobility, who wished to take possession of the property of the Church. In this manner the Reformation has been accounted for, by looking at the evil side of human nature and human affairs; by having recourse to the private interests and selfish passions of individuals.

On the other hand, the friends and partisans of the

Reformation have endeavored to account for it by the pure desire of effectually reforming the existing abuses of the Church. They have represented it as a redress of religious grievances, as an enterprise conceived and executed with the sole design of re-constituting the Church in its primitive purity. Neither of these explanations appears to me well founded. There is more truth in the latter than in the former; at least, the cause assigned is greater, and in better proportion to the extent and importance of the event; but, still, I do not consider it as correct. In my opinion, the Reformation neither was an accident, the result of some causal circumstance, or some personal interests, nor arose from unmingled views of religious improvement, the fruit of Utopian humanity and truth. It had a more powerful cause than all these; a general cause, to which all the others were subordinate. It was a vast effort made by the human mind to achieve its freedom; it was a new-born desire which it felt to think and judge, freely and independently, of facts and opinions which, till then, Europe received, or was considered bound to receive, from the hands of authority. It was a great endeavor to emancipate human reason; and to call things by their right names, it was an insurrection of the human mind against the absolute power of spiritual order. Such, in my opinion, was the true character and leading principle of the Reformation.

When we consider the state of the human mind, at this time, on one hand, and the state of the spiritual power of the Church, which had the government of the human mind, on the other, a double fact presents itself to our notice.

In looking at the *human mind*, we observe much greater activity, and a much greater desire to develop its powers, than it had ever felt before. This new activity was the result of various causes which had been accumulating for ages. For example, there were ages in which heresies sprang up, subsisted for a time, and then gave way to others; there were other ages in which philosophical opinions ran just the same course as heresies. The labors of the human mind, whether in the sphere of religion or of philosophy, had been accumulating from the eleventh to the sixteenth century; and the time was now come when they must necessarily have a result. Besides this, the means of instruction created or favored in the bosom of the Church itself, had brought forth fruit. Schools had been instituted; these schools had produced men of considerable knowledge, and their number had daily increased. These men began to wish to think for themselves, for they felt themselves stronger than they had ever been before. At last came that restoration of the human mind to a pristine youth and vigor, which the revival of the learning and arts of antiquity brought about, the progress and effects of which I have already described.

These various causes combined, gave, at the beginning of the sixteenth century, a new and powerful impulse to the human mind, an imperious desire to go forward.

The situation of the *spiritual power*, which then had the government of the human mind, was totally different; it, on the contrary, had fallen into a state of imbecility, and remained stationary. The political influence of the Church and Court of Rome was much diminished. European society had passed from the dominion of Rome to that of temporal governments. Yet in spite of all this, the spiritual power still preserved its pretensions, splendor, and outward importance. The same thing happened to it which has so often happened to long established governments. Most of the complaints made against it were now almost groundless. It is not true, that in the sixteenth century, the Court of Rome was very tyrannical; it is not true, that its abuses were more numerous and crying than they had been at former periods. Never, perhaps, on the contrary, had the government of the Church been more indulgent, more tolerant, more disposed to let things take their course, provided it was not itself implicated, provided that the rights it had hitherto enjoyed were acknowledged even though left unexercised, and that it was assured of its usual existence, and received its usual tributes. It would willingly have left the human mind to itself, if the human mind had been as tolerant toward its offences. But it usually happens, that just when governments have begun to lose their influence and power, just when they are comparatively harmless, that they are most exposed to attack; it is then that, like the sick lion, they may be attacked with impunity, though the attempt would have been desperate when they were in the plenitude of their power.

It is evident, therefore, simply from the consideration of the state of the human mind at this period, and of the power which then governed it, that the Reformation must have been, I repeat it, a sudden effort made by the human mind to achieve its liberty, a great insurrection of human intelligence. This, doubtless, was the leading cause of the Reformation, the cause which soared above all the rest; a cause superior to every interest either of sovereigns or of nations, superior to the need of reform properly so called, or of the redress of the grievances which were complained of at this period.

Let us suppose, that after the first years of the Reformation had passed away, when it had made all its demands, and insisted on all its grievances—let us suppose, I say, that the spiritual power had conceded everything, and said, "Well, be it so; I will make every reform you desire; I will return to a more legal, more truly religious order of affairs. I will suppress arbitrary exactions and tributes; even in matters of belief I will modify my doctrines, and return to the primitive standard of Christian faith. But, having thus redressed all your grievances, I must preserve my station, and retain, as formerly, the government of the human mind, with all the powers and all the rights which I have hitherto enjoyed." Can we believe that the religious revolution would have been satisfied with these concessions, and would have stopped short in its course? I cannot think so; I firmly believe that it would have continued its career, and that after having obtained reform, it would have demanded liberty. The crisis of the sixteenth century was not merely of a reforming character; it was essentially revolutionary. It cannot be deprived of this character, with all the good and evil that belongs to it; its nature may be traced in its effects.

Let us take a glance at the destinies of the Reformation; let us see, more particularly, what it has produced in the different countries in which it developed itself. It can hardly escape observation that it exhibited itself in very different situations, and with very different chances of success; if then we find that, notwithstanding this diversity of situations and chances, it has always pursued a certain object, obtained a certain result, and preserved a certain character, it must be evident that this character, which has surmounted all the diversities of situation, all the inequalities of chance, must be the fundamental character of the event; and that this result must be the essential object of its pursuit.

Well, then, wherever the religious revolution of the sixteenth century prevailed, if it did not accomplish a complete emancipation of the human mind, it procured it a new and great *increase of liberty*. It doubtless left the mind subject to all the chances of liberty or thraldom which might arise from political institutions; but it abolished or disarmed the spiritual power, the systematic and formidable government of the mind. This was the result obtained by the Reformation, notwithstanding the infinite diversity of circumstances under which it took place. In Germany there was no political liberty; the Reformation did not introduce it; it rather strengthened than enfeebled the power of princes; it was rather opposed to the free institutions of the middle ages than favorable to their progress. Still, in spite of this, it excited and maintained in Germany a greater freedom of thought, probably, than in any other country. In Denmark too, a country in which absolute power predominated in the municipal institutions, as well as the general institutions of the state, thought was emancipated through the influence of the Reformation, and freely exercised on every subject. In Holland, under a republic; in England, under a constitutional monarchy, and in spite of a religious tyranny which was long very severe, the emancipation of the human mind was accomplished by the same influence. And lastly, in France, which seemed from its situation the least likely of any to be affected by this religious revolution, even in this country, where it was actually overcome, it became a principle of mental independence, of intellectual freedom. Till the year 1685, that is, till the revocation of the edict of Nantes, the Reformation enjoyed a legal existence in France. During this long space of time, the reformers wrote, disputed, and provoked their adversaries to write and dispute with them. This single fact, this war of tracts and disputations between the old and new opinions, diffused in France a greater degree of real and active liberty than is commonly believed; a liberty which redounded to the advantage of science and morality, to the honor of the French clergy, and to the benefit of the mind in general. Look at the conferences of Bossuet with Claude, and at all the religious controversy of that period, and ask yourselves if Louis XIV. would have permitted a similar degree of freedom on any other subject. It was between the reformers and the opposite party that the greatest freedom of opinion existed in the seventeenth century. Religious questions were treated in a bolder and freer spirit of speculation than political, even by Fenelon himself in his Telemachus. This state of things lasted till the revocation of the edict of Nantes. Now, from the year 1685 to the explosion of the human mind in the eighteenth century, there was not an interval of forty years; and the influence of the religious revolution in favor of intellectual liberty had scarcely ceased when the influence of the revolution in philosophy began to operate.

You see, then, that wherever the Reformation penetrated, wherever it acted an important part, whether conqueror or conquered, its general, leading, and constant result was an immense progress in mental activity and freedom; an immense step toward the emancipation of the human mind.

Again, not only was this the result of the Reformation, but *it was content with this result.* Wherever this was obtained, no other was sought for; so entirely was it the very foundation of the event, its primitive and fundamental character! Thus, in Germany, far from demanding political liberty, the Reformation accepted, I shall not say servitude, but the absence of liberty. In England, it consented to the hierarchical constitution of the clergy, and to the existence of a Church, as full of abuses as ever the Romish Church had been, and much more servile. Why did the Reformation, so ardent and rigid in certain respects, exhibit, in these instances, so much facility and suppleness? Because it had obtained the general result to which it tended, the abolition of the spiritual power, and the emancipation of the human mind. I repeat it; wherever the Reformation attained this object, it accommodated itself to every form of government, and to every situation.

Let us now test this fact by the opposite mode of proof; let us see what happened in those countries into which the Reformation did not penetrate, or in which it was early suppressed. We learn from history that, in those countries, the human mind was not emancipated; witness two great countries, Spain and Italy. While, in those parts of Europe into which the Reformation very largely entered, the human mind, during the last three centuries, has acquired an activity and freedom previously unknown;—in those other parts, into which it was never allowed to make its way, the mind, during the same period, has become languid and inert: so that opposite sets of facts, which happened at the same time, concur in establishing the same result.

The impulse which was given to human thought, and the

abolition of absolute power in the spiritual order, constituted, then, the essential character of the Reformation, the most general result of its influence, the ruling fact in its destiny.

I use the word *fact*, and I do so on purpose. The emancipation of the human mind, in the course of the Reformation, was a fact rather than a principle, a result rather than an intention. The Reformation, I believe, has in this respect, performed more than it undertook—more, probably, than it desired. Contrary to what has happened in many other revolutions, the effects of which have not come up to their design, the consequences of the Reformation have gone beyond the object it had in view; it is greater, considered as an event, than as a system; it has never completely known all that it has done, nor, if it had, would it have completely avowed it.

What are the reproaches constantly applied to the Reformation by its enemies? which of its results are thrown in its face, as it were, as unanswerable?

The two principal reproaches are, first, the multiplicity of sects, the excessive license of thought, the destruction of all spiritual authority, and the entire dissolution of religious society: secondly, tyranny and persecution. "You provoke licentiousness," it has been said to the Reformers; "you produced it; and, after having been the cause of it, you wish to restrain and repress it. And how do you repress it? By the most harsh and violent means. You take upon yourselves, too, to punish heresy, and that by virtue of an illegitimate authority."

If we take a review of all the principal charges which have been made against the Reformation, we shall find, if we set aside all questions purely doctrinal, that the above are the two fundamental reproaches to which they may all be reduced.

These charges gave great embarrassment to the reform party. When they were taxed with the multiplicity of their sects, instead of advocating the freedom of religious opinion, and maintaining the right of every sect to entire toleration, they denounced sectarianism, lamented it, and endeavored to find excuses for its existence. Were they accused of persecution? They were troubled to defend themselves; they used the plea of necessity; they had, they said, the right to repress and punish error, because they were in possession of the truth. Their articles of belief, they contended, and their institutions, were the only legitimate ones; and if the Church of Rome had not the right to punish the reformed party, it was because she was in the wrong and they in the right.

And when the charge of persecution was applied to the ruling party in the Reformation, not by its enemies, but by its own offspring; when the sects denounced by that party said, "We are doing just what you did; we separate ourselves from you, just as you separated yourselves from the Church of Rome," this ruling party were still more at a loss to find an answer, and frequently the only answer they had to give was an increase of severity.

The truth is, that while laboring for the destruction of absolute power in the spiritual order, the religious revolution of the sixteenth century was not aware of the true principles of intellectual liberty. It emancipated the human mind, and yet pretended still to govern it by laws. In point of *fact*, it produced the prevalence of free inquiry; in point of *principle* it believed that it was substituting a legitimate for an illegitimate power. It had not looked up to the primary motive, nor down to the ultimate consequences of its own work. It thus fell into a double error. On the one side it did not know or respect all the rights of human thought; at the very moment that it was demanding these rights for itself, it was violating them toward others. On the other side, it was unable to estimate the rights of authority in matters of reason. I do not speak of that coercive authority which ought to have no rights at all in such matters, but of that kind of authority which is purely moral, and acts solely by its influence upon the mind. In most reformed countries something is wanting to complete the proper organization of intellectual society, and to the regular action of old and general opinions. What is due to and required by traditional belief, has not been reconciled with what is due to and required by freedom of thinking; and the cause of this undoubtedly is, that the Reformation did not fully comprehend and accept its own principles and effects.

Hence, too, the Reformation acquired an appearance of inconsistency and narrowness of mind, which has often given an advantage to its enemies. They knew very well what they were about, and what they wanted; they cited the principles of their conduct without scruple, and avowed all its consequences. There never was a government more consistent and systematic than that of the Church of Rome. In point of *fact*, the Court of Rome made more compromises and concessions than the Reformation; in point of *principle*, it adhered much more closely to its system, and maintained a more consistent line of conduct. Great strength is gained by a thorough knowledge of the nature of one's own views and actions, by a complete and rational adoption of a certain principle and design: and a striking example of this is to be found in the course of the religious revolution of the sixteenth century. Everybody knows that the principal power instituted to contend against the Reformation was the order of the Jesuits. Look for a moment at their history; they failed everywhere; wherever they interfered, to any extent, they brought misfortune upon the cause in which they meddled; in England they ruined kings; in Spain, whole masses of the people. The general course of events, the development of modern civilization, the freedom of the human mind, all these forces with which the Jesuits were called upon to contend, rose up against them and overcame them. And not only did they fail, but you must remember what sort of means they were constrained to employ. There was nothing great or splendid in what they did; they produced no striking events, they did not put in motion powerful masses of men. They proceeded by dark and hidden courses; courses by no means calculated to strike the imagination, or to conciliate that public interest which always attaches itself to great things, whatever may be their principle and object. The party opposed to them, on the contrary, not only overcame, but overcame signally; did great things and by great means; overspread Europe with great men; changed, in open day, the condition and form of states. Everything, in short, was against the Jesuits, both fortune and appearances; reason, which desires success—and imagination, which requires *éclat*—were alike disappointed by their fate. Still, however, they were undoubtedly possessed of grandeur; great ideas are attached to their name, their influence, and their history. The reason is, that they knew what they did; and what they wished to accomplish; that they were fully and clearly aware of the principles upon which they acted, and of the object which they had in view. They possessed grandeur of thought and of will; and it was this that saved them from the ridicule which attends constant reverses, and the use of paltry means. Wherever, on the contrary, the event has been greater than the design, wherever there is an appearance of ignorance of the first principles and ultimate results of an action, there has always remained a degree of incompleteness, inconsistency, and narrowness of view, which has placed the very victors in a state of rational or philosophical inferiority, the influence of which has sometimes been apparent in the course of events. This, I think, in the struggle between the old and the new order of things, in matters of religion, was the weak side of the Reformation, which often embarrassed its situation, and prevented it from defending itself so well as it had a right to do.

I might consider the religious revolutions of the sixteenth century under many other aspects. I have said nothing, and have nothing to say, respecting it as a matter of doctrine —respecting its effect on religions, properly so called, or respecting the relations of the human soul with God and an eternal futurity; but I might exhibit it in its various relations with social order, everywhere producing results of immense importance. For example, it introduced religion into the midst of the laity, into the world, so to speak, of believers. Till then, religion had been the exclusive domain of the ecclesiastical order. The clergy distributed the proceeds, but reserved to themselves the disposal of the capital, and almost the exclusive right even to speak of it. The Reformation again threw matters of religious belief into general circulation, and again opened to believers the field of faith into which they had not been permitted to enter. It had, at the same time, a further result; it banished, or nearly so, religion from politics, and restored the independence of the temporal power. At the same moment that religion returned into the possession of believers, it quitted the government of society. In the reformed countries, in spite of the diversities of ecclesiastical constitutions, even in England, whose constitution is most nearly akin to the old order of things, the spiritual power has no longer any serious pretensions to the government of the temporal power.

I might enumerate many other consequences of the Reformation, but I must limit myself to the above general views; and I am satisfied with having placed before you its principal feature—the emancipation of the human mind, and the abolition of absolute power in the spiritual order; an abolition which, though, undoubtedly not complete, is yet the greatest step which, down to our own times, has ever been made toward the attainment of that object.

Before concluding, I pray you to remark, what a striking resemblance of destiny there is to be found, in the history of modern Europe, between civil and religious society, in the revolutions they have had to undergo.

Christian society, as we have seen when I spoke of the Church, was, at first, a state of society perfectly free, formed entirely in the name of a common belief, without institutions or government, properly so called; regulated, solely, by moral and variable powers, according to the exigencies of the moment. Civil society began, in like manner, in Europe, partly, at least, by bands of barbarians; it was a state of society perfectly free, in which every one remained, because he wished to do so, without laws or powers created by institutions. In emerging from that state which was inconsistent with any great social development, religious society placed itself under a government essentially aristocratic; its governors were the clergy, the bishops, the councils, the ecclesiastical aristocracy. A fact of the same kind took place in civil society when it emerged from barbarism; it was, in like manner, the aristocracy, the feudalism of the laity, which laid hold of the power of government. Religious society quitted the aristocratic form of government to assume that of pure monarchy; this was the rationale of the triumph of the Court of Rome over the councils and the ecclesiastical aristocracy of Europe. The same revolution was accomplished in civil society; it was, in like manner, by the destruction of the aristocratic power, that monarchy prevailed, and took possession of the European world. In the sixteenth century, in the heart of religious society, an insurrection broke out against the system of pure ecclesiastical monarchy, against absolute power in the spiritual order. This revolution produced, sanctioned, and established freedom of inquiry in Europe. In our own time we have witnessed a similar event in civil society. Absolute temporal power, in like manner, was attacked and overcome. You see, then, that the two orders of society have undergone the same vicissitudes and revolutions; only religious society has always been the foremost in this career.

We are now in possession of one of the greatest facts in the history of modern society—freedom of inquiry, the liberty of the human mind. We see, at the same time, the almost universal prevalence of political centralization. In my next lecture I shall consider the revolution in England; the event in which freedom of inquiry and a pure monarchy, both results of the progress of civilization, came, for the first time, into collision.

LECTURE XIII.

THE ENGLISH REVOLUTION.

We have seen, that during the course of the sixteenth century, all the elements, all the facts, of ancient European society had merged in two essential facts, the right of free examination, and centralization of power; one prevailing in religious society, the other in civil society. The emancipation of the human mind and absolute monarchy triumphed at the same moment over Europe in general.

It could hardly be conceived that a struggle between these two facts—the characters of which appear so contradictory—would not, at some time, break out; for while one was the defeat of absolute power in the spiritual order, the other was the triumph of absolute power in the temporal order; one forced on the decline of the ancient ecclesiastical monarchy, the other was the consummation of the ruin of the ancient feudal and municipal liberty. Their simultaneous appearance was owing, as I have already observed, to the circumstance that the revolutions of the religious society followed more rapidly than those of the civil; one had arrived at the point in which the freedom of individual thought was secured, while the other still lingered on the spot where the concentration of all the powers in one general power took place. The coincidence of these two facts, so far from being the consequence of their similitude did, not even prevent their contradiction. They were both advances in the march of civilization, but they were advances connected with different situations; advances of a different moral date, if I may be allowed the expression, although coincident in time. From their position it seemed inevitable that they must clash and combat before a reconciliation could be effected between them.

The first shock between them took place in England. The struggle of the right of free inquiry, the fruit of the Reformation, against the entire suppression of political liberty, the object aimed at by pure monarchy—the attempt to abolish absolute power in the temporal order, as had already been done in the spiritual order—this is the true sense of the English revolution; this is the part it took in the work of civilization.

But how, it may be asked, came it to pass, that this struggle took place in England sooner than anywhere else? How happened it that the revolutions of a political character coincided here with those of a moral character sooner than they did on the Continent?

In England, the royal power had undergone the same vicissitudes as it had on the Continent. Under the Tudors it had reached a degree of concentraton and vigor which it had never attained to before. I do not mean to say that the practical despotism of the Tudors was more violent and vexatious than that of their predecessors; there were quite as many, perhaps more, tyrannical proceedings, vexations, and acts of injustice, under the Plantagenets, as under the Tudors. Perhaps, too, at this very period the very government of pure monarchy was more severe and arbitrary on the Continent than in England. The new fact under the Tudors was, that absolute power became systematic; royalty laid claim to a primitive, independent sovereignty; it held a language which it had never held before. The theocratic claims of Henry VIII., Elizabeth, James I., and Charles I., are very different from those of Edward I. and III., although, in point of fact, the power of the two latter monarchs was nowise less arbitrary or extensive. I repeat, then, it was the principle, the rational system of monarchy, which changed in England, in the sixteenth century, rather than its practical power; royalty now declared itself absolute and superior to all laws, even to those which it declared itself willing to respect.

There is another point to be considered; the religious revolution had not been accomplished in England in the same way as on the Continent; it was here the work of the monarchs themselves. It must not be supposed that the seeds had not been sown, or that even attempts had not been made at a popular reform, or that one would not probably have soon broken out. But Henry VIII. took the lead; power became revolutionary; and hence it happened, at least in its origin, that, as a redress of ecclesiastical abuses, as an emancipation of the human mind, the reform in England was much less complete than upon the Continent. It was made, as might naturally be expected, in accordance with the interests of its authors. The king and the episcopacy, which was here continued, divided between themselves the riches and the power, of which they despoiled their predecessors, the popes. The effect of this was soon felt. The Reformation, people cried out, had been closed while the greater part of the abuses which had induced them to desire it, were still continued.

The Reformation reappeared under a more popular form; it made the same demands of the bishops that had already been made of the Holy See; it accused them of being so many popes. As often as the general fate of the religious revolution was compromised; whenever a struggle against the ancient Church took place, the various portions of the Reformation party rallied together, and made common cause against the common enemy; but this danger over, the struggle again broke out among themselves; the popular reform again attacked the aristocracy and royal reform, denounced its abuses, complained of its tyranny, called upon it to make good its promises, and not to usurp itself the power which it had just dethroned.

Much about the same time a movement for liberty took place in civil society; a desire before unknown, or at least but weakly expressed, was now felt for political freedom. In the course of the sixteenth century, the commercial prosperity of England had increased with amazing rapidity, while during the same time, much territorial wealth, much baronial property, had changed hands. The numerous divisions of landed property, which took place during the sixteenth century, in consequence of the ruin of the feudal nobility, and from various other causes which I cannot now stop to enumerate, form a fact which has not been sufficiently noticed. A variety of documents prove how greatly the number of landed properties increased; the estates going generally into the hands of the gentry, composed of the lesser nobility, and persons who had acquired property by trade. The high nobility, the House of Lords, did not, at the beginning of the seventeenth century, nearly equal, in riches, the House of Commons. There had taken place, then, at the same time in England, a great increase in wealth among the industrious classes, and a great change in landed property. While these two facts were being accomplished, there happened a third; a new march of mind.

The reign of Queen Elizabeth must be regarded as a period of great literary and philosophical activity in England, a period remarkable for bold and pregnant thought; the Puritans followed, without hesitation, all the consequences of a narrow, but powerful creed; other intellects, with less morality, but more freedom and boldness, alike regardless of principle or system, seized with avidity upon every idea, which seemed to promise some gratification to their curiosity, some food for their mental ardor. And it may be regarded as a maxim, that wherever the progress of intelligence is a true pleasure, a desire for liberty is soon felt, nor is it long in passing from the public mind to the state.

A feeling of the same kind, a sort of creeping desire for political liberty, almost manifested itself in some of the countries on the Continent in which the Reformation had made some way; but these countries, being without the means of success, made no progress; they knew not how to make their desire felt; they could find no support for it either in institutions, or in the habits and usages of the people; hence this desire remained vague, uncertain, and sought in vain for the means of satisfying its cravings. In England the case was widely different: the spirit of political liberty which showed itself here in the sixteenth century, as a sort of appendix to the Reformation, found both a firm support and the means of speaking and acting in the ancient institutions of the country, and indeed the whole frame-work of English society.

There is hardly any one who does not know the origin of the free institutions of England. How, in 1215, a coalition of the great barons wrested Magna Charta from John; but it is not quite so generally known, that this charter was renewed and confirmed, from time to time, by almost every king. It was confirmed upward of thirty times between the thirteenth and sixteenth centuries, besides which new statutes were passed to confirm and extend its enactments. Thus it lived, as it were, without gap or interval. In the meantime the House of Commons had been formed, and taken its place among the sovereign institutions of the country. Under the Plantagenets it had taken deep root and became firmly established; not that at this time it played any great part, or had even much influence in the government; it scarcely indeed interfered in this except when called upon to do so by the king, and then only with hesitation and regret; afraid rather of bringing itself into trouble and danger, than jealous of augmenting its power and authority But the case was different when it was called upon to defend private rights, the house or property of the citizens, or in short the rights and privileges of individuals; this duty the House of Commons performed with wonderful energy and perseverance, putting forward and establishing all those principles, which have become the basis of the English constitution. Under the Tudors the House of Commons, or rather the Parliament altogether, put on a new character. It no longer defended individual liberty so well as under the Plantagenets. Arbitrary detentions, and violations of private rights, which became much more frequent, were often passed in silence. But, as a counterbalance for this, the Parliament interfered to a much greater extent than formerly in the general affairs of government. Henry VIII., in order to change the religion of the country, and to regulate the succession, required some public support, some public instrument, and he had recourse to Parliament, and especially to the House of Commons, for this purpose. This, which under the Plantagenets had only been a means of resistance, a guarantee of private right, became now, under the Tudors, an instrument of government, of general policy; so that at the end of the sixteenth century, notwithstanding it had been the tool, and submitted to the will of nearly all sorts of tyrannies, its importance had greatly increased; the foundation of its power was laid, the foundation of that power upon which truly rests representative government.

In taking a view, then, of the free institutions of England at the end of the sixteenth century, we find them to consist: *first*, of maxims—of principles of liberty, which had been constantly acknowledged in written documents, and of which the legislation and country had never lost sight; *secondly*, of precedents, of examples of liberty; these, it is true, were mixed with a great number of precedents and examples of an opposite nature; still they were quite sufficient to maintain, to give a legal character to the claims of the friends of liberty, and to support them in their struggle against arbitrary and tyrannical government; *thirdly*, particular and local institutions, pregnant with the seeds of liberty, the jury, the right of holding public meetings, of bearing arms, to which must be added the independence of municipal administration and jurisdiction; *fourthly and finally*, the Parliament and its authority became more necessary now than ever to the monarchs, as these having dilapidated the greater part of their independent revenues, crown domains, feudal rights, etc., could not support even the expenses of their households, without having recourse to a vote of Parliament.

The political state of England then was very different to that of the Continent; notwithstanding the tyranny of the Tudors, notwithstanding the systematic triumph of absolute monarchy, there still remained here a firm support for the new spirit of liberty, a sure means by which it could act.

At this epoch, two national wants were felt in England: on one hand, a want of religious liberty and of a continuation of the reformation already begun; on the other, a want of political liberty, which seemed arrested by the absolute monarchy now establishing its power. These two parties formed an alliance: the party which wished to carry forward religious reform, invoked political liberty to the aid of its faith and conscience against the bishops and the crown. The friends of political liberty, in like manner, sought the aid of the friends of popular religious reform. The two parties joined their forces to struggle against absolute power, both spiritual and political, now concentrated in the hands of the king. Such is the origin and signification of the English revolution.

It appears, then, to have been essentially devoted to the defence or conquest of liberty. For the religious party it was a means, for the political party it was an end; but the object of both was still liberty, and they were determined to pursue it in common. Properly speaking, there had been no true quarrel between the Episcopal and Puritan party; the struggle was not about doctrines, about matters of faith, properly so called. I do not mean that these were not very positive, very important, and differences of great consequence between them; but this was not the main affair. What the Puritan party wished to obtain from the Episcopal was practical liberty; this was the object for which it struggled. It must, however, be admitted that there did exist at the same time, a religious party which had a system to found; a set of doctrines, a form of discipline, an ecclesiastic constitution, which it wished to establish—I mean the Presbyterians; but though it did its best, it had not the power to obtain its object. Acting upon the defensive, oppressed by the bishops, unable to take a step without the sanction of the political reformers, its necessary allies and chieftains, liberty naturally became its predominant interest; this was the general interest, the common desire of all the parties which concurred in the movement, however different in other respects might be their views. Taking these matters then altogether, we must come to the conclusion, that the English revolution was essentially political; it was accomplished in the midst of a religious people and a religious age; religious ideas and passions often became its instruments; but its primary intention and its definite object were decidedly political, a tendency to liberty, the destruction of all absolute power.

I shall now briefly run over the various phases of this revolution, and analyze it into the great parties that succeeded one another in its course. I shall afterward connect it with the general career of European civilization; I shall show its place and influence therein; and you will be satisfied, from the detail of facts as well as from its first aspect, that it was truly the first collision of free inquiry and pure monarchy, the first onset that took place in the struggle between these two great and opposite powers.

Three principal parties appeared upon the stage at this important crisis; three revolutions seem to have been contained within it, and to have successively appeared upon the scene In each party, in each revolution, two parties moved together in alliance, a political party and a religious party; the former took the lead, the second followed, but one could not go without the other, so that a double character seems to be imprinted upon it in all its changes.

The first party which appeared in the field, and under whose banners at the beginning marched all the others, was the high, pure-monarchy party, advocating legal reform. When the revolution began, when the long Parliament assembled in 1640, it was generally said, and sincerely believed by many, that a legal, a constitutional reform would suffice; that the ancient laws and practices of the country were sufficient to correct every abuse, to establish a system of government which would fully meet the wishes of the public.

This party highly blamed and earnestly desired to put a stop to illegal imposts, to arbitrary imprisonments—to all acts, indeed, contrary to the known law and usages of the country. But under these ideas, there lay hid, as it were, a belief in the divine right of the king, and in his absolute power. A secret instinct seemed to warn it that there was something false and dangerous in this notion; and on this account it appeared always desirous to avoid the subject. Forced, however, at last to speak out, it acknowledged the divine right of kings, and admitted that they possessed a power superior to all human origin, to all human control; and as such they defended it in time of need. Still, however, they believed that this sovereignty, though absolute in principle, was bound to exercise its authority according to certain rules and forms; that it could not go beyond certain limits; and that these rules, these forms, and these limits were sufficiently established and guarantied in Magna Charta, in the confirmative statues, in the ancient laws and usages of the country. Such was the political creed of this party. In religious matters, it believed that the episcopacy had greatly encroached; that the bishops possessed far too much political power; that their jurisdiction was far too extensive, that it required to be restrained, and its proceedings jealously watched. Still it held firmly to episcopacy, not merely as an ecclesiastical institution, not merely as a form of church government, but as a necessary support of the royal prerogative, and as a means of defending and maintaining the supremacy of the king in matters of religion. The absolute power of the king over the body politic, exercised according to the forms and within the limits legally acknowledged; the supremacy of the king as head of the Church, applied and sustained by the episcopacy, was the twofold system of the legal reform party. We may enumerate as its chiefs, Lord Clarendon, Colepepper, Capel, and, though a more ardent friend of public liberty, Lord Falkland; and into their ranks were enlisted nearly all the nobility and gentry not servilely devoted to the court.

Behind this party advanced a second, which I shall call the political-revolutionary party; it differed from the foregoing, inasmuch as it did not believe the ancient guarantees, the ancient legal barriers sufficient to secure the rights and liberties of the people. It saw that a great change, a genuine revolution was wanting, not only in the forms, but in the spirit and essence of the government; that it was necessary to deprive the king and his council of the unlimited power which they possessed, and to place the preponderance in the House of Commons; so that the government should, in fact, be in the hands of this assembly and its leaders. This party made no such open and systematic profession of its principles and intentions as I have done; but this was the real character of its opinions, and of its political tendencies. Instead of acknowledging the absolute sovereignty of the king, it contended for the sovereignty of the House of Commons as the representatives of the people. Under this principle was hid that of the sovereignty of the people; a notion which the party was as far from considering in its full extent, as it was from desiring the consequences to which it might ultimately lead, but which they nevertheless admitted when it presented itself to them in the form of the sovereignty of the House of Commons.

The religious party most closely allied to this political-revolutionary one was that of the Presbyterians. This sect wished to operate much the same revolution in the Church as their allies were endeavoring to effect in the state. They desired to erect a system of church government emanating from the people, and composed of a series of assemblies dove-tailed, as it were, into each other; and thus to give to their national assembly the same authority in ecclesiastical matters that their allies wished to give in political to the House of Commons; only that the revolution contemplated by the Presbyterians was more complete and daring than the other, forasmuch as it aimed at changing the form as well as the principles of the government of the Church; while the views of the political party went no farther than to place the influence, the preponderance, in the body of the people, without meditating any great alteration in the form of their institutions.

Hence the leaders of this political party were not all favorable to the Presbyterian organization of the Church. Hampden and Hollis, as well as some others, it appears, would have given the preference to a moderate episcopacy, confined strictly to ecclesiastical functions, with a greater extent of liberty of conscience. They were obliged, however, to give way, as they could do nothing without the assistance of their fanatical allies.

The third party, going much beyond these two, declared that a change was required not only in the form, but also in the foundation of the government; that its constitution was radcially vicious and bad. This party paid no respect to the past life of England; it renounced her institutions, it swept away all national remembrances, it threw down the whole fabric of English government, that it might build up another founded on pure theory, or at least one that existed only in its own fancy. It aimed not merely at a revolution in the government, but at a complete revolution of the whole social system. The party of which I have just spoken, the political-revolutionary party, proposed to make a great change in the relations in which the Parliament stood with the crown; it wished to extend the power of the two houses, particularly of the commons, by giving to it the nomination of the great officers of state, and the supreme direction of affairs in general; but its notions of reform scarcely went beyond this. It had no idea, for example, of changing the electoral system, the judicial system, the administrative and municipal systems of the country. The republican party contemplated all these changes, dwelt upon their necessity, wished, in a word, to reform not only the public administration, but the relations of society, and the distribution of private rights.

Like the two preceding, this party was composed of a religious sect, and a political sect. Its political portion were the genuine republicans, the theorists, Ludlow, Harrington, Milton, etc. To these may be added the republicans of circumstance, of interest, such as the principal officers of the army, Ireton, Cromwell, Lambert, etc., who were more or less sincere at the begining of their career, but were soon controlled and guided by personal motives and the force of circumstances. Under the banners of this party marched the religious republcians, all those religious sects which would acknowledge no power as legitimate but that of Jesus Christ, and who, awaiting his second coming, desired only the government of his elect. Finally, in the train of this party followed a mixed assemblage of subordinate freethinkers, fanatics, and revellers, some hoping for license, some for an equal distribution of property, and others for universal suffrage.

In 1653, after twelve years of struggle, all these parties had successively appeared and failed; they appear at least to have thought so, and the public was sure of it. The legal reform party quickly disappeared; it saw the old constitution and laws insulted, trampled under foot, and innovations forcing their way on every side. The political-revolutionary party saw the destruction of parliamentary forms in the new use which it was proposed to make them—it had seen the House of Commons reduced, by the successive expulsions of royalists and Presbyterians, to a few members, despised, detested by the public, and incapable of governing. The republican party appeared to have succeeded better; it seemed to be left master of the field and of power; the

House of Commons consisted of but fifty or sixty members, all republicans. They might fancy themselves, and call themselves, the rulers of the country; but the country rejected their government; they were nowhere obeyed; they had no power either over the army or the nation. No social bond, no social security was now left; justice was no longer administered, or if it was, it was controlled by passion, chance, or party. Not only was there no security in the relations of private life, but the highways were covered with robbers and companies of brigands. Anarchy in every part of the civil, as well as of the moral world, prevailed; and neither the House of Commons, nor the republican Council of State, had the power to restrain it.

Thus, the three great parties which had brought about the revolution, and which in their turn had been called upon to conduct it—had been called upon to govern the country according to their principles and their will—had all signally failed. They could do nothing—they could settle nothing. "Now it was," says Bossuet, "that a man was found who left nothing to fortune, which he could gain by counsel and foresight;" a remark which has no foundation whatever in truth, and which every part of history contradicts. No man ever left more to fortune than Cromwell. No one ever risked more—no one ever pushed forward more rashly, without design, without an aim, yet determined to go as far as fate would carry him. Unbounded ambition, and admirable tact for drawing from every day, from every circumstance, some new progress—the art of profiting by fortune without seeming ever to possess the desire to constrain it, formed the character of Cromwell. In one particular his career was singular, and differs from that of every individual with whom we are apt to compare him: he adapted himself to all the various changes, numerous as they were, as well as to the state of things they led to, of the revolution. He appears a prominent character in every scene, from the rise of the curtain to the close of the piece. He was now the instigator of the insurrection—now the abetter of anarchy—now the most fiery of the revolutionists—now the restorer of order and social re-organization; thus playing himself all the principal parts which, in the common run of revolutions, are usually distributed among the greatest actors. He was not a Mirabeau, for he failed in eloquence, and, though very active, he made no great figure in the first years of the long Parliament. But he was successively Danton and

Bonaparte. Cromwell did more than any one to overthrow authority; he raised it up again, because there was no other than he that could take it and manage it. The country required a ruler; all others failed, and he succeeded. This was his title. Once master of the government, Cromwell, whose boundless ambition had exerted itself so vigorously, who had so constantly pushed fortune before him, and seemed determined never to stop in his career, displayed a good sense, a prudence, a knowledge of how much was possible, which overruled his most violent passions. There can be no doubt of his extreme fondness for absolute power, nor of his desire to place the crown upon his own head and keep it in his family. He saw the peril of this latter design and renounced it; and though, in fact, he did exercise absolute authority, he saw very well that the spirit of the times would not bear it; that the revolution which he had helped to bring about, which he had followed through all its phases, had been directed against despotism, and that the uncontrollable will of England was to be governed by a parliament and parliamentary forms. He endeavored, therefore, despot as he was, by taste and by deeds, to govern by a parliament. For this purpose he had recourse to all the various parties; he tried to form a parliament from the religious enthusiasts, from the republicans, from the Presbyterians, and from the officers of the army. He tried every means to obtain a parliament able and willing to take part with him in the government; but he tired in vain; every party, the moment it was seated in St. Stephen's, endeavored to wrest from him the authority which he exercised, and to rule in its turn. I do not mean to deny that his personal interest, the gratification of his darling ambition was his first care; but it is no less certain that if he had abdicated his authority one day, he would have been obliged to resume it the next. Puritans or royalists, republicans or officers, there was no one but Cromwell who was in a state at this time to govern with anything like order or justice. The experiment had been made. It seemed absurd to think of leaving to parliaments, that is to say, to the faction sitting in parliament, a government which it could not maintain. Such was the extraordinary situation of Cromwell: he governed by a system which he knew very well was foreign and hateful to the country, he exercised an authority which was acknowledged necessary by all, but which was acceptable to none. No party looked upon his domination as a definitive government. Royalists, Presbyterians, republicans, even the army itself, which appears to have been the party most devoted to Cromwell, all looked upon his rule as transitory. He had no hold upon the affections of the people; he was more than a *pis-aller*, a last resort, a temporary necessity. The protector, the absolute master of England, was obliged all his life to have recourse to force to preserve his power; no party could govern so well as he, but no party liked to see the government in his hands; he was repeatedly attacked by them all at once.

Upon Cromwell's death, there was no party in a situation to seize upon the government except the republicans; they did seize upon it, but with no better success than before. This happened from no lack of confidence, at least, in the enthusiasts of the party. A spirited and talented tract, published at this juncture by Milton, is entitled " A Ready and Easy Way to Establish a Free Commonwealth." You may judge of the blindness of these men, who soon fell into a state which showed that it was quite as impossible for them to carry on the government now as it had been before. Monk undertook the direction of that event which all England now seemed anxious for. The Restoration was accomplished.

The restoration of the Stuarts was an event generally pleasing to the nation. It brought back a government which still dwelt in its memory, which was founded upon its ancient traditions, while, at the same time, it had some of the advantages of a new government, in that it had not recently been tried, in that its faults and its power had not lately been felt. The ancient monarchy was the only system of government which had not been decried, within the last twenty years, for its abuses and want of capacity in the administration of the affairs of the kingdom. From these two causes the restoration was extremely popular; it was unopposed by any but the dregs of the most violent factions, while the public rallied round it with great sincerity. All parties in the country seemed now to believe that this offered the only chance left of a stable and legal government, and this was what, above all things, the nation now desired. This also was what the restoration seemed especially to promise; it took much pains to present itself under the aspect of legal government.

The first royalist party, indeed, to whom, upon the return of Charles the Second, the management of affairs was intrusted, was the legal party, represented by its able leader, the Lord Chancellor Clarendon. From 1660 to 1677, Clarendon was prime minister, and had the chief direction of affairs: he and his friends brought back with them their ancient principles of government, the absolute sovereignty of the king, kept within legal bounds, limited by the House of Commons as regards taxation, by the public tribunals, in matters of private right, or relating to individual liberty—possessing, nevertheless, in point of government, properly so called, an almost complete independence and the most decided preponderance, to the exclusion or even in opposition to the votes of the majorities of the two houses, but particularly to that of the House of Commons. In other matters there was not much to complain of: a tolerable degree of respect was paid to legal order; there was a tolerable degree of solicitude for the national interests; a sufficiently noble sentiment of national dignity was preserved, and a color of morality that was grave and honorable. Such was the character of Clarendon's administration, during the seven years the government was commited to his charge.

But the fundamental principles upon which this administration was based—the absolute sovereignty of the king, and a government beyond the preponderating control of parliament—were now become old and powerless. Notwithstanding the temporary reaction which took place at the first burst of the restoration, twenty years of parliamentary rule against royalty had destroyed them for ever. A new party soon showed itself among the royalists; libertines, profligates, wretches who, imbued with the free opinions of the times, and seeing that power was with the commons—caring themselves but little about legal order, or the absolute power of the king—were only anxious for success, and to discover the means of influence and power in whatever quarter they were likely to be found. These formed a party, and allying themselves with the national, discontented party, Clarendon was discarded.

A new system of government now took place under that portion of the royalists I have just described; profligates and libertines formed the administration of the Cabal, and several others which followed it. What was their character? Without inquietude respecting principles, laws, or rights, or care for justice or truth, they sought the means of success upon every occasion, whatever these means might be; if success depended on the influence of the commons, the commons were everything; if it was necessary to cajole the commons, the commons were cajoled without scruple, even though they had to apologize to them the next day. At one moment they attempted corruption, at another they flattered the national wishes; no regard was shown for the general interests of the country, for its dignity or its honor; in a word, it was a government profoundly selfish and immoral, totally unacquainted with all theory, principle, or public object: but, withal, in the practical management of affairs, showing considerable intelligence and liberality. Such was the character of the Cabal ministry, of Earl Danby's, and of the English government from 1667 to 1679. Yet notwithstanding its immorality, notwithstanding its disdain of all principle, and of the true interests of the country, this government was not so unpopular, not so odious to the nation as that of Clarendon; and this simply because it adapted itself better to the times, better understood the sentiments of the people, even while it derided them. It was neither foreign nor antiquated, like that of Clarendon; and though infinitely more dangerous to the country, the people accommodated themselves better to it.

But this corruption, this servility, this contempt of public rights and public honor, were at last carried to such a pitch as to be no longer supportable. A general outcry was raised against this government of profligates. A patriotic party, supported by the nation, became gradually formed in the House of Commons, and the king was obliged to take the leaders of it into his council. Lord Essex, the son of him who had commanded the first parliamentary armies in the civil war, Lord Russel, and Lord Shaftesbury, who, without any of the virtues of the other two, was much their superior in political abilities, were now called to the management of affairs. The national party, to whom the direction of the government was now committed proved itself unequal to the task: it could not gain possession of the moral force of the country: it could neither manage the interests, the habits, nor the prejudices of the king, of the court, nor of any with whom it had to do. It inspired no party, either king or people, with any confidence in its energy or ability; and after holding power for a short time, this national ministry completely failed. The virtues of its leaders, their generous courage, the beauty of their death, have raised them to a distinguished niche in the temple of fame, and entitled them to honorable mention in the page of history; but their political capacities in no way corresponded to their virtues: they could not wield power, though they could withstand its corrupting influence, nor could they achieve a triumph for that glorious cause, for which they could so nobly die!

The failure of this attempt left the English restoration in rather an awkward plight; it had, like the English revolution, in a manner tried all parties without success. The legal ministry, the corrupt ministry, the national ministry, having all failed, the country court were nearly in the same situation as that which England had been in before, at the close of the revolutionary troubles in 1653. Recourse was had to the same expedient: what Cromwell had turned to the profit of the revolution, Charles II., now turned to the profit of the crown; he entered upon a career of asbolute power.

James II. succeeded his brother; and another question now became mixed up with that of despotism: the question of religion. James II. wished to achieve, at the same time, a triumph for popery and for absolute power: now again, as at the commencement of the revolution, there was a religious struggle and a political struggle, and both were directed against the government. It has often been asked, what course affairs would have taken if William III. had not existed, and come over to put an end to the quarrel between James and the people. My firm belief is that the same event would have taken place. All England, except a very small party, was at this time arrayed against James; and it seems very certain, that, under some form or other, the revolution of 1688 must have been accomplished. But at this crisis, causes even superior to the internal state of England conduced to this event. It was European as well as English. It is at this point that the English revolution links itself, by facts, and independently of the influence of its example, to the general course of European civilization.

While the struggle which I have just been narrating took place in England, the struggle of absolute power against religious and civil liberty—a struggle of the same kind, however different the actors, the forms, and the theatre, took place upon the continent—a struggle which was at bottom the same, and carried on in the same cause. The pure monarchy of Louis XIV. attempted to become universal monarchy, at least it gave the world every reason to fear it; and, in fact, Europe did fear it. A league was formed in Europe between various political parties to resist this attempt, and the chief of this league was the chief of the party that struggled for the civil and religious liberty of Europe—William, Prince of Orange. The Protestant republic of Holland, with William at its head, had made a stand against pure monarchy, represented and conducted by Louis XIV. The fight here was not for civil and religious liberty in the interior of states, but for the interior independence of the states themselves. Louis XIV. and his adversaries never thought of debating the questions which were debated so fiercely in England. This struggle was not one of parties, but of states; it was carried on, not by political outbreaks and revolutions, but by war and negotiation; still, at bottom, the same principle was the subject of contention.

It happened, then, that the strife between absolute power and liberty, which James II. renewed in England, broke out at the very moment that this general struggle was going on in Europe between Louis XIV. and the Prince of Orange, the representatives of these two great systems, as well in the affairs which took place on the Thames as on the Scheldt. The league against Louis was so powerful that many sovereigns entered into it, either publicly, or in an underhand, though very effective manner, who were rather opposed than not to the interests of civil and religious liberty. The Emperor of Germany and Innocent XI. both supported William against France. And William crossed the channel to England less to serve the internal interests of the country, than to draw it entirely into the struggle against Louis. He laid hold of this kingdom as a new force which he wanted, but of which his adversary had had the disposal, up to this time, against him. So long as Charles II. and James II. reigned, England belonged to Louis XIV.; he had the disposal of it, and had kept it employed against Holland. England then was snatched from the side of absolute and universal monarchy, to become the most powerful support and instrument of civil and religious liberty. This is the view which must be taken, as regards European civilization, of the revolution of 1688; it is this which gives it a place in the assemblage of European events, independently of the influence of its example, and of the vast effect which it had upon the minds and opinions of men in the following century.

Thus, I think, I have rendered it clear, that the true sense, the essential character of this revolution is, as I said at the outset of this lecture, an attempt to abolish absolute power in the temporal order, as had already been done in the spiritual. This fact appears in all the phases of the revolution, from its first outbreak to the restoration, and again in the crisis of 1688: and this not only as regards its interior progress, but in its relations with Europe in general.

It now only remains for us to study the same great event, the struggle of free inquiry and pure monarchy, upon the Continent, or at least the causes and preparation of this event. This will be the object of the next and final lecture.

LECTURE XIV.

THE FRENCH REVOLUTION.

I ENDEAVORED, at our last meeting, to ascertain the true character and political object of the English revolution. We have seen that it was the first collision of the two great facts to which, in the course of the sixteenth century, all the civilization of primitive Europe tended—monarchy on the one hand, and free inquiry on the other. These two powers came to blows, if I may use the expression, for the first time in England. It has been attempted, from this circumstance, to deduce a radical difference between the social state of England and that of the Continent; it has been contended, that no comparison could be made between countries so differently situated; and it has been affirmed, that the English people had lived in a sort of moral separation from the rest of Europe, analogous to its physical insulation.

It is true that between the civilization of England, and that of the Continental states, there has been a material difference which it is important that we should rightly understand. You have already had a glimpse of it in the course of these lectures. The development of the different principles, the different elements of society, took place, in some measure, at the same time, at least much more simultaneously than upon the Continent. When I endeavored to determine the complexion of European civilization as compared with the civilization of ancient and Asiatic nations, I showed that the former was varied, rich, and complex, and that it had never fallen under the influence of any exclusive principle; that, in it, the different elements of the social state had combined, contended with, and modified each other, and had continually been obliged to come to an accommodation, and to subsist together. This fact, which forms the general character of European civilization, has in an especial manner been that of the civilization of England; it is in that country that it has appeared most evidently and uninterruptedly; it is there that the civil and religious orders, aristocracy, democracy, monarchy, local and central institutions, moral and political development, have proceeded and grown up together, if not with equal rapidity at least but at a little distance from each other. Under the reign of the Tudors, for example, in the midst of the most remarkable progress of pure monarchy, we have seen the democratic principle, the popular power, make its way and gain strength almost at the same time. The revolution of the seventeenth century broke out; it was at the same time religious and political. The feudal aristocracy appeared in it in a very enfeebled state, and with all the symptoms of decay; it was, however, still in a condition, to preserve its place in this revolution, and to have some share in its results. The same thing has been the case in the whole course of English history; no ancient element has ever entirely perished, nor any new element gained a total ascendency; no particular principle has ever obtained an exclusive influence. There has always been a simultaneous development of the different forces, and a sort of negotiation or compromise between their pretensions and interests.

On the Continent the march of civilization had been less complex and complete. The different elements of society, the civil and religious orders, monarchy, aristocracy, democracy, have developed themselves, not together, and abreast, as it were, but successively. Every principle, every system, has in some measure had its turn. One age, for example, has belonged, I shall not say exclusively, but with a decided predominance, to the feudal aristocracy; another to the principle of monarchy; another to the principle of democracy. Compare the middle ages in France, with the middle ages in England; the eleventh, twelfth, and thirteenth centuries of our history with the corresponding centuries on the other side of the channel; you will find in France, at that epoch, feudalism in a state of almost absolute sovereignty, while monarchy and the democratic principle scarcely had an existence. But turn to England, and you will find, that although the feudal aristocracy greatly predominated, that monarchy and democracy possessed, at the same time, strength and importance. Monarchy triumphed in England under Elizabeth, as in France under Louis XIV.; but what precautions it was constrained to take! how many restrictions, sometimes aristocratic, sometimes democratic, it was obliged to submit to! In England every system, every principle, has had its time of strength and success; but never so completely and exclusively as on the Continent: the conqueror has always been constrained to tolerate the presence of his rivals, and to leave them a certain share of influence.

To this difference in the march of these two civilizations there are attached advantages and inconveniences which are apparent in the history of the two countries. There is no doubt, for example, that the simultaneous development of the different social elements has greatly contributed to make England arrive more quickly than any of the Continental states, at the end and aim of all society, that is to say, the establishment of a government at once regular and free. It is the very nature of a government to respect all the interests, all the powers of the state, to conciliate them and make them live and prosper in common: now such was, beforehand, and by the concurrence of a multitude of causes, the despotism and mutual relation of the different elements of English society; and, therefore, a general and somewhat regular government had the less difficulty in establishing itself. In like manner the essence of liberty is the simultaneous manifestation and action of every interest, every kind of right, every force, every social element. England, therefore, had made a nearer approach to liberty than most other states. From the same causes, national good sense and intelligence of public affairs must have formed themselves more quickly than elsewhere; political good sense consists in undertaking and appreciating every fact, and in assigning to each its proper part; in England it has been a necessary consequence of the state of society a natural result of the course of civilization.

In the states of the Continent, on the contrary, every system, every principle, having had its turn, and having had a more complete and exclusive ascendency, the development took place on a larger scale, and with more striking circumstances. Monarchy and feudal aristocracy, for example, appeared on the Continental stage with more boldness, extent, and freedom. Every political experiment, so to speak, was broader and more complete. The result was, that political ideas—I speak of general ideas, and not of good sense applied to the conduct of affairs—that political ideas and doctrines took a greater elevation, and displayed themselves with much greater vigor. Every system having, in some sort, presented itself singly, and having remained a long time on the stage, people could contemplate it in its general aspect, ascend to its first principles, pursue it into its remotest consequences, and lay bare its entire theory. Whoever observes with some degree of attention the genius of the English nation, will be struck with a double fact; on the one hand, its steady good sense and practical ability; on the other, its want of general ideas, and of elevation of thought upon theoretical questions. Whether we open an English work on history, jurisprudence, or any other subject, we rarely find the great and fundamental reason of things. In every subject, and especially in the political sciences, pure philosophical doctrines—science properly so called—have prospered much more on the Continent, than in England; their flights, at least, have been bolder and more vigorous. Indeed, it cannot be doubted that the different character of the development of civilization in the two countries has greatly contributed to this result.

At all events, whatever may be thought of the inconveniences or advantages which have been produced by this difference, it is a real and incontestable fact, and that which most essentially distinguishes England from the Continent. But, though the different principles, the different social elements, have developed themselves more simultaneously there, and more successively in France, it does not follow that, at bottom, the road and the goal have not been the same. Considered generally, the Continent and England have gone through the same great phases of civilization; events have followed the same course; similar causes have led to similar effects. You may have convinced yourselves of this by the view I have given you of civilization down to the sixteenth century; you will remark it no less in studying the seventeenth and eighteenth centuries. The development of free inquiry, and that of pure monarchy, almost simultaneous in England, were accomplished on the Continent at pretty long intervals; but they were accomplished; and these two powers, after having successively exercised a decided predominance, came also into collision. The general march of society, then, on the whole, has been the same; and, though the differences are real, the resemblance is still greater. A rapid sketch of modern times will leave you no doubt on this subject.

The moment we cast our eyes on the history of Europe in the seventeenth and eighteenth centuries, we cannot fail to perceive that France marches at the head of European civilization. At the beginning of this course, I strongly affirmed this fact, and endeavored to point out its cause. We shall now find it more strikingly displayed than it has ever been before.

The principle of pure and absolute monarchy had predominated in Spain, under Charles V. and Philip II., before its development in France under Louis XIV. In like manner the principle of free inquiry had reigned in England in the seventeenth century, before its development in France in the eighteenth. Pure monarchy, however, did not go forth from Spain, nor free inquiry from England, to make the conquest of Europe. The two principles or systems remained, in some sort, confined within the countries in which they sprang up. They required to pass through France to extend their dominion; pure monarchy and liberty of inquiry were compelled to become French before they could become European. That communicative character of French civilization, that social genius of France, which has displayed itself at every period, was peculiarly conspicuous at the period which now engages our attention. I shall not dwell upon this fact; it has been expounded to you, with equal force of argument and brilliancy, in the lectures in which your attention has been directed to the influence of the literature and philosophy of France in the eighteenth century. You have seen how the philosophy of France had, in regard to liberty, more influence on Europe than the liberty of England. You have seen how French civilization showed itself much more active and contagious than that of any other country. I have no occasion, therefore, to dwell upon the details of this fact; I avail myself of it only in order to make it my ground for making France comprehend the picture of modern European civilization. There were, no doubt, between French civilization at this period, and that of the other states of Europe, differences in which I ought to lay great stress, if it was my attention at present to enter fully into this subject; but I must proceed so rapidly, that I am obliged to pass over whole nations, and whole ages, I think it better to confine your attention to the course of French civilization, as being an image, though an imperfect one, of the general course of things in Europe.

The influence of France in Europe, in the seventeenth and eighteenth centuries, appears under very different aspects. In the first of these centuries, it was the French government which acted upon Europe, and took the lead in the march of general civilization. In the second, it was no longer to the French government, but to the French society, to France herself, that the preponderance belonged. It was at first Louis XIV. and his court, and then France herself, and her public opinion, that attracted the attention, and swayed the minds of the rest of Europe. There were, in the seventeenth century, nations, who, as such, made a more prominent appearance on the stage, and took a greater share in the course of events, than the French nation. Thus, during the thirty years' war, the German nation, and the revolution of England, the English nation played, within their respective spheres, a much greater part than the French nation, at that period, played within theirs. In the eighteenth century, in like manner, there were stronger, more respected, and more formidable governments than that of France. There is no doubt that Frederick II. and Maria Theresa had more activity and weight in Europe than Louis XV. Still, at both of these periods, France was at the head of European civilization, first through her government, and afterward through herself; at one time through the political action of her rulers, at another through her own intellectual development To understand thoroughly the predominant influence on the course of civilization in France, and consequently in Europe, we must therefore study, in the seventeenth century, the French government, and in the eighteenth, the French nation. We must change our ground and our objects of view, according as time changes the scene and the actors.

Whenever the government of Louis XIV. is spoken of, whenever we attempt to appreciate the causes of his power and influence in Europe, we have little to consider beyond his splendor, his conquests, his magnificence, and the literary glory of his time. We must resort to exterior causes in order to account for the preponderance of the French government in Europe.

But this preponderance, in my opinion, was derived from causes more deeply seated, from motives of a more serious kind. We must not believe that it was entirely by means of victories, festivals, or even master-pieces of genius, that Louis XIV. and his government played, at that period, the part which no one can deny them.

Many of you may remember, and all of you have heard of the effect which, twenty-nine years ago, was produced by the consular government in France, and the state in which it found our country. Abroad, foreign invasion impending, and continual disasters in our armies; at home, the elements of government and society in a state of dissolution; no revenues, no public order; in short, a people beaten, humbled, and disorganized—such was France at the accession of the consular government. Who is there that does not remember the prodigious and successful activity of that government, an activity which, in a short time, secured the independence of our territory, revived our national honor, re-organized the administration of government, re-modeled our legislation, in short, gave society, as it were, a new life under the hand of power?

Well—the government of Louis XIV., when it began, did something of the same kind for France; with great differences of times, of proceedings and of forms, it prosecuted and attained very nearly the same results.

Remember the state into which France had fallen after the government of Cardinal Richelieu, and during the minority of Louis XIV.: the Spanish armies always on the frontiers, and sometimes in the interior; continual danger of invasion; internal dissensions carried to extremity, civil war, the government weak, and decried both at home and abroad. There never was a more miserable policy, more despised in Europe, or more powerless in France, than that of Cardinal Mazarin. In a word, society was in a state, less violent perhaps, but very analogous to ours before the 18th of Brumaire. It was from that state that the government of Louis XIV. delivered France. His earliest victories had the effect of the victory of Marengo; they secured the French territory and revived the national honor. I am going to consider this government under its various aspects, in its wars, its foreign relations, its administration, and its legislation; and you will see, I believe, that the comparison which I speak of, and to which I do not wish to attach a puerile importance (for I care very little about historical comparisons), you will see, I say, that this comparison has a real foundation, and that I am fully justified in making it.

I shall first speak of the wars of Louis XIV. European wars were originally (as you know, and as I have several times had occasion to remind you) great popular movements; impelled by want, by some fancy, or any other cause, whole populations, sometimes numerous, sometimes consisting of mere bands, passed from one territory to another. This was the general character of European wars, till after the crusades, at the end of the thirteenth century.

After this another kind of war arose, but almost equally different from the wars of modern times: these were distant wars, undertaken, not by nations, but by their governing powers, who went, at the head of their armies, to seek, at a distance, states and adventures. They quitted their country, abandoned their own territory. and penetrated, some into Germany, others into Italy, and others into Africa, with no other motive save their individual fancy. Almost all the wars of the fifteenth, and even a part of the sixteenth century, are of this character. What interest—and I do not speak of a legitimate interest—but what motive had France for wishing that Charles VIII. should possess the kingdom of Naples? It was evidently a war dictated by no political considerations; the king thought he had personal claims on the kingdom of Naples; and, for this personal object, to satisfy his own personal desire, he undertook the conquest of a distant country, which was by no means adapted to the territorial conveniences of his kingdom, but which, on the contrary, only endangered his power abroad and his repose at home. Such, again, was the case with regard to the expedition of Charles V. into Africa. The last war of this kind was the expedition of Charles XII. against Russia.

The wars of Louis XIV. were not of this description; they were the wars of a regular government—a government fixed in the centre of its dominions, endeavoring to extend its conquests around, to increase or consolidate its territory; in short, they were political wars. They may have been just or unjust, they may have cost France too dear;—they may be objected to on many grounds—on the score of morality or excess; but, in fact, they were of a much more rational character than the wars which preceded them; they were no longer fanciful adventures; they were dictated by serious motives; their objects were to reach some natural boundary, some population which spoke the same language, and might be annexed to the kingdom, some point of defence against a neighboring power. Personal ambition, no doubt, had a share in them; but examine the wars of Louis XIV., one after the other, especially those of the early part of his reign, and you will find that their motives were really political; you will see that they were conceived with a view to the power and safety of France.

This fact has been proved by results. France, at the present day, in many respects, is what the wars of Louis XIV. made her. The provinces which he conquered, Franche-Comte, Flanders, and Alsace, have remained incorporated with France. There are rational conquests as well as foolish ones; those of Louis XIV. were rational; his enterprises have not that unreasonable, capricious character, till then so general; their policy was able, if not always just and prudent.

If I pass from the wars of Louis XIV. to his relations with foreign states, to his diplomacy properly so called, I find an analogous result. I have already spoken of the origin of diplomacy at the end of the fifteenth century. I have endeavored to show how the mutual relations of governments and states, previously accidental, rare, and transient, had at that period become more regular and permanent, how they had assumed a character of great public interest; how, in short, at the end of the fifteenth and during the first half of the sixteenth century, diplomacy had begun to perform a part of immense importance in the course of events. Still, however, it was not till the seventeenth century that it became really systematic; before then, it had not brought about long alliances, great combinations, and especially combinations of a durable nature, directed by fixed principles, with a steady object, and with that spirit of consistency which forms the true character of established governments. During the course of the religious revolution, the foreign relations of states had been almost completely under the influence of religious interests; the Protestant and Catholic leagues had divided Europe between them. It was in the seventeenth century, under the influence of the government of Louis XIV., that diplomacy changed its character. On the one hand, it got rid of the exclusive influence of the religious principle; alliances and political combinations took place from other considerations. At the same time it became much more systematic and regular, and was always directed toward a certain object, according to permanent principles. The regular birth of the system of the balance of power in Europe, took place at this period. It was under the government of Louis XIV. that this system, with all the considerations attached to it, really took possession of the politics of Europe. When we inquire what was, on this subject, the general idea or ruling principle of the policy of Louis XIV., the following seems to be the result.

I have spoken of the great struggle which took place in Europe between the pure monarchy of Louis XIV., pretending to establish itself as the universal system of monarchy, and civil and religious liberty, and the independence of states, under the command of the Prince of Orange, William III. You have seen that the great European fact, at that epoch, was the division of the powers of Europe under these two banners. But this fact was not then understood as I now explain it; it was hidden, and unknown even to those by whom it was accomplished. The repression of the system of pure monarchy, and the consecration of civil and religious liberty, was necessarily, at bottom, the result of the resistance of Holland and her allies to Louis XIV.; but the question between absolute power and liberty was not then thus absolutely laid down. It has been frequently said that the propagation of absolute power was the ruling principle in the diplomacy of Louis XIV. I do not think so. It was at a late period, and in his old age, that this consideration assumed a great part in his policy. The power of France, her preponderance in Europe, the depression of rival powers —in short, the political interest and strength of the state, was the object which Louis XIV. always had in view, whether he was contending against Spain, the Emperor of Germany, or England. He was much less actuated by a wish for the propagation of absolute power, than by a desire for the aggrandizement of France and his own government. Among many other proofs of this, there is one which emanates from Louis XIV. himself. We find in his *Memoirs*, for the year 1666, if I remember rightly, a note conceived nearly in these terms:—

"This morning I had a conversation with Mr. Sidney, an English gentleman, who spoke to me of the possibility of reviving the republican party in England: Mr. Sidney asked me for £400,000 for this purpose. I told him I could not give him more than £200,000. He prevailed on me to send to Switzerland for another English gentleman, called Mr. Ludlow, that I might converse with him upon the same subject."

We find accordingly, in Ludlow's Memoirs, about the same date, a paragraph to the following import:—

"I have received from the French government an invitation to go to Paris, to have some discussion on the affairs of my country; but I distrust this government."

And, in fact, Ludlow did remain in Switzerland.

You see that the object of Louis XIV. at that time was to weaken the royal power of England. He fomented internal dissensions, he labored to revive the republican party, in order to hinder Charles II. from becoming too powerful in his own country. In the course of Barillon's embassy to England, the same fact is constantly apparent. As often as the authority of Charles II. seems to be gaining the ascendency, and the national party on the point of being overpowered, the French ambassador turns his influence in that direction, gives money to the leaders of the opposition, and, in short, contends against absolute power, as soon as that becomes the means of weakening a rival of France. When ever we attentively examine the conduct of foreign relations under Louis XIV., this is the fact which we are struck with.

We are also surprised at the capacity and ability of the French diplomacy at this period. The names of Torcy, D'Avaux, and Bonrepaus, are known to all well-informed persons. When we compare the despatches, the memorials, the skill, the management of these counsellors of Louis XIV., with those of the Spanish, Portugese, and German negotiators, we are struck with the superiority of the French ministers; not only with their serious activity and application to business, but with their freedom of thought These courtiers of an absolute king judge of foreign events, of parties, of the demands for freedom, and of popular revolutions, much more soundly than the greater part of the English themselves of that period. There is no diplomacy in Europe in the seventeenth century which appears equal to the diplomacy of France, except perhaps that of Holland. The ministers of John de Witt and William of Orange, those illustrious leaders of the party of civil and religious liberty, are the only ones who appear to have been in a condition to contend with the servants of the great absolute king.

You see, that, whether we consider the wars of Louis XIV., or his diplomatic relations, we arrive at the same results. We can easily conceive how a government which conducted in such a manner its wars and negotiations, must have acquired great solidity in Europe, and assumed not only a formidable, but an able and imposing aspect.

Let us now turn our eyes to the interior of France, and the administration and legislation of Louis XIV.; we shall everywhere find new explanations of the strength and splendor of his government.

It is difficult to determine precisely what ought to be understood by administration in the government of a state. Still, when we endeavor to come to a distinct understanding on this subject, we acknowledge, I believe, that, under the most general point of view, administration consists in an assemblage of means destined to transmit, as speedily and surely as possible, the will of the central power into all departments of society, and, under the same conditions, to make the powers of society return to the central power, either in men or money. This, if I am not mistaken, is the true object, the prevailing character, of administration. From this we may perceive that, in times where it is especially necessary to establish union and order in society, administration is the great means of accomplishing it—of bringing together, cementing, and uniting scattered and incoherent elements. Such, in fact, was the work of the administration of Louis XIV. Till his time, nothing had been more difficult, in France as well as in the rest of Europe, than to cause the action of the central power to penetrate into all the parts of society, and to concentrate into the heart of the central power the means of strength possessed by the society at large. This was the object of Louis's endeavors, and he succeeded in it to a certain extent, incomparably better, at least, than preceding governments had done. I cannot enter into any details; but take a survey of every kind of public service, the taxes, the highways, industry, the military administration, and the various establishments which belong to any branch of administration whatever; there is hardly any of them which you will not find to have either been originated, developed, or greatly meliorated, under the reign of Louis XIV. It was as administrators that the greatest men of his time, such as Colbert and Louvois, displayed their genius and exercised their ministerial functions. It was thus that his government acquired a comprehensiveness, a decision, and a consistency, which were wanting in all the European governments around him.

The same fact holds with respect to this government, as regards its legislative capacity. I will again refer to the comparison I made in the outset to the legislative activity of the Consular government, and its prodigious labor in revising and remodelling the laws. A labor of the same kind was undertaken under Louis XIV. The great ordinances which he passed and promulgated—the ordinances on the criminal law, on forms of procedure, on commerce, on the navy, on waters and forests—are real codes of law, which were constructed in the same manner as our codes, having been discussed in the Council of State, sometimes under the presidency of Lamoignon. There are men whose glory it is to have taken a share in this labor and those discussions— M. Pussort, for example. If we had to consider it simply in itself, we should have a great deal to say against the legislation of Louis XIV. It is full of faults which are now evident, and which nobody can dispute; it was not conceived in the spirit of justice and true liberty, but with a view to public order, and to give regularity and stability to the laws. But even that alone was a great progress; and it cannot be doubted that the legislative acts of Louis XIV., very superior to the previous state of legislation, powerfully contributed to the advancement of French society in the career of civilization.

Under whatever point of view, then, we regard this government, we can at once discover the means of its strength and influence. It was, in truth, the first government which presented itself to the eyes of Europe as a power sure of its position, which had not to dispute for its existence with domestic enemies, which was tranquil in regard to its territory and its people, and had nothing to think of but the care of governing Till then, all the European governments had been incessantly plunged into wars which deprived them of security as well as leisure, or so assailed by parties and enemies at home, that they passed their time in fighting for their existence. The government of Louis XIV. appeared to be the first that was engaged solely in managing its affairs like a power at once definitive and progressive, which was not afraid of making innovations, because it reckoned upon the future. In fact, few governments have been more given to innovation. Compare it with a government of the same nature, with the pure monarchy of Philip II. in Spain, which was more absolute than that of Louis XIV., and yet was less regular and tranquil. How did Philip II. succeed in establishing absolute power in Spain? By stifling every kind of activity in the country; by refusing his sanction to every kind of improvement, and thus rendering the state of Spain completely stationary. The government of Louis XIV., on the contrary, was active in every kind of innovation, and favorable to the progress of letters, arts, riches—favorable, in a word, to civilization. These were the true causes of its preponderance in Europe—a preponderance so great, that it was, on the Continent, during the seventeenth century, not only for sovereigns, but even for nations, the type and model of governments.

It is frequently asked, and it is impossible to avoid asking, how a power so splendid and well established—to judge from the circumstance I have pointed out to you, should have fallen so quickly into a state of decay? how, after having played so great a part in Europe, it became in the following century so inconsiderable, so weak, and so little respected? The fact is undeniable: in the seventeenth century, the French government stood at the head of European civilization. In the eighteenth century it disappeared; it was the society of France, separated from its government, and often in a hostile position toward it, which led the way and guided the progress of the European world.

It is here that we discover the incorrigible vice and infallible effect of absolute power. I shall not enter into any detail respecting the faults of the government of Louis XIV.; and there were great ones. I shall not speak either of the war of the succession in Spain, or the revocation of the edict of Nantes, or the excessive expenditure, or many other fatal measures which affected its character. I will take the merits of the government, such as I have described them. I will admit that, probably, there never was an absolute power more completely acknowledged by its age and nation, or which has rendered more real services to the civilization of its country as well as to Europe in general. It followed, indeed, from the single circumstance, that this government had no other principle than absolute power, and rested entirely on this basis, that its decay was so sudden and deserved. What was essentially wanting to France in Louis XIV.'s time was institutions, political powers, which were independent and self-existent, capable, in short, of spontaneous action and resistance. The ancient French institutions, if they deserve the name, no longer subsisted; Louis XIV. completed their destruction. He took care not to replace them by new institutions; they would have constrained him, and he did not choose constraint. The will and action of the central power were all that appeared with splendor at that epoch. The government of Louis XIV. is a great fact, a powerful and brilliant fact, but it was built upon sand. Free institutions are a guarantee, not only for the prudence of governments, but also for their stability. No system can endure otherwise than by institutions. Wherever absolute power has been permanent, it has been based upon, and supported by, real institutions; sometimes by the division of society into *castes*, distinctly separated, and sometimes by a system of religious institutions. Under the reign of Louis XIV., power, as well as liberty, needed institutions. There was nothing in France, at that time, to protect either the country from the illegitimate action of the government, or the government itself against the inevitable action of time. Thus, we behold the government assisting its own decay. It was not Louis XIV. only who grew old, and became feeble, at the end of his reign; it was the whole system of absolute power. Pure monarchy was as much worn out in 1712, as the monarch himself. And the evil was so much the more serious, that Louis XIV. had destroyed political habits as well as political institutions. There can be no political habits without independence. He only who feels that he is strong in himself, is always capable either of serving the ruling power, or of contending with it. Energetic characters disappear along with independent situations, and a free and high spirit arises from the security of rights.

We may, then, describe in the following terms the state in which the French nation and the power of the government were left by Louis XIV.: in society there was a great development of wealth, strength, and intellectual activity of every kind; and, along with this progressive society, there was a government essentially stationary, and without means to adapt itself to the movement of the people; devoted, after half a century of great splendor, to immobility and weakness, and already fallen, even in the lifetime of its founder, into a decay almost resembling dissolution. Such was the situation of France at the expiration of the seventeenth century, and which impressed upon the subsequent period so different a direction and character.

It is hardly necessary for me to remark that a great movement of the human mind, that a spirit of free inquiry, was the predominant feature, the essential fact of the eighteenth century. You have already heard from this chair a great deal on this topic; you have already heard this momentous period characterized, by the voices of a philosophic orator and an eloquent philosopher. I cannot pretend, in the small space of time which remains to me, to follow all the phases of the great revolution which was then accomplished; neither, however, can I leave you without calling your attention to some of its features which perhaps have been too little remarked.

The first, which occurs to me in the outset, and which, indeed, I have already pointed out, is the almost entire disappearance (so to speak) of the government in the course of the eighteenth century, and the appearance of the human mind as the principal and almost sole actor. Excepting in what concerned foreign relations, under the ministry of the Duke de Choiseul, and in some great concessions made to the general bent of the public mind, in the American war, for example;—excepting, I say, in some events of this kind, there perhaps never was a government so inactive, apathetic, and inert, as the French government of that time. In place of the ambitious and active government of Louis XIV., which was everywhere, and at the head of everything, you have a power whose only endeavor, so much did it tremble for its own safety, was to slink from public view—to hide itself from danger. It was the nation which, by its intellectual movement, interfered with everything, and alone possessed moral authority, the only real authority.

A second characteristic which strikes me in the state of the human mind in the eighteenth century, is the universality of the spirit of free inquiry. Till then, and particularly in the sixteenth century, free inquiry had been exercised in a very limited field; its object had been sometimes religious questions, and sometimes religious and political questions conjoined; but its pretensions did not extend much further. In the eighteenth century, on the contrary, free inquiry became universal in its character and objects: religion, politics, pure philosophy, man and society, moral and physical science—everything became, at once, the subject of study, doubt, and system; the ancient sciences were overturned; new sciences sprang up. It was a movement which proceeded in every direction, though emanating from one and the same impulse.

This movement, moreover, had one peculiarity, which perhaps can be met with at no other time in the history of the world; that of being purely speculative. Until that time, in all great human revolutions, action had promptly mingled itself with speculation. Thus, in the sixteenth century, the religious revolution had begun by ideas and discussions purely intellectual; but it had, almost immediately, led to events. The leaders of the intellectual parties had very speedily become leaders of political parties; the realities of life had mingled with the workings of the intellect. The same thing had been the case, in the seventeenth century, in the English revolution. In France, in the eighteenth century, we see the human mind exercising itself upon all subjects—upon ideas which from their connexion with the real interests of life necessarily had the most prompt and powerful influence upon events. And yet the promoters of, and partakers in, these great discussions, continued to be strangers to every kind of practical activity, pure speculators, who observed, judged, and spoke without ever proceeding to practice. There never was a period in which the government of facts, and external realities was as completely distinct from the government of thought. The separation of spiritual from temporal affairs has never been real in Europe, except in the eighteenth century. For the first time, perhaps, the spiritual world developed itself quite separately from the temporal world; a fact of the greatest importance, and which had a great influence on the course of events. It gave a singular character of pride and inexperience to the mode of thinking of the time: philosophy was never more ambitious of governing the world, and never more completely failed in its object. This necessarily led to results; the intellectual movement necessarily gave, at last, an impulse to external events; and, as they had been totally separated, their meeting was so much the more difficult, and their collision so much the more violent.

We can hardly now be surprised at another character of the human mind at this epoch, I mean its extreme boldness. Prior to this, its greatest activity had always been restrained by certain barriers; man had lived in the midst of facts, some of which inspired him with caution, and repressed, to a certain degree, his tendency to movement. In the eighteenth century, I should really be at a loss to say what external facts were respected by the human mind, or exercised any influence over it; it entertained nothing but hatred or contempt for the whole social system; it considered itself called upon to reform all things; it looked upon itself as a sort of creator; institutions, opinions, manners, society, even man himself—all seemed to require to be re-modeled, and human reason undertook the task. Whenever, before, had the human mind displayed such daring boldness?

Such, then, was the power which, in the course of the eighteenth century, was confronted with what remained of the government of Louis XIV. It is clear to us all that a collision between these two unequal forces was unavoidable. The leading fact of the English revolution, the struggle between free inquiry and pure monarchy, was therefore sure to be repeated in France. The differences between the two cases, undoubtedly, were great, and necessarily perpetuated themselves in the results of each; but, at bottom, the general situation of both was similar, and the event itself must be explained in the same manner.

I by no means intend to exhibit the infinite consequences of this collision in France. I am drawing toward the close of this course of lectures, and must hasten to conclude. I wish, however, before quitting you, to call your attention to the gravest, and, in my opinion, the most instructive fact which this great spectacle has revealed to us. It is the danger, the evil, the insurmountable vice of absolute power, wheresoever it may exist, whatsover name it may bear, and for whatever object it may be exercised. We have seen that the government of Louis XIV. perished almost from this single cause. The power which succeeded it, the human mind, the real sovereign of the eighteenth century, underwent the same fate; in its turn, it possessed almost absolute power; in its turn, its confidence in itself became excessive. Its movement was noble, good, and useful; and, were it necessary for me to give a general opinion on the subject, I should readily say that the eighteenth century appears to me one of the grandest epochs in the history of the world, that perhaps which has done the greatest service to mankind, and has produced the greatest and most general improvement. If I were called upon, however, to pass judgment upon its ministry (if I may use such an expression), I should pronounce sentence in its favor. It is not the less true, however, that the absolute power exercised at this period by the human mind, corrupted it, and that it entertained an illegitimate aversion to the subsisting state of things, and to all opinions which differed from the prevailing one;—an aversion which led to error and tyranny. The proportion of error and tyranny, indeed, which mingled itself in the triumph of human reason at the end of the century—a proportion, the greatness of which cannot be dissembled, and which ought to be exposed instead of being passed over—this infusion of error and tyranny, I say, was a consequence of the delusion into which the human mind was led at that period by the extent of its power. It is the duty, and will be, I believe, the peculiar event of our time, to acknowledge that all power, whether intellectual or temporal, whether belonging to governments or people, to philosophers or ministers, in whatever cause it may be exercised—that all human power, I say, bears within itself a natural vice, a principle of feebleness and abuse, which renders it necessary that it should be limited. Now, there is nothing but the general freedom of every right, interest, and opinion, the free manifestation and legal existence of all these forces—there is nothing, I say, but a system which ensures all this, can restrain every particular force or power within its legitimate bounds, and prevent it from encroaching on the others, so as to produce the real beneficial subsistence of free inquiry. For us, this is the great result, the great moral of the struggle which took place at the close of the eighteenth century, between what may be called temporal absolute power and spiritual absolute power

I am now arrived at the end of the task which I undertook. You will remember, that, in beginning this course, I stated that my object was to give you a general view of the development of European civilization, from the fall of the Roman Empire to the present time. I have passed very rapidly over this long career; so rapidly that it has been quite out of my power even to touch upon everything of importance, or to bring proofs of those facts to which I have drawn your attention. I hope, however, that I have attained my end, which was to mark the great epochs of the development of modern society. Allow me to add a word more. I endeavored, at the outset, to define civilization, to describe the fact which bears that name. Civilization appeared to me to consist of two principal facts, the development of human society and that of man himself; on the one hand, his political and social, and on the other, his internal and moral advancement. This year I have confined myself to the history of society. I have exhibited civilization only in its social point of view. I have said nothing of the development of man himself. I have made no attempt to give you the history of opinions—of the moral progress of human nature. I intend, when we meet again here, next season, to confine myself especially to France; to study with you the history of French civilization, but to study it in detail and under its various aspects. I shall try to make you acquainted not only with the history of society in France, but also with that of man; to follow, along with you, the progress of institutions, opinions, and intellectual labors of every sort, and thus to arrive at a comprehension of what has been, in the most complete and general sense, the development of our glorious country. In the past, as well as in the future, she has a right to our warmest affections.

THE END.

www.ingramcontent.com/pod-product-compliance
Lightning Source LLC
Chambersburg PA
CBHW031956230426
43672CB00010B/2176